Great Escapes

Motorcycle Touring in New Zealand

Peter Mitchell

Foreword by Garrick Tremain

Longacre Press

Author acknowledgements appear on page 7.

Drawings on pages 5 & 24 by Garrick Tremain.

Photographs not credited belong to the author Peter Mitchell
and book designer Jenny Cooper.

ISBN 1 877135 45 3

First published by Longacre Press, 2000
9 Dowling Street, Dunedin, New Zealand

Book and cover design by Jenny Cooper
Maps drawn by Peter Mitchell and Christine Buess
Printed by PrintLink, Wellington, New Zealand

Contents

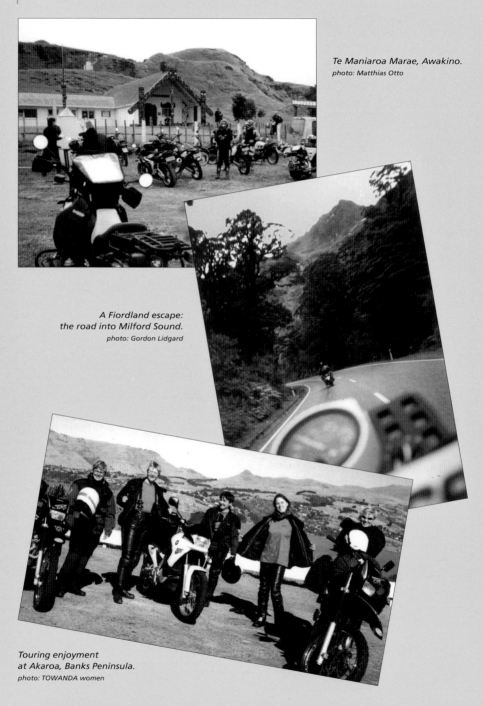

Te Maniaroa Marae, Awakino.
photo: Matthias Otto

A Fiordland escape:
the road into Milford Sound.
photo: Gordon Lidgard

Touring enjoyment
at Akaroa, Banks Peninsula.
photo: TOWANDA women

Foreword

by Garrick Tremain

Like Peter Mitchell, my motorcycling life divides into two halves... adolescent motorcycling, for reasons of economic necessity, and geriatric motorcycling, to recapture the fun and freedom.

At 16 years of age I worked on a Hawkes Bay farm but wished to travel home on days off. A motorcycle was the only affordable transport alternative to infrequent and often inconvenient bus services. That a dark-eyed, young telephonist in the Takapau exchange was an hour away on foot or ten minutes by bike may have had some bearing on my eagerness to purchase my first machine, a Triumph Thunderbird. It was delivered to our gate. The fellow took me through the rudiments of starting, operating clutch, throttle and brake, and left me to it.

I stood proudly astride the bike in the middle of the street, revving enthusiastically to attract neighbourly attention. Satisfied with my audience, I opened the throttle and released the clutch.

I stood dumbfounded as the machine roared forty feet along the road and collapsed into the gutter. I had forgotten to lower my weight onto the bike.

Once I cottoned onto the idea that the bike and I should do things together it was a lot of fun and served me well. There was a freedom to motorcycling then we no longer enjoy. Helmets, for example, were an option, not a legal imposition. And because motorbikes were the choice of those who could not yet afford four wheels, motorcyclists were almost invariably youthful.

In my twenties, living well in Kuala Lumpur and driving an Alpha Romeo Spider, I bought myself a 250cc Yamaha. I had a hankering to return to the spirit of two-wheel travel. The bike was my toy and Malaysia's excellent roads my playground.

For the following 20 years I was bikeless but in my forties, I again felt the urge to experience the joys of travel with the wind in one's face and the smells of the landscape. A new Harley Softail joined the family.

The intervening years have seen changes in biking. Our roads have improved in number and variety as have bikes. And, noticeably, bikers are more mature. When the helmets come off, it is still a surprise to discover the bikers I've shared the last few miles with are frequently as bald, grey and wrinkled as myself.

Nor, in earlier days, were there volumes to turn to for the extensive and invaluable information contained in Peter Mitchell's **Great Escapes**.

August, 2000

Author's Introduction

In my youth a motorcycle was merely economical, efficient transport, and perhaps a sign of youthful rebellion. As the responsibilities of raising a family approached, the motorcycle was sold (but never forgotten). Much later, when my children had grown up, my thoughts returned again to the joys of motorcycling. Eventually I purchased another motorcycle, and found that many things had changed:

- Motorcycles have become more powerful, more reliable, and safer.
- Roads have become better.

In light of these discoveries I found that I especially enjoyed motorcycle touring holidays, ideally in the company of friends. I rapidly learned that although I thought I knew New Zealand like the back of my hand, my motorcycling friends seemed to know New Zealand better. I was constantly amazed by the routes taken by the more experienced riders. I was also surprised at the quality of the roads, and the beauty of the scenery. Often these routes had an added advantage – they were not busy. Gone were the cars and trucks that clog our main arterial routes. Gone also were the prying speed cameras, and the revenue collectors that our traffic police have become.

It was like discovering a *new* New Zealand.

To paraphrase Robert Pirsig in *Zen and the Art of Motorcycle Maintenance*, in a car the emphasis is on the quickest way between A & B. On a motorcycle the emphasis is on the most *enjoyable* way between A & B. In a car the emphasis is on making good time, on a motorbike the emphasis is on *having* a good time.

A motorcyclist will typically choose a longer secondary route, particularly if it offers more corners, more hills and less traffic – for it is in these conditions that a motorcycle excels. Often these routes have the added advantage of offering scenery better than that seen from the busy major routes.

I learned of the Ulysses Motorcycle Club – a club established for 'born-again' riders aged over forty, like myself. It does not foster any one make of motorbike, but rather revels in diversity and promotes the joys and pleasures of motorcycle riding with other like-minded riders. In this club I learned the joys of 'formation flying', and it was from this club that I learned more about the intriguing routes favoured by motorcyclists over car drivers.

A questionnaire was prepared and sent to the club's regional coordinators throughout New Zealand, requesting details about their club members' favourite one or two day 'escape' runs. The results were extremely encouraging. Not only did over 70% of those contacted respond, but many went to great efforts to describe and promote the attractions of their chosen run, and their unique part of New Zealand.

Armed with the results of these surveys, and a year of much riding, this Guide slowly took shape. In it I have been able to collect for the first time in one publication, more than 40 of New Zealand's favoured motorcycling 'escape' runs for all to enjoy. I have graded the runs to provide a comparison by rating road quality, scenery, diversity of terrain, lack of traffic, and safety. I have also endeavoured to explore some of the myths surrounding motorcycles and their riders, in an effort to portray the joys of motorcycle touring in a manner hopefully more understandable to all.

In my other work (providing tourist accommodation at Castlewood, Dunedin, to over 1,000 guests each year), I get to learn about New Zealand as seen from an international perspective. I hear many compliments on the quality of New Zealand roads, the general lack of traffic and our world-class scenery. It's not surprising that many visitors believe New Zealand has some of the best motorcycling roads in the world. I invite you to use this book to discover these roads and the joys of motorcycling for yourself.

Peter Mitchell

BLUE WING HONDA

A vote of thanks

I stress that the effort of preparing this book has not been all mine. I greatly appreciate the support of the Ulysses club members and several others for revealing their secret escape roads. Other thanks must go to Blue Wing Honda, without whose assistance this book may have languished. My special thanks to Clive Cooper-Smith, General Manager of Blue Wing Honda Ltd. The team at Longacre Press have also been very supportive. Particular thanks to fellow rider Jenny Cooper of Longacre who from an early stage shared the vision. It is to the good fortune of this book that Jenny's riding skills are matched by her computer layout skills. Special thanks to Christine Buess who worked magic with my maps; editor Paula Boock who knew when enough is enough, plus Barbara Larson and Annette Riley who coordinated throughout.

For some memorable photos that grace these pages my special thanks to Judy Voullaire, Kennedy Warne, Len Chilcott, Murray Hawke, Fred King, Matthias Otto, Gordon Lidgard (NZ Motorcycle Rentals), Tina Hartung (TOWANDA women), and David Wall.

To fellow Otago Ulyssians: Jenny Cook, Harold Fennell, William Glendenning, and Michael Ingham, my appreciation for assistance and guidance along the way. To Bill, Jason and Dean Veitch of McIver & Veitch Ltd, my sincere appreciation for your efforts in assisting this book.

To Web-Enz (www.web-enz.co.nz), thanks for making *Great Escapes* Internet-friendly and providing www.mcycle.co.nz to facilitate updates and feedback.

Special thanks to Donna, my soul mate and fellow rider on so many adventures, and our daughters Ami and Holly. This book is dedicated to our journeys together.

Notes

Visitor Information Network ('VIN'), Accommodation and Attractions

This guide is primarily for motorcycle touring and does not claim to be a comprehensive guide to accommodation and attractions. I highly recommend New Zealand's Visitor Information Network (or 'VIN') to obtain the best and most up-to-date information, tailored to your individual needs. Local VIN Internet sites, where available, are detailed in this guide, also 'motorcycle friendly' recommended attractions, accommodation, restaurants and bars. However, as owners come and go and standards can change, no guarantees are expressed or implied.

City maps

This guide is about touring, so we trust you will spend as little time as possible in cities. As most major routes in and out of city centres are clearly signposted, city maps are not included in this guide; if needed, they are available at VIN offices. Follow the International 'i' signs to the local VIN office, and/or follow directions to the City Centre where the VIN office is usually located.

State Highways

New Zealand's roads are known as 'State Highways' and each has its own route number. In this guide the initials 'S.H.' followed by a number refer to the 'state highway' route number. For example, the main road route from the top of the North Island to the bottom of the South Island is known as S.H. 1 (State Highway 1).

The term 'state highway' is used in this book as convention dictates; however, in the author's opinion, it is a misnomer as 'highway' is rather a grand name for 80% of the roads so named.

Useful Internet Sites

www.purenz.com

General New Zealand touring information and addresses of regional VIN offices (just follow the prompts to relevant information).

www.doc.govt.nz.

New Zealand's National Parks are managed by the Department of Conservation (often referred to as 'DOC'). This site provides information on the National Parks and New Zealand's extensive walkways.

www.aaguides.co.nz

Useful information provided by the Automobile Association ('AA') on most accommodation options, particularly motels, hotels and camping grounds.

www.bnb.co.nz

www.travelwise.co.nz

New Zealand's extensive Bed & Breakfast facilities are often too small to warrant listing in the (more expensive) AA Guide, so the above sites are recommended for those seeking this unique way to sample New Zealand life.

Updates and New Routes

We have established an internet site for readers to record their thoughts, and to provide up-to-date information on NZ motorcycle road routes, attractions, accommodation and eateries. Your input is welcome via this site:

www. mcycle.co.nz.

Distances and times

New Zealand's roading network is constantly changing. 'Trouble spots' are identified and re-engineered and improvements such as new passing lanes are ongoing. Every effort has been made to provide accurate distances and travel times, but we suggest you take the times as a guide only (allow a plus or minus factor of around 10%). Our estimates provide for comfortable travel within speed limits, and adequate refreshment stops. If there has been any doubt we tend to over estimate, rather than under estimate. We would rather that you have too much time rather than too little – and too much petrol, than too little!

'Round the Block'

When motorcyclists were asked to name their favourite run we received many showing good imagination, but we noticed that several were favoured by the name 'round the block'. Perhaps many motorcyclists leave home saying, 'won't be long dear – just going round the block'. To differentiate 'round the block' runs, we have included the name of the area or town from where the run originates.

A word on diversity

Most motorcyclists have their favourite brand, model or type – a reflection of the diverse tastes of individuals. When asked, almost without exception they will proudly expound the attributes that led them to choose and identify with that particular brand of motorcycle – rarely is their choice anything but the 'best in the world'.

However, when carried to extremes, brand loyalty can lead to prejudice and hostility. Strive to avoid such prejudice. Treat every motorcycle and every rider as an individual, and learn from their varied experiences. The people you meet are your teachers in the school of life; treat all people with an open mind and you will learn much. Close your mind to certain people, and certain brands or types of motorcycles, and it will be your loss. Celebrate diversity and you will enjoy your motorcycling more.

> ***Repetition:*** Each 'Escape' in this guide is compiled as a stand-alone unit. For ease of reference, some repetition is necessary where routes share attractions and diversions.

GRIN FACTORS

Runs in this guide are graded according to the following system of 'Grin Factors' :

☺	Best left to cars and trucks, therefore not featured here.
☺☺	A welcome escape from the ordinary.
☺☺☺	More than just an escape. Good scenery, variety, and challenging riding.
☺☺☺☺	You are almost in Heaven. Plenty of twists, undulations, challenges, plus great scenery. Just a few niggles, like occasional heavy traffic, render such runs a fraction less than perfect.
☺☺☺☺☺	Heaven on wheels, with world-beating scenery. Surely joy riding doesn't get any better; more smiles per mile.

What Makes a Motorcyclist?

Throughout much of southern Europe, Asia and South America, the motorcycle is the preferred transport medium of the masses. From Bangkok to Rome, small mopeds and scooters carry out the duties conducted by cars in more 'advanced' countries.

From early New Zealand motorcycling days until well into the 1950s motorcycling was the chosen form of transport for those who could not afford a motorcar. It became the workhorse of the working class and some of the lower socio-economic status that was associated with this remains today. It was perhaps from such roots that the James Dean rebel image also became linked to motorcycling, developing into the gang image of the1960s and 1970s.

Since the 1980s, cars have become more affordable, and whilst the motorcycle is still a workhorse in many farm and rural New Zealand situations (where it has all but replaced the horse), elsewhere it is seen more as a recreation tool and a lifestyle choice, however perverse.

The common motivation for recreational motorcycle riders is now the adventure or 'fun factor'. It seems there is a similarity between the motorcyclist and the downhill skier, the bungy jumper, the surfer, the snow boarder, the hang glider, and the parapenter. Such people are seen by less enthusiastic observers to put their bodies at risk in the pursuit of thrills and the associated endomorphine or adrenalin release. Noted New Zealand motorcycle racer, Loren Poole, holder of the 1994 speed record achieved on the famed Britten V1000, talked of the 'wicked buzz' that achieving the 303 kph mark gave him. In the same interview he described his experience on the Isle of Man racing course as *'the most exciting thing you can do… for an adrenalin rush or buzz, it is just outrageous'.* [1]

The words of noted blind author, Helen Keller (1880-1968), are particularly relevant: *'Life is either a daring adventure or nothing.'*

Motorcyclists are careful to take calculated risks, and take nothing for granted. For them life is sweeter when one appreciates that life is transitory and can quickly end. The joy of motorcycle riding is one of careful risk-taking, the 'daring adventure' in a life otherwise filled with dreary occupations and television escapism.

* * *

Others see motorcycling in different terms. Robert Pirsig in his best selling *Zen and the Art of Motorcycle Maintenance* describes the joys of motorcycling:

'In a car you're … always in a compartment, and … through the car window everything you see is just more TV.

… On a [motor] cycle … you're completely in contact with it all. You're in the scene, not just watching it anymore.'

On a motorcycle airconditoning is free and not an optional extra. On a motorcycle you feel the air, you smell the air, you are suspended in the air. It blows, it buffets. You no longer take air for granted; you no longer take life for granted.

* * *

[1] *The Sunday Times,* 16 Jan 2000

Pirsig also mentions another motivation for motorcyclists, that of the fascination of things mechanical. There is little doubt that some people find the relatively raw and elemental mechanics of motorcycling more appealing than a modern car which contains more silicon-chips than spark-plugs. While some motorcyclists, typified by Pirsig's character John Sutherland, 'just get on and ride', others (like the hero of the book) take immense interest in adjusting, checking and fiddling with their motorcycle. As Pirsig notes, the mechanics of a motorcycle hold an almost Zen-like fascination to them; 'the motorcycle... is almost impossible to understand unless you already know how one works'.

* * *

Judy Voullaire, a writer, who with four others toured New Zealand's North Island and wrote of her experiences in *Southern Skies* (Dec 1999), gives a female perspective: 'The Dream Ride is about escapism, freedom, and never growing old'.

And if you do need to grow old then the motto of the Ulysses Club sums up the feelings of over 4,000 40-plus-year-old New Zealand riders when it cries, 'Grow old disgracefully'!

In the May 2000 issue of *NZ Goldwing News*, Marie (Super-Gran) Black describes how she discovered the joys of pillion riding at the age of 48.

'One day in a moment of madness I said he could take me for a little ride as long as he went in a straight line, and not around any corners... well, from the first moment I was hooked. The sights, smells, fresh air in the brain cells, sheer exhilaration of speeding along the straight roads, the sheer terror of going around a bend which I coped with by shutting my eyes and praying hard, have opened a new aspect of life to me. The feeling of actually being alive is very addictive.

* * *

photo: Len Chilcott

Whatever the motivation, today's recreational riders come from all walks of life. You quickly learn that you can't judge a motorcyclist from the outside. Clad almost uniformly in black leather the similarity is deceptive and it's tempting to stereotype. However, if you take the time to chat — and many do — you will find real people, with some interesting views on life. The people I have ridden with in the last twelve months include engineers, computer programmers, teachers, graphic designers, butchers, policemen, farmers, managers, receptionists, probation officers, furniture restorers, pilots and restaurateurs. The appeal of motorcycling, it seems, is almost universal.

It is hoped that this book, as well as giving the reader an insight into some of the best motorcycling roads in the world, will also encourage others to experience the pleasures of riding a motorcycle. Drive safely, and we hope that like Marie, you will find that 'the feeling of actually being alive is very addictive'.

photo: Blue Wing Honda Ltd

Riding Skills

Like most motorcyclists, when offered my first ride I just got on and more or less did everything I had learned when riding a bicycle. Sure, corners came at me more quickly, and braking did rather strange things, but I got by with only a few minor scrapes (mostly slow speed manoeuvres while parking etc.) However, when I started riding with others I noticed that while I could keep up with them on the straights, I was left behind on the corners.

I started listening to other riders discussing techniques and heard such novel terms as 'counter steering'. I learned that there is an important distinction between 'turning' and 'cornering' and resolved to find out more, but I was amazed at how little information on motorcycle riding skills is available in published literature.

Eventually, by exploring the Internet and asking skilled riders, I learned more about motorcycle riding skills and the more I learned the better I became. While I'm still no expert or skilled racer, I trust the following will help improve your riding skills.

The Physics of Motorcycling

Motorcycles are strange beasts. Left on their own, without a stand or a rider to hold them, they will fall over. In a stationary or slow-moving situation without momentum, the laws of inertia apply and motorcycles are extremely vulnerable. It is at this time the majority of small motorcycling accidents occur and a motorcycle will often simply, (in the words of their rider) 'fall over'.

It is this vulnerability that is fundamental to understanding motorcycle riding.

Upset the delicate physics and geometry of a motorcycle and it will fall over. But just how does a motorcycle work? What are the physics that keep it upright?

As a child, you may remember twirling a bucket of water and being amazed that the water in the bucket did not spill. You may recall a spinning top, revolving on a small axis, and toppling over the moment its speed slows. The laws of momentum and centrifugal force are too complex to explain in detail here, but these are the laws of physics at work. They keep the water in the bucket and the top spinning on its axis, and they also keep a moving motorcycle on the road and allow it to lean into a corner without falling over.

Turning

In motorcycling there is a vast difference between 'turning' and 'cornering', and the distinction is very important. When riding a motorcycle at slow speeds 'turning' is carried out much as in a car, by turning the handle bar (or steering wheel) and pointing the front wheel in the direction of the turn. However, unlike a car, such 'turning' applies only for slow speed manoeuvering or parking. Once road speed is attained, 'turning' a motorcycle becomes 'cornering' and changing direction is more a function of leaning the motorcycle in the direction one wishes to turn with little or no 'turning' of the handle bars. Frequently, novice riders will fear leaning into a corner until they gain confidence, but it is an important and fundamental riding skill.

Cornering

Good cornering skills are what motorcyclists strive to achieve. They thrive on testing their skills on tight and twisty roads. Correct, smooth cornering equates to a constant challenge, and when achieved, the satisfaction is momentary, before the hunt is on for the next corner, the next challenge and the next buzz of adrenalin. Good cornering is akin to a motorcyclist's nirvana.

Ask an accomplished motorcyclist to define good and bad cornering and frequently the answer will be along these lines: Good cornering is smooth, with the various transitions from approach to exit flowing in progression. In a succession of corners a rhythm is established much akin to that achieved by a good downhill skier. The rider is feeling cool, calm, relaxed and somewhat impartial. Although intimately connected to the corner, and watching for every nuance, the rider seemingly observes his or her progress in a form of relaxed slow motion.

By contrast, bad cornering is somewhat erratic and the feeling is akin to panic. Speed into the corner is frequently too fast, and last-minute braking is required. This in turn unsettles the motorcycle and upsets the flow. Smooth, fast acceleration out of the corner is hampered by being in the wrong gear, and this can create unsteady, erratic movement.

Defensive Cornering

An inherent fault in all motorcycles is their inability to change direction suddenly – where the car driver can twitch the steering wheel to dodge sharply to left or to right, even at fairly high speeds the motorcyclist can only lean his (or her) bike over and swerve rather than turn when the speedometer registers anything over 10 k.p.h.[1]

With this in mind, the best way to stay in control on a moving motorcycle is to avoid abrupt changes such as sudden braking, sudden turning, and bad gear changing, which can all effect the delicate balance of riding. In order to do so, a motorcyclist must plan ahead and anticipate defensive requirements much more than is required by a car driver.

Riding to your skill level is crucial. Do not be tempted to keep up with others unless you are skilled enough to do so. If they can corner faster, so be it. It is better to corner at your own speed and rhythm than to worry about keeping up with others.

However, if riding in a group, it is useful to watch other riders and see the lines they are taking, and where, or if, they are braking. You can learn a lot this way.

Defensive Cornering is the result of understanding the following concepts *(Vanishing Point, Entry, Apex, Exit)* and using them along with technical skills *(Counter Steering, Braking)* to read the road, and judge the appropriate motorcycle speed for the situation.

Vanishing Point

Most motorcyclists will know the feeling: you have approached a corner at what you judge is the correct speed, and in the correct gear, when all of a sudden the corner becomes tighter. Alarm bells ring. You brake, the motorcycle's stability alters as it slows, and if you are lucky you emerge from the corner unscathed but feeling chagrined and rather lucky to have survived.

Advanced Motorcycling,
Institute of Advanced Motorists

All corners have a vanishing point, and the use of this point to adjust your speed in accordance with your skills is crucial to good cornering. The vanishing point in any corner is the point where the two kerbs (or road edges) appear to meet.

Vanishing
Point

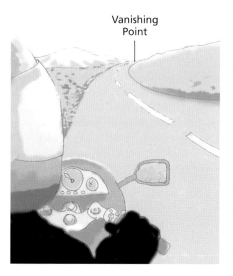

If the vanishing point is coming towards you, this means that the corner is getting tighter. The speed with which the vanishing point comes toward you will determine how much you need to slow down. As the vanishing point comes closer, slow, and stay wide of the apex, until the vanishing point starts moving away. At this point you can see the exit, you can accelerate, and chase the vanishing point out of the corner, by leaning into the corner more and cutting close to the corner's apex.

If the vanishing point is constant, i.e. not moving towards you or away from you, then your speed is consistent with the corner. Maintain course and speed and wait for the corner either to open out and the vanishing point to move away or the corner to tighten (as above). The feeling is one of relaxed awareness and anticipation.

With experience, you become adept at judging appropriate road speed to the vanishing point. Road signs will indicate advisory corner speed and should be noted, but other clues are often available. Telegraph poles, hedges and trees all help determine the direction of the vanishing point. A rippling in the tarmac, or brake marks, or loose gravel indicate that other motorists have found the corner a bit more tricky than anticipated and signal the alert rider to slow down more.

Entry–Apex–Exit

All corners go through three stages – an entry point, an apex, and an exit. Reading these points in addition to the vanishing point will allow the motorcyclist to judge their speed more effectively, and achieve a smooth flowing transition between each stage. The keys to good cornering are to go in slow, to exit at speed, and to spend as much time in the corner with the 'power on' as possible. Your eyes should always be looking as far ahead as vision allows.

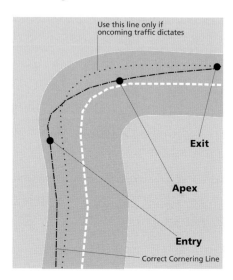

Use this line only if oncoming traffic dictates

Exit

Apex

Entry

Correct Cornering Line

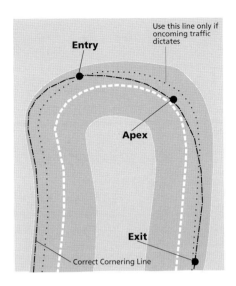

Use this line only if oncoming traffic dictates

Entry

Apex

Exit

Correct Cornering Line

Entry

By the time you reach the entry point of a corner, you will have noted advisory warning signs, traffic density, road conditions and vanishing point and had time to adjust your speed by easing off the throttle, changing into a lower gear and only braking as a last resort. Your motorcycle will be positioned wide from the corner's apex and your eyes will be looking well ahead for an exit point. The aim is to go into a corner relatively slow and to come out of the corner relatively fast.

Apex

The apex is the point where you cut closest to the corner or the centre line. By the time you reach this point you will have seen the vanishing point start moving away, and determined the corner's exit point. More importantly, you will have determined if any dangers lie ahead such as loose gravel, cow poo, or an approaching car to take into consideration as you perhaps cut closer to a centre line apex. You will be beginning to accelerate, and as the thrust comes on, you will lean more acutely into the corner.

The trick is to spend as little time with the throttle closed after entry into a corner, but rather to 'power through' the corner at the correct speed relative to the exit and vanishing points.

Exit

Here your motorcycle is accelerating – you change up to a higher gear and chase the vanishing point smoothly out of the corner. As you exit the corner you will position your bike in readiness for the next corner, either right or left of the centre point in your lane, and the motorcycle will become more upright.

Counter Steering

Remember, cornering a *moving* motorcycle is *not* a matter of turning the handle bars. Cornering is achieved by leaning or by shifting the rider's weight from side to side with minimal directional pressure on the handle bars. In fact, if there is pressure on the handle bars, the required pressure is called 'counter pressure,' or 'counter steering' and paradoxically it is almost the opposite to what you would do to turn the motorcycle at slow speeds, such as when parking.

Try this simple experiment to learn the Counter Steering paradox:

Choose a quiet traffic-free straight road, and when travelling at a steady road speed of at least 40 k.p.h. in a straight line, give a gentle push away from you on, say, the right handle bar. You will find the motorcycle will lean slightly to the right; keep up the pressure and the motorcycle will also begin to veer (or turn) to the right. Next, gently push the left side handle bar away from you. Now the motorcycle will veer to the left. Next, try each side in succession and the motorcycle will slalom or weave from left to right depending on which side you push.

For the mechanically minded, counter steering is a result of the motorcycle's steering geometry and the effect of the rake angle of the front forks, the principles of 'gyroscopic precession' and 'camber thrust'.

While the causes are complicated, the effect is not. Counter steering makes your turning quicker and more precise, and requires much less effort or weight shift than it does to lean a motorcycle into a corner.

To put these theories into cornering practise, choose a familiar 70-80 k.p.h. corner and approach it in your normal manner; however, just prior to the apex (the point where you wish to turn), push on the handle bar on the side to which you wish to turn. Push left for a left hand turn; push right for a right hand turn. You will find the motorcycle leans into the turn more easily, and cornering becomes much easier. As you exit the bend, accelerate smoothly and look for another corner to test your skills on.

Once you become familiar with it you will find that counter steering is a useful tool for changing direction quickly, eg; to avoid a sudden pot-hole. Counter steering is also extremely useful to counteract the effect of strong wind gusts. If a wind suddenly pushes your motorcycle across the road, simply apply counter pressure to push the motorcycle back into the wind, and back on path.

Braking

The old adage for braking a motorcycle used to be, '75% pressure on the front brake and 25% on the rear brake' (in wet conditions adjusted to 50/50 braking). This rule dates back to the days when motorcycles had hub or drum brakes, and were designed to prevent the rear wheel getting into a slide which will almost always lead to a serious spill. However, hub or drum brakes have increasingly been replaced by disc brakes. Modern motor-

cycles typically have double disc brakes on the front wheel and a single disc brake on the rear. This in effect achieves the desired result of the '75/25 rule'.

In addition, some modern motorcycles have linked front and rear brakes, particularly Honda CBR models and Moto Guzzi. These innovations have the effect of applying braking to the above rule, without the rider even having to think about the process. Another modern innovation is the use of anti-skid or ABS braking found on some BMW motorcycles. With ABS no matter which brake is applied, or how hard, the pressure is pulsed to avoid wheel lock-up and skidding.

The result of these innovations has meant the '75/25' rule is out of step with modern bikes, particularly when it comes to slow manoeuvring or turning below 20 k.p.h. At such times relatively small pressure to a front disc brake will see the front forks dive and the rider thrown forward. So the new rule is one of 'balanced braking'.

Advocates of 'balanced braking' recommend the following stages when braking from normal road speeds:

- **Apply both brakes gradually with almost equal force.**

- **As the motorcycle slows and weight transfers forwards, the front forks compress. At this stage, most braking pressure can be transferred to the front brake.**

- **As the motorcycle slows more, the front forks rise back, and the rider then transfers braking to the rear brake.**

- **Thus at slow speeds (say, under 15 k.p.h.) all braking is on the rear wheel.**

> If in doubt, remember the simple dictum that most modern motorcycle braking is a balance between front and rear, with the front brake used more at road speeds, while the rear bake is used more for slow speed manoeuvring and turning.

Each individual motorcycle will have its own braking requirements. The skilled rider will take time to become familiar with their vehicle's braking characteristics well before taking any risks or requiring 'emergency braking'.

What you see is what you get

Your eyes should constantly be scanning the road ahead. If you see a problem, don't fixate on the problem, otherwise you will ride straight into it. Instead, let your eyes find the solution (the gap, or the way out) and you will amazingly find that you instead ride straight to the solution. **Simple but true. In an emergency, if you look at it, you'll hit it. If you don't, you won't.**

Always look ahead as far as you can see. This is particularly true when cornering. You will never achieve a smooth line around a corner if you don't look far enough ahead. Let your eyes chase the Vanishing Point.

Good cornering is smooth, with the various transitions from approach to exit flowing in progression. In a succession of corners a rhythm is established.

photo: Blue Wing Honda Ltd

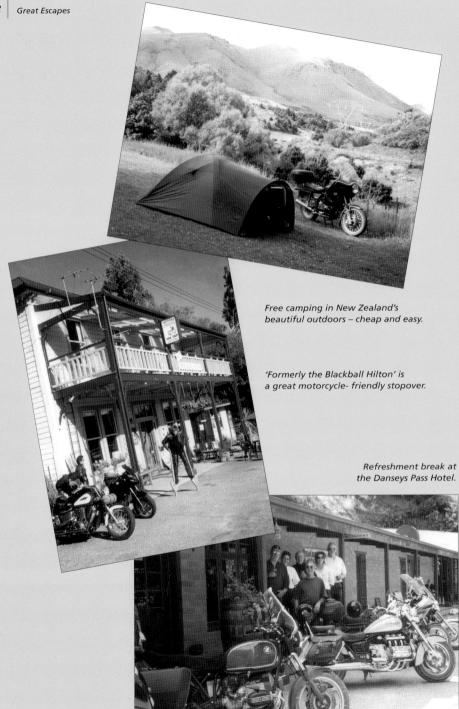

Free camping in New Zealand's
beautiful outdoors – cheap and easy.

'Formerly the Blackball Hilton' is
a great motorcycle- friendly stopover.

Refreshment break at
the Danseys Pass Hotel.

Accommodation Options

This section examines the accommodation options for motorcyclists in New Zealand. I strongly recommend using New Zealand's extensive Visitor Information Network (VIN) to obtain up-to-date information and bookings. Details of local VIN offices accompany the selected motorcycle tours in this book, as do some recommended 'motorcycle friendly' accommodation. For those not familiar with the accommodation options in New Zealand, the following descriptions are intended to help you make the best choice for your needs.

> **NOTE: prices are in $NZ**

Free Camping

Nothing could be more simple. Throw your tent and camping gear on the back of your motorcycle and escape. Free camping is an attractive option in New Zealand where numerous public facilities abound and where many roadside rest areas and reserves offer scenic camping locations.

New Zealand's unique Queen's Chain legislation means that about 70% of the waterways and coastline allow a distance of one chain (approx. 20 metres) from the water's edge to be regarded as part of the public estate. By using some discretion, such marginal strips may be suitable for free camping. If ever in any doubt about land access, ask permission from the nearest farmer or landowner.

Wherever you camp, be extremely careful to observe New Zealand's 'clean and green' codes of behaviour:

- Only light fires in designated fire places, and observe any local fire warning restrictions or bans. When leaving an open fire, ensure it is fully extinguished.

- While tap water is usually safe to drink, it is best to treat stream water by boiling it prior to drinking.

- Take care not to leave behind any rubbish, and use only designated rubbish bins.

- Use only designated toilet areas. If necessary elsewhere, bury your waste carefully.

- Leave all farm gates as you find them.

In some areas such as National Parks, the Bay of Islands, the Coromandel Peninsula, and in water catchment areas, free camping is not encouraged – local 'no camping' signs will warn you of this. Respect the signs and choose another accommodation option.

Motor Camps

Motor camps are plentiful throughout New Zealand and offer a good range of basic accommodation and prices. Some motor camps have very scenic locations, and during the peak summer season advance bookings may be required. Typically, facilities such as cooking, ablutions and a guests' TV lounge are communal. Prices range from $3 up to $10 per person per night to pitch a tent, whilst a cabin or caravan can be rented for up to $15 per person per night (bedding not included).

Backpackers and Hostels

New Zealand's Youth Hostel network is extensive, and since the 1990s there has been a large increase in the number of privately operated backpacker hostels. The standard can vary markedly, from very attractive to very run-down. Typically you will be offered either shared dormitory rooms or private rooms. Cooking, ablution and guest lounge facilities are usually shared and prices can range from $10 to $25 per night per person (allow extra if you require bedding supplied). Due to their communal nature backpackers and hostels offer a good opportunity to meet other like-minded travellers; however, the same communal facilities mean that you should exercise care with your personal security. In many cases parking is 'on the street' and motorcyclists are advised to check the security of the parking options.

Motels

Along with the advent of the motorcar and motorcycle came motor hotels, or motels. Today New Zealand has an extensive motel network which ranges from the more basic 1 or 2 star (often dating back to the 1960s), to more modern, 5 star luxury ratings. Motels offer more private and secure personal accommodation with your own cooking and ablution facilities. There are usually 1 or 2 bedroom options which can sleep up to 4 adults. Motels generally offer more secure off-street parking and prices typically range from $50 to $90 per person per night. Bedding is supplied.

For further information AA and Jasons Accommodation Guides are useful. Refer: www.aaguides.co.nz

Bed & Breakfast, Homestay, Farmstay

In recent years a widespread Bed & Breakfast and Homestay or Farmstay accommodation network has become very popular in New Zealand. Anecdotal information suggests that the NZ B&B network rates second only to Ireland in both quality and quantity. For the overseas visitor the option provides relatively cheap accommodation, as well as the opportunity to experience living with a 'typical' New Zealander in their own home (with the exception of some of the larger, more commercial B&Bs). The Homestay/Farmstay option will usually include breakfast, and in some (often more isolated) locations offer the opportunity of a home-cooked evening meal. Prices typically range from $30 to $70 per person per night.

The New Zealand Bed & Breakfast Book offers the most comprehensive range of such accommodation, and can be viewed on the internet at www. bnb.co.nz (or) www.travelwise.co.nz

Hotels and Lodges

The range of hotels throughout New Zealand is extensive, and many country hotels offer considerable character and reasonably priced meals. The AA and Jasons Accommodation Guides provide further information on this option.

The following distinctions should be noted to aid your selection:

Private Hotels are generally not licensed to serve alcohol. The absence of a bar may put some people off, but it also often means relatively quiet and safe accommodation. Usually there will be a choice of either private or shared ablution facilities, with prices ranging from $25 per person per night. There may be limited parking options.

Public Hotels (or Pubs) generally offer accommodation, alcohol, plus dining facilities. This can be either an advantage or a disadvantage depending on your needs and views.

Lodges are usually viewed as the more exclusive or expensive accommodation option with prices ranging from $80 to $500 per person per night. For further information the *Friars Guide to NZ Accommodation for the Discerning Traveller* is recommended.

New Zealand Weather

Motorcyclists are obviously more exposed to variations in weather than those motorists secure within metal cans. Accordingly, it is hoped that this section will assist those not familiar with New Zealand's weather patterns to avoid the worst extremes.

There is a New Zealand saying, 'if you don't like the weather… wait an hour and it will change'. Almost constant change typifies New Zealand's weather, and whilst it may take longer than an hour to change, change it will – just give it a day (or two).

Unlike continental Europe and America where climatic changes are slow and generally follow the seasons, New Zealand, by virtue of its mid-ocean location and long narrow shape, is subject to considerable weather variation. Weather can change dramatically and quickly, although threatening cloud formations usually give the rider a 1-2 hour warning to head for cover.

For motorcycle touring in New Zealand, it is highly recommended to be prepared for adverse weather at all times by carrying:

a) **An extra layer of slip-over extreme wet weather gear.**

b) **An extra pair of thermal underwear.**

c) **A thermal balaclava to slip on under your helmet (this alone can make a huge difference to your warmth).**

d) **An additional thermal lining to put on under your gloves.**

At any given time New Zealand's weather pattern is made up of many quite different micro-climates, often located within a day's ride of each other. So if bad weather threatens one area, it is relatively easy to modify your touring plans and find an alternative route that will be less affected.

The following information may help a visitor to understand New Zealand weather patterns a little more:

- Motorcycling can take place throughout most of the year, however in winter months (June, July, August) greater care is needed, particularly in frost-prone inland and higher altitude areas of both islands.

- December, January and February are regarded as peak summer months.

- March, April, and May are the autumn (fall) months (particularly in the South Island) and can provide attractive South Island riding weather.

- September, October and November are the spring months.

- On a typical day, main centre temperatures will vary up to 5˚C from the warmer north to the colder south.

- Weather patterns generally come from the west, travelling in a west to east flow.

- Anticyclones or 'Highs' generally signal more settled, drier weather.

- 'Lows' or low pressure zones generally signal less desirable weather.

- The closer the isobars on the weather map, the greater the likelihood of strong winds in exposed areas.

Weather Maps

The following typical weather maps are annotated to assist you in interpreting those published daily in most newspapers. **As you tour New Zealand we suggest you check weather maps daily, and alter your route to avoid the worst weather.**

Typical SW Cold Front Approach

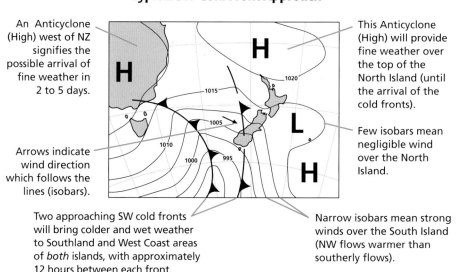

An Anticyclone (High) west of NZ signifies the possible arrival of fine weather in 2 to 5 days.

Arrows indicate wind direction which follows the lines (isobars).

This Anticyclone (High) will provide fine weather over the top of the North Island (until the arrival of the cold fronts).

Few isobars mean negligible wind over the North Island.

Two approaching SW cold fronts will bring colder and wet weather to Southland and West Coast areas of *both* islands, with approximately 12 hours between each front.

Narrow isobars mean strong winds over the South Island (NW flows warmer than southerly flows).

Typical Anticyclone (High) Fine Weather for great motorcycling

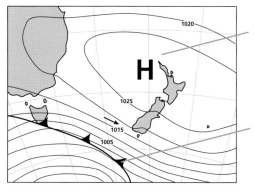

An Anticyclone (High) located over the North Island will extend clear, fine, calm weather over the majority of NZ. Great motorcycling weather!

A cold front should pass to the south of the South Island, and the westerly air flows may bring unsettled weather and some rain to the south west, Fiordland areas south of Haast Pass.

Typical NW Bad Weather Pattern

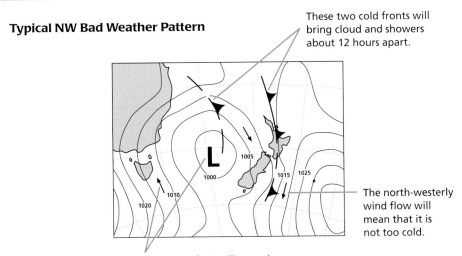

These two cold fronts will bring cloud and showers about 12 hours apart.

The north-westerly wind flow will mean that it is not too cold.

This low pressure zone west of NZ will spread onto the country preceeded by two cold fronts. Expect clouds, showers and colder weather when the southerly air flows reach NZ in, say, 2 days.

Typical Southerly Bad Weather Pattern

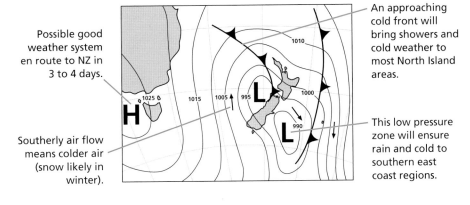

Possible good weather system en route to NZ in 3 to 4 days.

Southerly air flow means colder air (snow likely in winter).

An approaching cold front will bring showers and cold weather to most North Island areas.

This low pressure zone will ensure rain and cold to southern east coast regions.

Note: This weather pattern heralded the 20th Annual Brass Monkey Rally in June 2000, bringing showers and snow to 500 metres. While motorcyclists attending the Rally (held near Oturehua in Central Otago) escaped the worst of it, Wellington bore the brunt of atrocious weather. Surface flooding and wind gusts wreaked havoc on roads and at sea, while 7-metre waves in Cook Strait forced the cancellation of all ferry crossings.

Comparative NORTH ISLAND weather patterns

- Generally weather in the North Island is more humid, and warmer.
- The further north you go the more tropical the climate becomes.
- Rain is generally more tropical, i.e. more sudden, heavy, frequent and more short-lived.
- The west coast receives more rain than the east coast.
- East coast areas are generally drier, less humid, with more sunshine hours. The Hawkes Bay climate is particularly 'Mediterranean'.
- The central highlands represented by the Desert Plateau area from Taupo south to Taihape experience more extremes. In winter this means frosts and occasional snow. In summer there will be higher temperatures, less humidity, and colder nights.
- Western areas are more prone to strong winds, and this is particularly evident in the 'wind funnel' area south of Palmerston North to Wellington.

Comparative SOUTH ISLAND weather patterns

- Generally less humid, and comparatively cooler than the North Island.
- Rain is generally less heavy, but a soaking coastal drizzle may last a day or more.
- South Island West Coast has a mild temperate climate and avoids many of the major temperature extremes associated with the mountainous areas and central highlands south of Lake Tekapo.
- The Southern Alps provide a 'rain shadow' with more rain falling west of the central divide (up to 7,000 mm p.a.) with a comparatively dry climate east of the divide (typically up to 300 mm p.a.)
- East of the Southern Alps, particularly on the Canterbury Plains, north-west winds (referred to as 'nor-westers') can bring gusty hot dry winds. In such conditions you may appreciate why a Canterbury town is named Windwhistle!
- Blenheim, North Canterbury, and the Central South Island from Lake Tekapo to Queenstown are areas noted for having a hot dry summer and provide a useful refuge if coastal weather is unpleasant.

North Island

Whangarei	0	467	827	626	369	283	374	455	447	403	706	71	526	590	815	155	295	668	58	514	271	170
Whakatane		0	545	358	235	209	97	257	165	85	424	538	384	308	533	622	193	201	482	262	738	298
Wellington			0	198	473	586	546	371	400	460	145	898	355	321	102	982	532	538	842	344	1098	657
Wanganui				0	273	479	439	171	225	309	74	697	160	252	183	781	331	467	641	141	897	455
Waitomo					0	182	151	102	163	166	341	440	173	306	450	524	74	445	384	159	640	200
Thames						0	116	268	206	164	465	354	339	349	574	438	108	410	298	303	554	114
Tauranga							0	235	150	86	415	445	308	300	524	529	106	298	389	236	645	205
Taumarunui								0	117	172	239	526	183	260	348	610	160	449	470	59	726	286
Taupo									0	80	259	518	296	145	368	602	152	332	462	97	718	279
Rotorua										0	339	474	299	223	448	558	108	286	418	177	674	235
Palmerston North											0	777	234	178	109	861	411	393	721	223	977	537
Paihia												0	597	661	886	107	366	739	129	585	223	240
New Plymouth													0	412	343	681	231	585	541	242	797	357
Napier														0	233	748	295	215	605	240	861	421
Masterton															0	970	520	448	830	332	1086	646
Kaitaia																0	450	823	169	669	116	324
Hamilton																	0	394	310	219	566	126
Gisborne																		0	683	429	939	499
Dargaville																			0	529	285	184
Chateau Tongariro																				0	784	345
Cape Reinga																					0	440
Auckland																						0

DISTANCES BETWEEN NORTH ISLAND MAIN CENTRES

(in kilometres)

Source: Ministry of Transport Data

Great
Escapes

Cape Reinga

Mangonui

Kaitaia
Kerikeri

Paihia
Kawakawa

Opononi
8
6

Dargaville
WHANGAREI

Wellsford
*Great Barrier
Island*

Warkworth

Helensville
Orewa

Coromandel

AUCKLAND
Whitianga

1
2

Pukekohe
Pokeno
Thames

Paeroa
23
Waihi

9

Raglan
HAMILTON
TAURANGA

Te Awamutu
Cambridge
11
Hicks Bay

Tirau
Whakatane
5

4
Opotiki

Tokoroa
18
ROTORUA

Te Kuiti
16
Murupara
Tolaga
Bay

10
*Lake
Waikaremoana*

12
Gisborne

Taumarunui
*Lake
Taupo*
Taupo

NEW PLYMOUTH
3
Turangi
Wairoa
7

14
National
Park
13

Stratford
Ohakune

Raetihi
Waiouru

Hawera
NAPIER

20
Taihape
22
Hastings

WANGANUI
15
Waipukurau

Bulls
Feilding

**PALMERSTON
NORTH**
Woodville

17

Levin

*Kapiti
Island*
Masterton

Paraparaumu
19

21
Featherston

WELLINGTON
*Lake
Wairarapa*

NORTH ISLAND TOURS

1 Auckland - Coromandel Escape (Part 1)

A convenient one-day escape from Auckland around the Firth of Thames with attractive coastal vistas and some challenging riding. The route can be linked with Part 2 *(see p. 30)* to provide a more thorough exploration of the Coromandel Peninsula. Take a swimsuit with you.

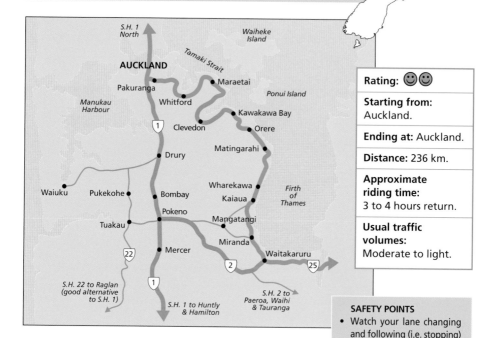

Rating: ☺☺
Starting from: Auckland.
Ending at: Auckland.
Distance: 236 km.
Approximate riding time: 3 to 4 hours return.
Usual traffic volumes: Moderate to light.

SAFETY POINTS
- Watch your lane changing and following (i.e. stopping) distances on S.H. 1.
- Between Orere Point and Kaiaua the road gets rather narrow and twisty.

Run Description

- From central **Auckland** take **S.H. 1** south, leaving the motorway at the 'Sth Eastern Highway & Airport' exit.
- Follow **Route 10** signs to **Pakuranga** and cross the Pakuranga Bridge.
- Turn right into **Te Rakau Drive (Route 8)** and follow this and **East Tamaki Road (Route 5)** until the intersection with **Whitford Road**.
- Follow **Whitford Road** to **Whitford** (38 km).
- At Whitford, take Maraetai Road to **Maraetai** (10 km).
- From Maraetai, continue south around the coast to **Clevedon** (14 km).
- At Clevedon turn left (north-east), following signs to **Kawakawa Bay***, **Orere*** (and a short diversion to Orere Point), **Matingarahi**, **Wharekawa**, **Kaiaua*** and **Miranda*** (with thermal pools), to **Waitakaruru** (66 km).

- At Waitakaruru turn **right** (south-west) on **S.H. 25** to return to **Auckland**, or if continuing to the Coromandel as per Part 2, turn **left** and follow the signs to **Thames** (26 km).
- If returning to **Auckland**, turn right at the intersection with S.H. 2 and follow **S.H. 2** to **Pokeno** (31 km).
- From Pokeno return north to **Auckland** on S.H. 1. (51 km).

---

* *A worthwhile stopover – see Highlights & Diversions.*

Highlights & Diversions

Auckland

(668 km from Wellington via Lake Taupo and S.H. 1; 171 km from Whangarei via S.H. 1.)

A city of two halves united by its spectacular harbour bridge, Auckland's southern landscape is dominated by several Maori pa sculptured extinct volcanoes of which One Tree Hill is perhaps the most symbolic. As befitting its fiery past, Auckland harbour is also dominated by another former volcano, Rangitoto Island. Northern Auckland is typically rolling hill country, with picturesque bays overlooking the Hauraki Gulf.

Fertile volcanic soils and an abundant harbour led to the area being settled by the early Maori some 700 years ago. After the arrival of European settlers and the 1840 Treaty of Waitangi, Auckland was chosen as the political capital of New Zealand; however, as the balance of pakeha wealth and settlement shifted south with the discovery of gold in Otago, the capital city status moved to Wellington in 1865. Despite this set-back the bountiful harbour, prolific soils and kind climate have combined to encourage a population and commercial growth in the region unequalled elsewhere in New Zealand. Today Auckland is New Zealand's most populous city. Modern 'downtown' Auckland is dominated by the Skytower Hotel and Casino which rises above the city and provides visitors with panoramic vistas of the city and surrounds. The Viaduct Basin harbour-side area has been made famous by New Zealand's successful year 2000 defence of yachting's prestigious America's Cup and is a popular area for visitors to gather. There is a wide variety of accommodation available with many budget hotels and backpackers available in the city centre near Queen Street.

For further information contact the Auckland Visitor Information Centre: 287 Queen Street, Auckland (follow signs to the city centre). Phone: (09) 979-2333. Email: reservations@aucklandnz.com

Maraeiti

(48 km from central Auckland; 10 km from Whitford.)

A sleepy seaside village with good beaches, boating, fishing and BBQ areas.

Ness Valley Winery

(32 km from Whitford.)

After Clevedon, look out for the short deviation to the Ness Valley Winery and a pleasant opportunity for a wee tipple. A further 6 km along the road is an oyster farm (open during business hours) which might just mix well with the wine you purchased.

Kawakawa Bay

(43 km from Whitford.)

A rather pretty little seaside resort.

Orere Point

(52 km from Whitford.)

Camping is available at the beach.

Kaiaua

(73 km from Whitford.)

The fish & chip shop here won the NZ title for the 'Best Fish & Chips' in 1980 and 1995.

Miranda Wildlife Reserve and Miranda Hot Springs

(78 km from Whitford; a further 7 km to the Hot Springs.)

The vast tidal mud flats around Miranda are noted for bird life with several species commuting here to avoid the worst of Arctic winters. The Naturalists' Trust offers clean and tidy accommodation for $15 per night (non members rate).

The Miranda Hot Thermal Springs is reputed to be the largest mineral pool complex in the southern hemisphere (open 9.00 am to 9.00 pm daily). Reasonably priced camping is available.

With thanks to Keith Lawrey of Ulysses Auckland, who recommended aspects of this run.

2 *Auckland - Coromandel Escape (Part 2)*

Add this run onto the Auckland – Coromandel Escape Part 1 and you have the makings of a memorable two or three-day holiday *(see p. 28).* The Coromandel has many pretty beaches, twisting roads, and varied camping and dining opportunities. The only negative is that during peak holiday times the area becomes a little too crowded. Go off-peak and enjoy some of the best beaches in New Zealand.

Rating: ☺ ☺ ☺ ☺ ☺
Starting from: Auckland or Waitakaruru – refer Part 1 for directions to reach Waitakaruru (128 km ex Auckland).
Ending at: Auckland.
Distance: 295 km (allow more for diversions).
Approximate riding time: Best spread over 2 days (3 hours riding per day.)
Usual traffic volumes: Moderate to light.

Run Description

- From **Waitakaruru**, turn left (east) on **S.H. 25** to Kopu, and thence to **Thames*** (24 km).
- From Thames continue north on S.H. 25 to **Ngarimu Bay**, **Thornton Bay**, **Waiomu**, **Tapu**, **Waikawau**, **Kereta**, **Manaia**, **Ahimia** to **Coromandel*** (54 km).
- From Coromandel you can either return back down the coast to Thames, or complete a circuit of the Coromandel by taking the inland route to **Te Rerenga**, **Kuaotunu** and **Whitianga*** (46 km to Whitianga). *Caution: this route included some 20 km of twisting gravel road that may not appeal to some riders, but as it may now be sealed you are advised to check locally.*

- From Whitianga, head south to **Coroglen** to **Whenuakite** (26 km).
  North of Whenuakite, watch for the diversion (22 km return) to **Cooks Beach**,
  and/or **Hot Water Beach*** (16 km return).
- From Whenuakite, head south to **Tairua*** and **Hikuai** (31 km).
- From Hikuai another diversion (22 km return) will take you to **Pauanui***.
- From Pauanui return to Hikuai and **S.H. 25A**; continue to **Kopu**, and west to
  Waitakaruru (47 km).
- If returning to Auckland, turn right at the intersection with S.H. 2 and follow
  S.H. 2 to **Pokeno** (40 km).
- From Pokeno return north to **Auckland** on
  S.H. 1 (51 km).

---

* *A worthwhile stopover – see Highlights & Diversions.*

SAFETY POINTS
- Take care on the gravel roads and hill routes.
- Roads can be crowded at key holiday periods.

Highlights & Diversions

Auckland

(668 km from Wellington via Lake Taupo and S.H.1; 171 km from Whangarei via S.H.1.)

A city of two halves united by its spectacular harbour bridge, Auckland's southern landscape is dominated by several Maori pa sculptured extinct volcanoes of which One Tree Hill is perhaps the most symbolic. As befitting its fiery past, Auckland harbour is also dominated by another former volcano, Rangitoto Island. Northern Auckland is typically rolling hill country, with picturesque bays overlooking the Hauraki Gulf.

Fertile volcanic soils and an abundant harbour led to the area being settled by the early Maori some 700 years ago. After the arrival of European settlers and the 1840 Treaty of Waitangi, Auckland was chosen as the political capital of New Zealand; however, as the balance of pakeha wealth and settlement shifted south with the discovery of gold in Otago, the capital city status moved to Wellington in 1865. Despite this set-back the bountiful harbour, prolific soils and kind climate have combined to encourage a population and commercial growth in the region unequalled elsewhere in New Zealand. Today Auckland is New Zealand's most populous city. Modern 'downtown' Auckland is dominated by the Skytower Hotel and Casino which rises above the city and provides visitors with panoramic vistas of the city and surrounds. The Viaduct Basin harbour-side area has been made famous by New Zealand's successful year 2000 defence of yachting's prestigious America's Cup and is a popular area for visitors to gather. There is a wide variety of accommodation available with many budget hotels and backpackers available in the city centre near Queen Street.

For further information contact the Auckland Visitor Information Centre: 287 Queen Street, Auckland (follow signs to the city centre). Phone: (09) 979-2333. Email: reservations@aucklandnz.com

Thames

(154 km from Auckland via Part 1 [see previous page]; 170 km from Hamilton via Whangamata.)

Providing a gateway to the scenic Coromandel, the architecture of Thames shows its rich gold mining heritage. The Historical Museum on the corner of Cochrane and Pollen Streets is worth a visit in order to appreciate the town's history. The Dickson Holiday Camp 3 km north of Thames provides a good overnight stopping point. On approaching Thames keep an eye out for signs denoting Totara Pa Cemetery (2.5 km south of Thames). This hill-top vantage point provides excellent views of Thames, and is the site of a bloody battle between Hongi Hika and the Ngati Maru tribe.

For further information contact the Visitor Information Office: 206 Pollen Street. Phone: (07) 868-7284. Email: thames@ihug.co.nz

Coromandel

(54 km from Thames; 49 km from Whitianga via Kuaotunu – approximately 20 km of which is gravel; 33 km from Whitianga via the Waiau River Valley gravel road route.)

Once a bustling town boasting a population of over 10,000 after the discovery of gold nearby in 1852. Today the population is nearer 1,000, sustained by tourism, crafts and alternative life-stylers. The Coromandel Mining & Historic Museum on Rings Road provides a glimpse of the colourful gold mining past. The Coromandel Visitor Information Centre is located at 355 Kapanga Road, phone (07) 866-8598, and provides useful maps on the many local walks as well as details of the Coromandel Craft Trail. It also offers information on the plentiful backpackers and motor camps plus a wide range of other accommodation.

www.webtrails.co.nz/coromandel/coromandeltown

Whitianga

(49 km from Coromandel via Kuaotunu or 33 km via Waiau Valley; 43 km from Tairua; 57 km from Hikuai.)

One of the most sheltered bays on the Coromandel, noted for its bountiful off-shore fishing and the absence of a sand bar, Whitianga is a popular boating resort. Polynesian explorer Kupe reputedly discovered the area in A.D. 950 and it was named 'Whitianga-a-kupe',meaning the 'crossing place of Kupe'. When Captain Cook visited the area in 1769 to view the Transit of Mercury (hence Mercury Bay), Whitianga Rock boasted an impressive Maori pa – part of which is now reputed to form the stone work of the present ferry landing. The ferry across Whitianga Harbour operates from 7.30 am to 6.30 pm with an hour's break at lunch time (winter hours). During the summer, operating hours are extended through to 10.30 pm. On the southern side of the harbour there are a variety of walks to Whitianga Rock and Shakespeare Cliff (1.5 km) reached from the ferry landing. There is an abundant choice of accommodation, and restaurants. During late December and January the resort is at its most crowded.

The Whitianga Visitor Information Office is located at 66 Albert Street, phone (07) 866-5555. Email: whitvin@ihug.co.nz

Personal thermal pools at Hot Water Beach.

Hahei and Hot Water Beach

(32 km south of Whitianga.)

These two charming beach resorts can be reached as a day's return ride from Whitianga, or alternatively via a bus that links up with the ferry from Ferry Landing. (For details enquire at the Visitor Information Centre.)

Hahei: Surrounded by off-shore islands, the pink hued sand beach is amongst the best of the Coromandel and features two Maori pa sites, one at the eastern end of the beach where the terracing and earthworks are still evident. The other, north of Hahei, is seen en route to Cathedral Cave whose gigantic cavern is accessible only at low tide (allow 2 hours return walk).

Hot Water Beach: For two hours either side of low tide, visitors dig holes in the sand to make their own personal thermal pools. Incoming seawater can be used to regulate temperatures. There is a motor camp for those wishing to stay longer in this interesting area.

Tairua and Pauanui

(43 km south of Whitianga on S.H.25; 45 km from Kopu and 51 km from Thames via S.H. 25a; 41 km from Whangamata.)

On the north side of the Tairua Harbour the sleepy township of Tairua contrasts with the suburban yuppiedom of Pauanui – a Queensland canal-style holiday resort just a ferry trip across the harbour. Alternatively, you can ride around the harbour to indulge in Pauanui (a 22 km return detour signposted 15 km south of Tairua).

Tairua has considerable appeal, and a walk to the top of the Maori pa sculptured slopes of the twin peaks of Paku (178m) is highly recommended.

*Auckland's Skytower Hotel
dominates the city skyline.*
photo above: Gordon Lidgard

Pauanui as seen from Paku, above Tairua.
photo: Jenny Cooper

Traversing the coastal border between the Taranaki and the Waikato Maori tribes this route was the scene of much ancient inter-tribal warfare; evidence remains in the many former pa sites that dot the coast (particularly around Urenui). This possible return route traverses the best of the New Plymouth to Te Kuiti road (S.H. 3) through quaint coastal fishing villages and the contrasting hill climb and twists of Mt Messenger (189 m above sea level).

From Awakino you have the option to carry on to Te Kuiti (73 km) via the highly recommended 4-star Awakino Gorge, or return to New Plymouth (101 km).

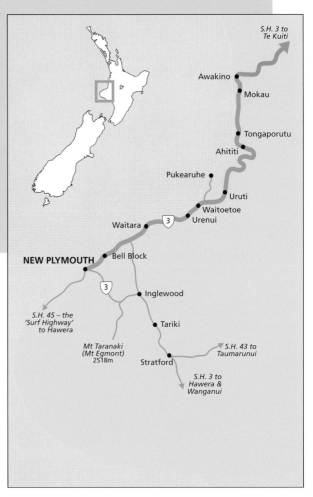

Rating: ☺☺☺	
Starting from: New Plymouth or Te Kuiti.	
Ending at: Te Kuiti or New Plymouth.	
Distance: 202 km return.	
Approximate riding time: 4 hours return	
Usual traffic volumes: Medium.	

Run Description

- From **New Plymouth*** head north east on **S.H. 3** to **Waitara, Motonui, Onaero, Urenui*, Waitoetoe, Uruti, Ahititi, Tongaporutu*, Mokau*** to **Awakino*** (101 km).
- Return via the same route, or carry on to Te Kuiti via the 4-star Awakino Gorge (73 km).

* *A worthwhile stopover – see Highlights & Diversions.*

Highlights & Diversions

New Plymouth

(160 km from Wanganui; 366 km from Hamilton; 163 km from Te Kuiti.)

Very much a rural service town for the rich dairy farmlands that surround Mt Taranaki, in recent times New Plymouth has also become the centre of New Zealand's petroleum and natural gas industry after the Kapuni natural gas field was discovered in 1962. The Taranaki Museum on Ariki Street is well worth a visit, particularly for those interested in the Maori history of the region. The museum houses a superb selection of Te Atiawa wood carvings as well as the fabled anchor stone of the Tokomaru canoe from which it is claimed that early Maori arrived from Polynesia some 600 years ago. For contemporary art lovers the Govett-Brewster gallery on the corner of Queen and King Streets is a pleasing surprise. Its selection of modern and abstract NZ art is one of the most comprehensive in New Zealand, and seems strangely out of place in the rural hinterland of New Plymouth. Nonetheless it exists, and is a tribute to the area's enlightened art patrons.

The New Plymouth Visitor Information Centre is located on the corner of Leach and Liardet Streets. Phone (06) 759-6080.
Email: info@newplymouth.govt.nz
Internet: www.newplymouthnz.com

Waitara

(26 km from New Plymouth; 136 km from Te Kuiti.)

An impressively carved Maori meeting house looks out over Waitara from the eastern side of the Waitara River.

Urenui

(32 km from New Plymouth; 131 km from Te Kuiti.)

The former Urenui Pa site is found north of Urenui township by following the signs to Urenui Beach which is a popular swimming spot. There is a motor camp for those wanting a stopover.

Whitecliffs Brewery

(36 km from New Plymouth; 127 km from Te Kuiti.)

A possible thirst quenching stop to sample 'real beer' from this fine boutique brewery.

Pukearuhe

(Turn-off 42 km from New Plymouth; 121 km from Te Kuiti.)

A 22 km return diversion from S.H. 3 to visit this strategic site. Once used by Maori as a pa site and later by Europeans as the site of a fort or blockhouse, now only a fireplace and some steps remain to mark the fighting that took place here.

Tongaporutu

(72 km from New Plymouth; 91 km from Te Kuiti.)

A rather picturesque fishing settlement where the sea has carved huge caverns into nearby sandstone cliffs. In one cavern early Maori rock drawings are still visible. (Entry is only possible at low tide, by following the river from Clifton Road. Allow 35 minutes return walk.)

Te Kawau

(80 km from New Plymouth; 83 km from Te Kuiti.)

An island at the mouth of the Kira-tahi Stream marks the site of a strategic pa.

Mokau

(88 km from New Plymouth; 75 km from Te Kuiti.)

Bounded by the pretty Mokau River which formed the border between Taranaki and Waikato tribes, the area around Mokau was subject to much inter-Maori warfare. Maniaroa Pa, 5 km north of the township, hosts what is claimed to be the anchor stone of the original Tainui canoe which in ancient times brought a human cargo from Polynesia. Mokau's White Bait Inn is a popular and tasty stopover.

Awakino

(90 km from New Plymouth; 73 km from Te Kuiti.)

A small coastal fishing settlement, with a pub popular with passing motorcyclists. The nearby café Hook, Line & Sinker, overlooking the river, serves delicious home-made pies and other delights.

SAFETY POINT
Stock effluent and early morning frosts on Mt Messenger can be hazardous.

With thanks to B. Bennetts of Ulysses Taranaki, who recommended aspects of this run.

4 Benneydale and Back

This one-day escape from Hamilton utilises quiet country roads to traverse a nice variety of interesting terrain – including the scenic Pureora Forest Park and the Waikato River's Lakes Maraetai and Waipapa, with some 5-star twisting challenges between Mangakino and Arohena.

Rating: ☺☺☺ +	
Starting from: Hamilton.	
Ending at: Hamilton.	
Distance: 240 km.	
Approximate riding time: 4 hours return.	
Usual traffic volumes: Medium and occasionally heavy on S.H. 3 and the approaches to Hamilton, but generally light from Te Kuiti back to Kihikihi.	

Run Description

- Head south from **Hamilton*** on **S.H. 3** to **Te Awamutu*** and **Otorohanga*** to **Te Kuiti*** (72 km).

- At Te Kuiti take **S.H. 30** to **Benneydale, Pureora*** (56 km).

- 20 km past Pureora (8 km before Whakamaru) **turn off left** (north) to **Mangakino*** (8 km).

- From Mangakino take **Waipapa Road** signposted to **Te Awamutu, Maraetai, Lake Waipapa,** and **Arohena** to **Rotongata** (45 km).

- At Rotongata turn left (on Waipapa Road) to **Wharepapa South** (6 km).

- At Wharepapa South turn right onto Owairaka Valley Road and follow this via **Parawera** and **Orakau** to **Kihikihi** (23 km).

- At Kihikihi, turn north-west on **S.H. 3** to **Te Awamutu** and **Hamilton** (30 km).

* *A worthwhile stopover – see Highlights & Diversions.*

Highlights & Diversions

Hamilton

(129 km south of Auckland.)

Initially a military settlement on the banks of the Waikato River, Hamilton is now New Zealand's fourth largest city, and a major trading centre for the rich agricultural area of the Waikato. To gain an insight to the region's rich history and the controversial Maori Wars, spend some time at the Waikato Museum of Art and History on the corner of Victoria and Grantham Streets. Hamilton boasts plentiful accommodation and a wide range of restaurants.

The Hamilton Visitor Information Centre is found on the corner of Ward and Angelsea Streets. Phone (07) 839-3580. Email: hamiltoninfo@wave.co.nz

Te Awamutu

(23 km from Hamilton.)

A small town servicing the fertile South Waikato farmlands, Te Awamutu is famed for its roses – displayed to spectacular effect in the Rose Gardens on Gorst Avenue and Arawa Street. Te Awamutu and nearby Kihikihi were centres for much fighting during the 1860s Maori Wars. Te Awamutu's District Museum in Roche Street has much information on the period (as well as an exhibition celebrating Neil and Tim Finn of Split Enz and Crowded House fame). Nearby Kihikihi's main street (4 km south) hosts the grave of Rewi Maniapoto, hero of the battle known (and filmed) as 'Rewi's Last Stand'. In the 1864 battle, Rewi and 300 of his tribe including women and children were surrounded by a force of 2,000 soldiers. After three days of fighting Rewi was called upon to surrender, but refused, and in subsequent fighting managed to lead about half of his tribe to safety.

Otorohanga

(52 km from Hamilton.)

The Kiwi and Native Bird Centre in Alex Telfer Drive (off Kakamutu Road) is highly recommended, and the special nocturnal kiwi houses make sure visitors will see the nocturnal kiwi at whatever time of day they call.

Waitomo Caves Diversion

(16 km from Otorohanga; 68 km from Hamilton.)

A major tourist attraction of international repute, a visit to the Waitomo Caves is thoroughly recommended. Spectacular limestone formations and the ethereal glow-worms provide a memorable display as your tour boat glides gently deep into the cave system. Guided tours last about 45 minutes and generally operate between 9.00 am and 5.30 pm. Return to S.H. 3 and continue 12 km south to Te Kuiti.

Te Kuiti

(72 km from Hamilton.)

A bustling rural service town, Te Kuiti boasts the splendid Maori meeting house called Te Tokanganui-a-Noho, which was built in 1878 for the Maori leader Te Kooti. The front porch is noted for its fine carvings. (Located on the main road near the railway crossing; permission must be sought before entering.) Just 4 km from Te Kuiti on the road to Mangakino is the Mangaokewa Scenic Reserve – a lovely picnic spot, featuring native bush and limestone cliffs.

Pureora Forest Park

(20 km east of Benneydale.)

The Pureora Forest Park contains some of the finest stands of native rimu, matai, and totara to be found in the North Island, and stretches over 83,000 hectares. Rare native birds also find shelter in the forest. To find out more, a visit to the Department of Conservation's office at Pureora is recommended.

Mangakino

(158 km from Hamilton via this route.)

Primarily a Ministry of Works town erected during the construction of Waikato River hydroelectric system, Mangakino still bears much of this rather unremarkable architecture.

The Waikato River Lakes

The Waikato River at 354 km is New Zealand's longest river and the most highly developed for electricity generation, with ten hydro-electric dams, two thermal dams and one coal-powered generator encroaching on its banks.

SAFETY POINTS
- Care needed on tight, twisting corners between Mangakino and Arohena.
- Care required with ice and grit on shaded portions during winter.

With thanks to Greg Bailey of Ulysses Hamilton, who recommended aspects of this run.

East Cape Circuit

Rating: ☺☺☺☺☺
Starting from: either Whakatane or Gisborne.
Ending at: either Gisborne or Whakatane.
Distance: 592 km.
Approximate riding time: 8 hours return. Best spread over two days.
Usual traffic volumes: Generally light, but during summer and school holidays expect moderate traffic.

The scenic East Coast is the spiritual heartland for many Maori and has achieved almost legendary status amongst motorcyclists for its scenery, twists, undulations and hospitality. The run can be completed from either Whakatane or Gisborne, with the twisty Waioeka Gorge providing a return option if the route is to be completed as a circuit.

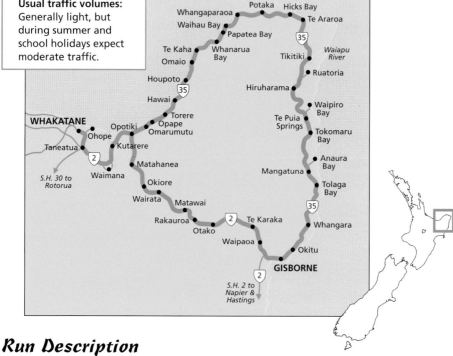

Run Description

- Head south from **Whakatane*** and turn left (west) on **S.H. 2** to **Opotiki*** (58 km).
- From Opotiki take **S.H. 35** to **Te Kaha***, **Waihau Bay***, **Whangaparaoa***, **Hicks Bay***, **Te Araroa***, **Tikitiki***, **Tokomaru Bay***, **Tolaga Bay*** to **Gisborne*** (340 km).
- Return to Whakatane via **S.H. 2** via **Te Karaka**, **Matawai** and the **Waioeka River Gorge** to **Opotiki*** (136 km).
- Take S.H. 2 from Opotiki to **Whakatane*** (58 km).

* *A worthwhile stopover – see Highlights & Diversions.*

Highlights & Diversions

Whakatane

(92 km from Rotorua; 398 km from Gisborne via the East Coast; 194 km from Gisborne via S.H. 2.)

Blessed by one of the sunniest climates in the North Island and some beautiful beaches, Whakatane is reputedly the arrival point for Toi te Huatahi, an early Polynesian explorer. The site of his pa at Kohi Point and some of New Zealand's earliest defensive earthworks can be found via the Nga Tapuwae O Toi Walkway (3 to 4 hrs). Maps and details of the walk can be obtained from the Visitor Information Office in Boon Street. Phone (07) 308-6058. Email: whakataneinfo@xtra.co.nz

Kohi Point can also be reached by motorcycle by taking Kohi Point Lookout Road, off the road to Ohope Beach. Also on Boon Street is the Whakatane Museum, which is well worth a visit. The Whakatane Motor Camp on McGarvey Road is a popular stopping point.

Opotiki

(58 km from Whakatane; 136 km from Gisborne via S.H. 2; or 340 km via East Coast.)

A rather unremarkable town that serves as a gateway and refuelling stop to the East Coast. There are plenty of hotels, motels and a motor camp. However, if you are looking to overnight in the area, Opape Motor Camp 12 km from Opotiki on the East Coast road offers beach frontage and considerable charm.

Opotiki to Te Kaha on the East Coast route: One of the most scenic stretches of road in New Zealand; take it easy and enjoy the views, undulations and twists. North of Hawai the road climbs 218 metres to the Parunui lookout. White sand beaches – often fringed with pohutukawa trees – leave a lasting impression. Traffic is usually light, but over the December/January period is moderate. Take care.

Te Kaha

(127 km from Whakatane; 271 km from Gisborne.)

A former whaling settlement and site of an early Maori pa, Te Kaha is set in a picturesque bay and is the largest town until Te Araroa. The ornately carved meeting house opposite the Post Office is worthy of closer examination, but do seek permission before entering.

Te Kaha to Whangaparaoa: The stunning coastline continues as the road hugs the shoreline most of the way to Whangaparaoa. There are numerous camp and picnic sites along the way. At Waihau Bay there is a small settlement as well as a camping ground with views across to Cape Runaway.

Whangaparaoa

(174 km from Whakatane; 224 km from Gisborne.)

Whangaparaoa marks the traditional arrival site of two of the great canoes (Arawa and Tainui) that brought Maori ancestors from Polynesia some 600 years ago. From such origins, the entire East Coast abounds in Maori heritage. From Whangaparaoa the road heads inland through undulating farmland for 33 km to Hicks Bay and a further 12 km to Te Araroa.

Big game fishing competition at Te Kaha.

Hicks Bay

(200 km from Whakatane; 190 km from Gisborne.)

An old wharf and the derelict shell of a freezing works provides a hint to a bustling past. Elsewhere there are plentiful camping spots on what is a very picturesque bay popular for fishing. The Maori meeting house near the Post Office is well worth closer inspection, with internal carvings dating back to 1872. (Seek permission before entering.)

Coastline near Te Araroa.

Te Araroa

(223 km from Whakatane; 175 km from Gisborne.)

Take a look at the rather grand pohutukawa on the foreshore near the hotel; it is said to be over 600 years old. From Te Araroa the road turns south and inland with a series of hills and descents into picturesque valleys for 23 km to Tikitiki.

Tikitiki

(250 km from Whakatane, 148 km from Gisborne.)

This small roadside settlement features St Mary's Church, reputedly one of the most richly carved Maori churches in New Zealand.

Te Puia Springs

(296 km from Whakatane; 102 km from Gisborne.)

A pretty little town noted for its thermal pools.

Tokomaru Bay

(306 km from Whakatane; 92 km from Gisborne.)

Another landing point for Maori ancestors, Tokomaru is named after their canoe. Yet another abandoned freezing works suggests a more prosperous past.

Anaura Bay

(A short diversion, 330 km from Whakatane; 69 km from Gisborne.)

A very appealing option for a stopover, Anaura Bay was a landing point for Captain James Cook. Today there is good picnicking and camping, with a pleasant 3.5 km walkway located at the northern end of the bay.

Tolaga Bay

(343 km from Whakatane; 55 km from Gisborne.)

Another very attractive option for a stopover, with good swimming and fishing. The motor camp with cabins is located near the wharf.

Gisborne

(398 km from Whakatane via the East Coast; 194 km from Whakatane via S.H. 2.)

Noted for its sun and surf, Gisborne is a pretty port with plentiful accommodation for visitors. It was here that Captain Cook first landed in 1769, and the Cook National Historic Reserve affords good views of the city. The Maori history of the area is extensive and often bloody and is depicted in the local museum at 18 Stout Street. Nearby Kaiti Hill provides a natural site for the Titirangi Pa and offers extensive views of the city. The Waikanae Beach Holiday Park, located on the seaward end of Grey Street, is centrally placed to both city and surf.

Gisborne Visitor Information Centre:
209 Grey Street. Phone (06) 868-6139.
Email: info@eastland.tourism.co.nz
Internet: www.eastland.tourism.co.nz

SAFETY POINTS
- Take care as East Coast drivers are unique (to say the least).
- Watch for logging trucks around Tolaga Bay and Ruatoria.
- Fuel up at Opotiki or Gisborne as there is scant 96-octane fuel available on the coast.

With thanks to I. Davison of Ulysses Whakatane, who recommended aspects of this run.

Weaving through a selection of major and minor roads, this route allows riders to experience the joys of the far north with a minimum of repetition and a maximum of diverse riding. Along the way you will experience a northern 'heartland' whose history and scenery has left an indelible mark on the soul of many a visitor. The relatively warm temperatures in the 'winterless north' mean this route is an ideal winter escape and much less crowded than during the summer.

In addition, the Auckland to Wellsford section offers a convenient 'If-I-can't-think-of anywhere-else-to-ride' escape (approximately 200 km or 2 to 3 hours).

Rating: ☺☺☺☺☺	
Starting from: Auckland.	
Ending at: Auckland.	
Distance: *Day 1:* 441 km. *Day 2:* 433 km. (Allow 221 km extra for a return diversion to Cape Reinga.)	
Approximate riding time: 2 days, approximately 5 hours riding per day. (Allow 3 days if you wish to take in Cape Reinga and the Bay of Islands.)	
Usual traffic volumes: Medium on S.H. 1; heavy approaching Auckland.	

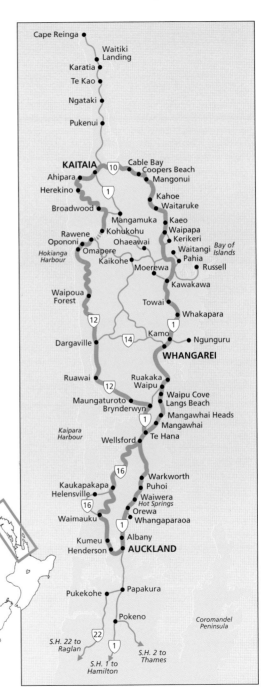

Run Description

DAY ONE:

- From central **Auckland*** head north west on **S.H. 16** (The Great North Western Motorway) to **Henderson** and **Kumeu** (22 km).

- 9 km west from Kumeu, at **Waimauku**, there is an option to turn left for a 20 km (return) scenic diversion to **Muriwai Beach***.

- Return to Waimauku, turn north on a minor road signposted as **Taylor Road** and **Peak Road** to **Kaukapakapa** (24 km).

- At Kaukapakapa take **S.H. 16** which skirts the Kaipara Harbour and continue north-east to **Wellsford** (50 km).

- At Wellsford turn left (north) on **S.H. 1** to the **Brynderwyn Hills** junction (27 km).

- At Brynderwyn Junction, turn left (west) on **S.H. 12** to **Maungaturoto**, **Ruawai**, and **Dargaville** (70 km). Refuel at Dargaville.

- From Dargaville head north on **S.H. 12** via the Waipoua Forest and **Tane Mahuta*** to **Opononi*** and the **Hokianga Harbour***, **Omapere**, **Opononi** and **Rawene** (113 km). *After 318 km travelled, an overnight stopover to explore the Hokianga from Omapere or Opononi is an option.*

- At Rawene take the ferry, which operates hourly from about 7.30 am to 6.00 pm, to **Kohukohu** and continue via minor roads following the signs to **Te Karae**, **Orawau**, **Broadwood**, **Awaroa**, **Herekino**, to **Ahipara** (70 km). Ahipara is an overnight option, but if not suitable continue to **Kaitaia** (14 km). *From Kaitaia there is a 220 km return option to travel to Cape Reinga.*

- From Kaitaia turn left (north) to **Awanui** (8 km).

- At Awanui turn right (east) on **S.H. 10** to **Kaingaroa**, **Cable Bay**, **Coopers Beach**, and **Mangonui** (31 km). *At over 441 km travelled, these resorts offer a picturesque option for an overnight stopover and a base from which to explore Cape Reinga.*

DAY TWO:

- From Mangonui continue south on S.H. 10 to **Kahoe**, **Waitaruke**, **Kaeo**, to **Waipapa** (57 km).

- At Waipapa a 10 km diversion to **Kerikeri*** and the historic Stone Store is recommended.

- Return to S.H. 10 and continue to **Puketona Junction** (7 km).

- At Puketona Junction turn left (east) to **Paihia***, **Waitangi*** (14 km) where there is an optional diversion via the ferry to **Russell***.

- Continue south via S.H. 10 to **Kawakawa*** (16 km).

- At Kawakawa take **S.H. 1** to **Whangarei*** (54 km). At **Kamo** on the northern outskirts of Whangarei there is an optional diversion to turn left (east) to **Ngunguru*** seaside resort (52 km return).

- From Whangarei return via S.H. 1 to **Waipu** (39 km).

- At Waipu turn left (east) and follow the minor coastal road to **Waipu Cove**, **Langs Beach**, **Mangawhai Heads** and **Mangawhai**, and continue on to rejoin S.H. 1 near **Te Hana** (56 km).

- Continue on S.H. 1 to **Wellsford** (7 km) and on to **Warkworth**, **Puhoi**, and **Waiwera*** where a soak in the thermal pools would be enjoyable (39 km).

- From Waiwera continue on S.H. 1 to **Orewa*** (6 km). *Here a diversion to **Whangaparaoa*** is optional (10 km return).*

- From Orewa continue south on S.H. 1 to **Albany** and **Auckland** (53 km).

---

* *A worthwhile stopover – see Highlights & Diversions.*

Highlights & Diversions

Auckland

(668 km from Wellington via Lake Taupo and S.H.1; 171 km from Whangarei via S.H.1.)

A city of two halves united by its spectacular harbour bridge, Auckland's southern landscape is dominated by several Maori pa sculptured extinct volcanoes of which One Tree Hill is perhaps the most symbolic. As befitting its fiery past, Auckland harbour is also dominated by another former volcano, Rangitoto Island. Northern Auckland is typically rolling hill country, with picturesque bays overlooking the Hauraki Gulf.

Fertile volcanic soils and an abundant harbour led to the area being settled by the early Maori some 700 years ago. After the arrival of European settlers and the 1840 Treaty of Waitangi, Auckland was chosen as the political capital of New Zealand; however, as the balance of pakeha wealth and settlement shifted south with the discovery of gold in Otago, the capital city status moved to Wellington in 1865. Despite this set-back the bountiful harbour, prolific soils and kind climate have combined to encourage a population and commercial growth in the region unequalled elsewhere in New Zealand. Today Auckland is New Zealand's most populous city. Modern 'downtown' Auckland is dominated by the Skytower Hotel and Casino which rises above the city and provides visitors with panoramic vistas of the city and surrounds. The Viaduct Basin harbour-side area has been made famous by New Zealand's successful year 2000 defence of yachting's prestigious America's Cup and is a popular area for visitors to gather. There is a wide variety of accommodation available with many budget hotels and backpackers available in the city centre near Queen Street.

For further information contact the Auckland Visitor Information Centre: 287 Queen Street, Auckland (follow signs to the city centre). Phone (09) 979-2333. Email: reservations@aucklandnz.com

Muriwai Beach

(44 km from Auckland.)

A classic West Coast beach, perhaps not as spectacular as the more southern Piha Beach, but more convenient to include on this tour, and nonetheless a classic icon well worth a visit. Walks are plentiful, and the nearby gannet colony is claimed as one of only two known mainland nesting sites in the world.

Helensville

(50 km from Auckland.)

A rather sleepy ex-kauri timber town, today best noted for the nearby Parakai thermal pools, signposted 3 km north of the town.

Dargaville

(58 km from Whangarei.)

Dargaville owes its origins to the trading of Kauri timber and gum from the Kaipara Harbour, and today is known as the 'Kumara Capital of NZ' for its famed ability to grow this native potato. Selwyn Park motor camp on Onslow Street offers reasonable accommodation as does the Greenhouse Backpackers Hostel on Portland Street. The Dargaville Maritime Museum in Harding Park makes interesting viewing for those with the sea in their blood.

Waipoua Kauri Forest

(63 km north of Dargaville on S.H. 12.)

The 9,000-plus hectare forest park was established in 1952 to protect three quarters of New Zealand's last remaining stands of its oldest and largest native tree, the kauri. Take the 10 minute return walk (signposted from S.H. 12) to view 'Tane Mahuta' (God of the Forest) with a height of 51m and estimated to be 1,200 years old.

'Tane Mahuta' – largest kauri tree in Waipoua Forest.

The Hokianga Harbour and Opononi

(90 km north of Dargaville.)

The famed Hokianga Harbour attracted early Maori for its bountiful sea harvest, and is reputed to be the departure point used by the Polynesian explorer Kupe when returning to his homeland after exploring New Zealand. The first pakeha settlers began arriving in the early 1800s, attracted initially by the harbour and the kauri trees that grew to the water's edge.

Omapere: Savour the spectacular views of the Hokianga Harbour as you descend into Omapere from the south. Noted for its fishing, Omapere also offers a spectacular blow-hole (best at high tide) that can be reached by a 30 minute return walk to the heads.

Opononi: A possible stopover site, Opononi offers a variety of harbour trips to view dolphins and the harbour. One particularly friendly dolphin, 'Opo', is commemorated with a statue located on the shore opposite the hotel.

Rawene and its ferry: The pretty township of Rawene is worth a visit, even if not contemplating using the ferry to cross the harbour and carry on north to Kaitaia. However, the ferry crossing is strongly recommended. Clendon House on the Esplanade is also well worth a visit. The Boat Shed Café and Hokianga Brewery offer interesting and diverse hospitality. The Rawene ferry operates hourly from about 7.30 am to 6.00 pm. (The minor tar-sealed road north to Ahipara Bay and Kaitaia covers 79 km and will take you about an hour.)

Ahipara

(71 km from the Hokianga ferry via this route.)

Situated on the southern shores of Ninety Mile Beach, Ahipara is noted for both its huge sand dunes and the nearby kauri gum fields. If walking is not your thing, quad-bike tours operate to both the gum fields and the sand dunes and are based at Adriaan Lodge.

Kaitaia

(85 km from the Hokianga ferry via this route; 157 km from Whangarei via S.H. 1.)

The centre of the 'winterless north' Kaitaia is also the tourist centre from which a variety of tours of the nearby Ninety Mile Beach and Cape Reinga depart. If you wish to drive to Cape Reinga (the northern-most tip of NZ) allow an additional 220 km return or 3 hours. The town reflects strong links to both the Maori and Dalmatian cultures as many of the early Dalmatian settlers made a hard living extracting kauri gum from the surrounding gum fields.

The Kaitaia Visitor Information Centre is located at Jaycee Park, off South Road. Phone (09) 408-0879. Email: fndckta@xtra.co.nz

Coopers Beach and Mangonui

(30 km from Kataia; 77 km from Paihia via S.H. 10.)

The charming white sand beaches of Doubtless Bay, fringed with pohutukawa trees, make the area an ideal holiday stop. The Bay is said to have been first discovered by the great Polynesian explorer Kupe, whose descendants (the relatives of today's Maori) followed several hundred years later. The English explorer Captain Cook discovered the area in 1769.

Coopers Beach, with a Maori pa at each end of the sweep of the bay, has considerable appeal while Mangonui and its collection of restored old kauri weatherboard buildings offers a variety of accommodation. The nearby motor camp is very popular. A walk to Rangikapiti Pa reserve, located between Mangonui and Coopers Beach, offers extensive views of Doubtless Bay from its terraced slopes.

The Bay of Islands, Russell, Waitangi and Paihia

(77 km from Mangonui; 71 km from Whangarei via this route.)

The appropriately named bay, dotted with over 150 islands, has a charm that endures and is justifiably world renowned. An overnight stay, or longer, is thoroughly recommended. The history of the Bay of Islands is almost as fascinating as the area is beautiful. First discovered by Kupe, the Bay of Islands was settled by early Maori after the arrival of Toi some 200 years after Kupe. Pakeha settlers first arrived in the 1770s when the French explorer Marion du Fresne visited the area and 'lost' 36 of his crew in rather controversial and bloody circumstances. Across the Bay, **Russell** was settled in the 1820s by sealers and their drunken exploits gave the area an extremely sordid reputation. Today, however, the town has great charm and is also the centre of a flourishing boating and big-game fishing scene. The ferry ride across from Paihia to visit Russell is a strongly recommended diversion.

Waitangi: The Waitangi National Reserve, with the cottage built by James Busby in 1832, became the focus of national attention with the signing of the Treaty of Waitangi on the sweeping lawns overlooking the Bay in 1840. The Treaty is widely regarded as the symbolic commencement of

Maori carving at Waitangi.

Bay of Islands boat cruise through 'the hole in the rock': Piercy Island off Cape Brett.

modern New Zealand history and British Rule; however, to many Maori it also marks the commencement of much controversy and grievances in the shape of claimed subsequent breaches of the Treaty. Many of these grievances continue today.

Paihia is the centre of commerce for the Bay of Islands, boasting a wide variety of accommodation and restaurants.

The Paihia Visitor Information Centre is located on Marsden Road. Phone (09) 402-7345. Email: visitorinfo@fndc.govt.nz

Kawakawa

(16 km from Paihia; 31 km from Kaikohe; 55 km from Whangarei.)

The best place in New Zealand to go to the toilet is Kawakawa whose public toilet is the only building in the Southern Hemisphere designed by brilliant Austrian architect and artist, Frederick Hundertwasser. Enjoy the creativity of this magic space as you gain some relief. The town also is noted for a railway line which shares the main street, which can be a bit of a trap for motorcycle wheels, especially in wet weather. A recommended diversion is the Ruapekapeka Pa site, signposted 16 km south of Kawakawa on S.H. 1. Here famed Maori leader, Hone Heke, was defeated by Sir George Grey who, after heavy bombardment, surprised the defenders by attacking on a Sunday which the Ngapuhi Maori had expected would be a 'day of rest'. The pa site was one of the largest in Northland and covered over 5,000 square metres, with palisades up to six metres high.

SAFETY POINTS
- Railway tracks on the main street in Kawakawa can catch motorcycle wheels and be slippery when wet.
- Take care through the twists of Waipoua Forest.
- Watch following distances on S.H. 1 north of Auckland.
- The straights on S.H. 1 south of Whangarei around Ruakaka are a notorious accident 'black spot' with many fatalities. Take care.

Whangarei

(169 km from Auckland.)

Whangarei owes much of its commercial strength to one of the deepest harbours in New Zealand which has attracted New Zealand's largest oil refinery and a talented boat building industry. Whangarei means 'Cherished Harbour'. Offshore, the Poor Knights Island Marine Reserve provides some of New Zealand's best skin diving opportunities. The town is also noted for Clapham's Clock Museum located in the Rose Gardens on Water Street.

The Whangarei Visitor Information Centre is located at 92 Otaika Road. Phone (09) 438-1079. Email: whangarei@clear.net.nz

Waiwera

(129 km south of Whangarei; 48 km north of Auckland.)

Located in a sheltered and picturesque bay, Waiwera's thermal pools are well known for their therapeutic benefits. Indeed, Maori call the springs Te Rata ('the doctor'). The pools are generally open from 9.00 am to 10.00 pm.

With thanks to Fred Ullness of Ulysses Auckland, who recommended aspects of this run.

❼ Gisborne - Wairoa - Mahia Round the Block

This one-day run offers plenty of interesting features and contrasts, travelling from Gisborne via the pretty and twisty Wairoa River valley to emerge along the Hawkes Bay coast to Mahia, and return through Wharerata Forest and Muriwai. The optional diversions to Lake Waikaremoana and the Mahia Peninsula allow you to turn this run into an overnight excursion. Pack your swimsuit and enjoy the Morere thermal pools.

Rating: ☺☺☺	
Starting from: Gisborne.	
Ending at: Gisborne.	
Distance: 190 km return. Allow extra for diversions to Lake Waikaremoana (86 km return) and Mahia (20 km return).	
Approximate riding time: 3 hours return.	
Usual traffic volumes: Light.	

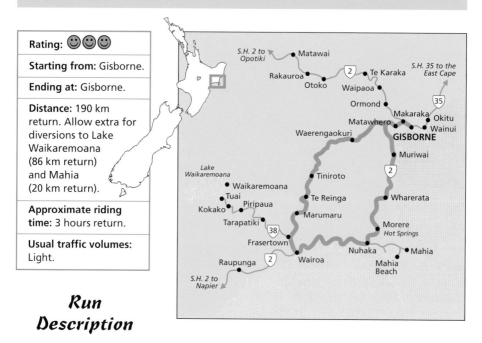

Run Description

- From **Gisborne*** travel west on **S.H. 2** to **Makaraka** (6 km) and **Matawhero** (11 km).
- After Matawhero take the minor road on your right (west) signposted to **Waerengaokuri, Tiniroto, Te Reinga, Marumaru,** to **Frasertown** (84 km).
- At Frasertown turn left (south) on **S.H. 38** to **Wairoa** (7 km). *An optional diversion is to turn right (west) for the 86 km return ride to **Lake Waikaremoana***. Note: this diversion involves 30 km of twisting good quality gravel road.*
- At Wairoa turn right (east) on **S.H. 2** to **Nuhaka** (31 km). At Nuhaka there is an optional diversion to **Mahia*** (20 km return).
- From Nuhaka continue north on S.H. 2 to **Morere*, Wharerata, Muriwai** and **Gisborne*** (57 km).

---

* *A worthwhile stopover – see Highlights & Diversions.*

Highlights & Diversions

Gisborne

(398 km from Whakatane via the East Coast; 194 km from Whakatane via S.H. 2.)

Noted for its sun and surf, Gisborne is a pretty port with plentiful accommodation for visitors. It was here that Captain Cook first landed in 1769, and the Cook National Historic Reserve affords good views of the city. The Maori history of the area is extensive and often bloody and is depicted in the local museum at 18 Stout Street. Nearby Kaiti Hill provides a natural site for the Titirangi Pa and offers extensive views of the city. The Waikanae Beach Holiday Park, located on the seaward end of Grey Street, is centrally located to both city and surf.

The Gisborne Visitor Information Centre is located at 209 Grey Street. Phone: (06) 868-6139.
Email: info@eastland.tourism.co.nz
Internet: www.eastland.tourism.co.nz

SAFETY POINT
Care is needed on the tight corners and gravel of the road into Lake Waikaremoana.

Lake Waikaremoana

(138 km from Gisborne via this route; 64 km N.W. of Wairoa.)

Set in the mystical forests of Te Urewera National Park, this beautiful lake evokes an almost spiritual response, and has long featured in Maori folk-lore. More recently the lake and its surrounds have been harnessed to generate hydroelectricity, but this doesn't detract from the charm. There are ample camping spots and some very scenic walks if further attractions are needed. A highly recommended walk is the Hinerau track (30 minutes return) which begins at the Department of Conservation's Aniwaniwa visitor centre.

Mahia Peninsula

(43 km from Wairoa; 57 km south of Gisborne via S.H. 2.)

Once an island, over time the peninsula has become joined to the mainland. To enjoy the lovely beaches there are camping grounds and picnic spots at Waikokopu, and Mahia Beach. The area is renowned for fishing.

Morere

(50 km south of Gisborne via S.H. 2.)

A quaint township nestled amongst native forest and groves of nikau palms; the main attraction is the public thermal pools which are open to the public from 10.00 am to 6.00 pm. There is limited accommodation available.

With thanks to Des Chiles of Gisborne Ulysses, who recommended aspects of this run.

Lake Waikaremoana in Te Urewera National Park.

8 *Hokianga Heartland Run*

Rating: ☺ ☺ ☺ ☺ ☺
Starting from: Whangarei. (To complete this run ex Auckland, allow another 4 hours or 338 km.)
Ending at: Whangarei.
Distance: 271 km return.
Approximate riding time: 4 hours return.
Usual traffic volumes: Light. Medium on S.H. 1.

From the tall kauri trees of Waipoua Forest, to the laid back coastal delights of the famed Hokianga Harbour, this trail is spiced with New Zealand heartland's scenic icons – not the least of which is a toilet stop at Kawakawa to delight in the eccentricity of architect Frederick Hundertwasser's final work.

Cape Reinga
Waitiki Landing
Karatia
Te Kao
Ngataki
Pukenui
KAITAIA (10) Cable Bay
Coopers Beach
Ahipara
Mangonui
Herekino (1)
Kahoe
Broadwood
Waitaruke
Mangamuka Kaeo
Rawene Kohukohu Waipapa
Opononi Kerikeri
Hokianga Omapere Ohaeawai Waitangi Bay of
Harbour Kaikohe Pahia Islands
Moerewa Russell
Waipoua Kawakawa
Forest Towai
(12) Whakapara
(1)
Dargaville (14) Kamo Ngunguru
S.H. 12 to WHANGAREI
Auckland S.H. 1 to
Auckland

Run Description

- From **Whangarei*** travel south-west on **S.H. 14** to **Dargaville*** (58 km).
- From Dargaville head north on **S.H. 12** via the Waipoua Forest and **Tane Mahuta*** to **Opononi*** and the **Hokianga Harbour*** (90 km).
- Continue on S.H. 12 to **Kaikohe** and **Ohaeawai** (65 km).
- From Ohaeawai return to Whangarei via **Kawakawa*** and **S.H. 1** (48 km).

---

* *A worthwhile stopover – see Highlights & Diversions.*

Highlights & Diversions

Whangarei

(169 km from Auckland.)

Whangarei owes much of its commercial strength to one of the deepest harbours in New Zealand which has attracted New Zealand's largest oil refinery and a talented boat building industry. Whangarei means 'Cherished Harbour'. Offshore, the Poor Knights Island Marine Reserve provides some of New Zealand's best skin diving opportunities. The town is also noted for Clapham's Clock Museum located in the Rose Gardens on Water Street.

The Whangarei Visitor Information Centre is located at 92 Otaika Road. Phone (09) 438-1079. Email: whangarei@clear.net.nz

SAFETY POINTS
- Railway tracks on the main street in Kawakawa can catch motorcycle wheels and be slippery when wet.
- Take care through the twists of Waipoua Forest.

Whangarei Falls.

Rawene and its ferry: The pretty township of Rawene is worth a visit, even if not contemplating using the ferry to cross the harbour and carry on north to Kaitaia. However, the ferry crossing is strongly recommended. Clendon House on the Esplanade is also well worth a visit. The Boat Shed Café and Hokianga Brewery offer interesting and diverse hospitality. The Rawene ferry operates hourly from about 7.30 am to 6.00 pm. (The minor tar-sealed road north to Ahipara Bay and Kaitaia covers 79 km and will take you about an hour.)

Dargaville

(58 km from Whangarei.)

Dargaville owes its origins to the trading of kauri timber and gum from the Kaipara Harbour, and today is known as the 'Kumara Capital of NZ' for its famed ability to grow this native potato. Selwyn Park motor camp on Onslow Street offers reasonable accommodation as does the Greenhouse Backpackers Hostel on Portland Street. The Dargaville Maritime Museum in Harding Park makes interesting viewing for those with the sea in their blood.

Waipoua Kauri Forest

(63 km north of Dargaville on S.H. 12.)

The 9,000-plus hectare forest park was established in 1952 to protect three quarters of New Zealand's last remaining stands of its oldest and largest native tree, the kauri. Take the 10 minute return walk (signposted from S.H. 12.) to view 'Tane Mahuta' (God of the Forest) with a height of 51m and estimated to be 1,200 years old.

The Hokianga Harbour and Opononi

(90 km north of Dargaville.)

The famed Hokianga Harbour attracted early Maori for its bountiful sea harvest, and is reputed to be the departure point used by the Polynesian explorer Kupe when returning to his homeland after exploring New Zealand. The first pakeha settlers began arriving in the early 1800s, attracted initially by the harbour and the kauri trees that grew to the water's edge.

Omapere: Savour the spectacular views of the Hokianga Harbour as you descend into Omapere from the south. Noted for its fishing, Omapere also offers a spectacular blow-hole (best at high tide) that can be reached by a 30 minute return walk to the heads.

Opononi: A possible stopover site, Opononi offers a variety of harbour trips to view dolphins and the harbour. One particularly friendly dolphin, 'Opo', is commemorated with a statue located on the shore opposite the hotel.

Kaikohe

(87 km from Whangarei.)

Named after kai (food) of the Kohekohe upon which the local Maori tribe was once forced to subsist while under attack from an adjoining tribe, Kaikohe is today a rural service town noted for the nearby Ngawha Hot Springs. Found 8 km from town on S.H. 12, the spring's waters are said to be beneficial to numerous skin disorders.

Kawakawa

(31 km from Kaikohe; 55 km from Whangarei.)

The best place in New Zealand to go to the toilet is Kawakawa whose public toilet is the only building in the Southern Hemisphere designed by brilliant Austrian architect and artist, Frederick Hundertwasser. Enjoy the creativity of this magic space as you gain some relief. The town also is noted for a railway line which shares the main street, which can be a bit of a trap for motorcycle wheels, especially in wet weather. A recommended diversion is the Ruapekapeka Pa site, signposted 16 km south of Kawakawa on S.H. 1. Here famed Maori leader, Hone Heke, was defeated by Sir George Grey who, after heavy bombardment, surprised the defenders by attacking on a Sunday which the Ngapuhi Maori had expected would be a 'day of rest'. The pa site was one of the largest in Northland and covered over 5,000 square metres, with palisades up to six metres high.

With thanks to Nick Corbin of Far North Ulysses, who recommended aspects of this run.

Kawhia - Raglan Fish & Chip Run

This break from Hamilton incorporates a multitude of testing tortuous twisties linking scenic treasures such as the Waitomo Caves and the west coast seaside resorts of Kawhia and Raglan. An extra 70 km (return) diversion is required to include the side trip to the surfing mecca of Raglan.

Rating: ☺☺☺ +

Starting from: Hamilton. (Can be accessed from Taupo via Mangakino, and Wharepapa South.)

Ending at: Hamilton.

Distance: 254 km (allow an extra 70 km return to include Raglan).

Approximate riding time: 4 hours.

Usual traffic volumes: Medium and occasionally heavy on S.H. 3 and the approaches to Hamilton, but light after the Waitomo Caves.

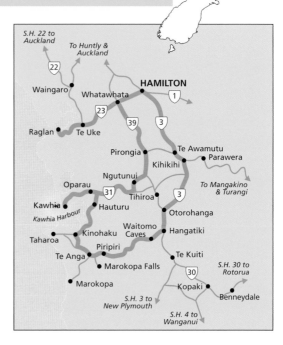

Run Description

- Travel south from **Hamilton*** on **S.H. 3** to **Te Awamutu*** and **Otorohanga*** (52 km).
- At Otorohanga continue south on S.H. 3 to **Hangatiki** (8 km).
- Leave S.H. 3 at Hangatiki and follow the signs to **Waitomo Caves*** (8 km).
- Continue on this minor road following signs to **Marokopa*** to **Te Anga** (32 km).
- At Te Anga take the option signposted to **Kawhia** via Kinohaku and Hauturu – turning left at **S.H. 31** (56 km).
- From Kawhia return towards **Hamilton** on S.H. 31; after 36 km take the left (north) option and follow signs to **Pirongia**, joining **S.H. 39** after 7 km (56 km).
- Continue towards Hamilton via **S.H. 31/39** to the junction with **S.H. 23** near **Whatawhata** (26 km).
- At Whatawhata you can either divert left (west) to **Raglan*** (70 km return) or turn right (east) and take **S.H. 23** to **return to Hamilton*** (13 km).

* *A worthwhile stopover – see Highlights & Diversions.*

Waitomo Caves entrance.

Highlights & Diversions

Hamilton

(129 km south of Auckland.)

Initially a military settlement on the banks of the Waikato River, Hamilton is now New Zealand's fourth largest city, and a major trading centre for the rich agricultural area of the Waikato. Spend some time at the Waikato Museum of Art and History on the corner of Victoria and Grantham Streets and gain an insight to the region's rich history and the controversial Maori Wars. Hamilton boasts plentiful accommodation and a wide range of restaurants.

The Hamilton Visitor Information Centre is found on the corner of Ward and Angelsea Streets. Phone (07) 839-3580. Email: hamiltoninfo@wave.co.nz

Te Awamutu

(23 km from Hamilton.)

A small town servicing the fertile South Waikato farmlands, Te Awamutu is famed for its roses – displayed to spectacular effect in the Rose Gardens on Gorst Avenue and Arawa Street. Te Awamutu and nearby Kihikihi were centres for much fighting during the 1860s Maori Wars. Te Awamutu's District Museum in Roche Street has much information on the period (as well as an exhibition celebrating Neil and Tim Finn of Split Enz and Crowded House fame). Nearby Kihikihi's main street (4 km south) hosts the grave of Rewi Maniapoto, hero of the battle known (and filmed) as 'Rewi's Last Stand'. In the 1864 battle, Rewi and 300 of his tribe including women and children were surrounded by a force of 2,000 soldiers. After three days of fighting Rewi was called upon to surrender, but refused, and in subsequent fighting managed to lead about half of his tribe to safety.

SAFETY POINT
Take care from Waitomo to Kawhia as the road is often one-way, with uneven surfaces and occasional loose gravel on corners.

Otorohanga

(52 km from Hamilton.)

The Kiwi and Native Bird Centre in Alex Telfer Drive (off Kakamutu Road) is highly recommended, and the special nocturnal kiwi houses make sure visitors will see the nocturnal Kiwi at whatever time of day you call.

Waitomo Caves

(16 km from Otorohanga; 68 km from Hamilton.)

A major tourist attraction of international repute, a visit to the Waitomo Caves is thoroughly recommended. Spectacular limestone formations and the ethereal glow-worms provide a memorable display as your tour boat glides gently deep into the cave system. Guided tours last about 45 minutes and generally operate between 9.00 am and 5.30 pm. Return to S.H. 3 and continue 12 km south to Te Kuiti.

Marokopa Falls

(24 km from Waitomo.)

Here a 10 minute walk takes you to where the Marokopa River descends in a series of smaller falls, leading to a spectacular 36-metre waterfall. A nearby picnic spot provides a welcome spot for a break.

Colonial cottage at Raglan.

The harbour at Kawhia.

Kawhia

(94 km from Hamilton; or 152 km via this route.)

Turn back the clock – a visit to Kawhia transports you to another time. Blessed by one of the finest natural harbours on the North Island's west coast, Kawhia is thought to mark the spot where the Tainui canoe arrived bringing some of the first Polynesian settlers to Aotearoa. Maori land owners expelled the pakeha settlers for some 20 years during the Maori land wars. As a result, this charming area has remained in somewhat of a time-warp ever since. The nearby Te Puia (Hot Water) beach features hot springs which allow visitors to fashion their own spa pools in the sand. At the end of Karewa Street stands one of Maoridom's most revered pohutukawa trees (Tangi te Korowhiti), said to mark the mooring of the Tainui canoe. The Kawhia Fish & Chip shop provides the excuse for this run. There are two camping grounds, one with cabins for those inclined to stay longer.

Raglan

(A 70 km return diversion west from Whatawhata; 96 km return from Hamilton.)

Raglan is world renowned for its surfing, thanks to the cult surf movie 'The Endless Summer'. This once sleepy seaside fishing town is now becoming quite a trendy mecca for both surfers and those Hamiltonians wanting to escape to the coast. It provides a highly recommended stopover, and welcome alternative to Hamilton. Manu Bay, 8 km west of Raglan, is said to have the longest left hand surf break in the world. There is quite a vibrant restaurant and accommodation scene. The Tongue and Groove Café on Bow Street offers great coffee and hearty meals (fully licensed to sell liquor). Raglan Wagon Cabins, phone (07) 825-8268, offers a series of old railway wagons as funky and affordable accommodation from around $18 per person. The main camping ground has a convenient location, just a harbour bridge walk from the town centre.

For further information contact the Visitor Information Office on Bow Street. Phone (07) 825-0556.

With thanks to Greg Bailey of Ulysses Hamilton, who recommended aspects of this run.

A rather short but nonetheless intriguing run that gives an insight into parts of the King Country that are largely unknown and unappreciated. The central location of this escape means it can be easily accessed from Hamilton, New Plymouth, Wanganui, Taupo and Rotorua.

Rating: 😊 😊

Starting from: either Te Kuiti, Hamilton or Taupo.

Ending at: either Te Kuiti, Hamilton or Taupo.

Distance: 150 km.

Approximate riding time: 3 to 4 hours return.

Usual traffic volumes: Light.

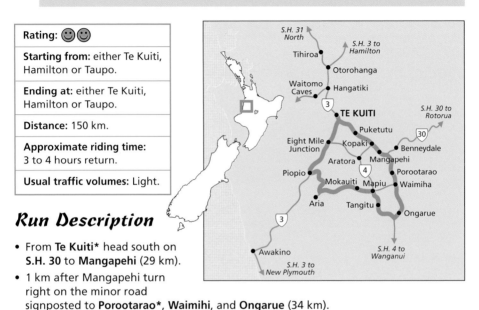

Run Description

- From **Te Kuiti*** head south on **S.H. 30** to **Mangapehi** (29 km).
- 1 km after Mangapehi turn right on the minor road signposted to **Porootarao***, **Waimihi**, and **Ongarue** (34 km).
- Following Ongarue, turn right (north) at **S.H. 4** and continue to **Tangitu** and **Mapiu** (23 km).
- At Mapiu turn left on a minor road signposted to **Mokauiti***, **Aria**, **Piopio** and **S.H. 3** (38 km).
- At Piopio turn right (north-east) on **S.H. 3** and return to **Te Kuiti** (23 km).

---

* *A worthwhile stopover – see Highlights & Diversions.*

Highlights & Diversions

Te Kuiti

(72 km from Hamilton.)

A bustling rural service town, Te Kuiti boasts the splendid Maori meeting house called Te Tokanganui-a-Noho, which was built in 1878 for the Maori leader Te Kooti. The front porch is noted for its fine carvings. (Located on the main road near the railway crossing; permission must be sought before entering.) Just 4 km from Te Kuiti on the road to Mangakino is the Mangaokewa Scenic Reserve – a lovely picnic spot, featuring native bush and limestone cliffs.

SAFETY POINT
Beware of frosts and ice on shaded parts of the road in winter.

Porootarao Rail Tunnel

There are picturesque views south from this area.

The Mokauiti Valley

A pretty part of the world, with attractive hydro-electric generating dams between Aria and Piopio.

With thanks to Grant Mansell of Ulysses King Country, who recommended aspects of this run.

⑪ *Rotorua Lakes Circuit*

The lakes around Rotorua are cloaked with Maori heritage and provide scenic, twisty riding through a mixture of forest and hill country roads. This escape can be easily accessed from either Tauranga, Whakatane or from Hamilton, and can be completed as a circuit, or as a through route to and from the access points.

Rating: ☺☺☺
Starting from: either Whakatane, Tauranga, Hamilton or Rotorua.
Ending at: either Whakatane, Tauranga, Hamilton or Rotorua.
Distance: 178 km.
Approximate riding time: 2 to 3 hours return.
Usual traffic volumes: Moderate.

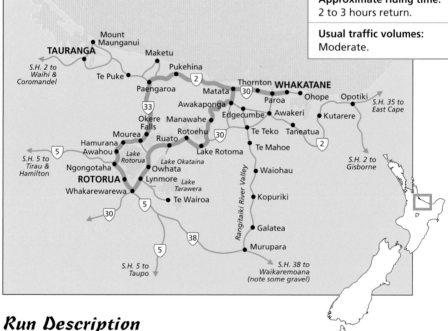

Run Description

- From **Whakatane*** head west on **S.H. 30** to **Matata** (25 km).
  (If beginning from Tauranga head east on S.H. 2 to Matata.)
- At Matata turn south on **S.H. 2** to **Awakaponga** (4 km).
- At Awakaponga turn right on a minor road signposted to **Manawahe** and **Lake Rotoma*** (23 km).
- At Lake Rotoma turn right (west) on **S.H. 30** to **Lake Rotoiti***, **Rotokawa**, **Owhata**, **Lynmore** to **Rotorua*** (48 km).
- From Rotorua take **S.H. 5** to **Ngongotaha** (6 km).
- At Ngongotaha turn right (north) taking the minor road, following edge of Lake Rotorua signposted to **Awahou**, **Hamurana** and **Okere Falls** (15 km).
- At Mourea turn left (north) on **S.H. 33** to **Okere Falls** and **Paengaroa** (32 km).

- From Paengaroa take **S.H. 2** *either* **left** to Te Puke and **Tauranga*** *or* **right** to Matata and **Whakatane*** (37 km).

*Note: An interesting alternative is to travel south from **Rotorua** on **S.H. 5** and 21 km from Rotorua turn left on **S.H. 38** to **Murupara**. At Murupara turn north on the minor road signposted to **Galatea** and continue down the Rangitaiki River valley via Kopuriki, Waiohau, Te Mahoe to **Te Teko** and thence to **Whakatane** (113 km) or **Tauranga** (185 km).*

* *A worthwhile stopover –*
see Highlights & Diversions.

Highlights
& Diversions

Whakatane

(92 km from Rotorua; 398 km from Gisborne via the East Coast; 194 km from Gisborne via S.H. 2.)

Blessed by one of the sunniest climates in the North Island and some beautiful beaches, Whakatane is reputedly the arrival point for Toi te Huatahi, an early Polynesian explorer. The site of his pa at Kohi Point and some of New Zealand's earliest defensive earthworks can be found via the Nga Tapuwae O Toi Walkway (3 to 4 hrs). Maps and details of the walk can be obtained from the Visitor Information Office in Boon Street. Phone (07) 308-6058.
Email: whakataneinfo@xtra.co.nz

Kohi Point can also be reached by motorcycle by taking Kohi Point Lookout Road, off the road to Ohope Beach. Also on Boon Street is the Whakatane Museum, which is well worth a visit. The Whakatane Motor Camp on McGarvey Road is a popular stopping point.

The Rotorua Museum of Art and History.

Rotorua

(100 km from Whakatane via this route; 80 km from Tauranga via Te Puke; or 104 km from Hamilton.)

A major tourism icon for the North Island set amidst rolling hills beside a beautiful lake, Rotorua has long been a centre of Maori culture and home to the Arawa tribe, who utilised the naturally occurring thermal pools for bathing, cooking and heating. Early pakeha settlers noted Rotorua's beauty, and were also attracted by its thermal pools and the nearby Pink and White Terraces which, before their destruction by a volcanic eruption in 1886, were considered one of the wonders of the world. The town expanded as a spa resort and in 1908 the imposing Tudor bath house set in the Gardens off Hinemoa Street was built. The bath house now hosts the Rotorua Museum of Art and History. A visit to the famous thermal reserve of Te Whakarewarewa, 2 km south of Rotorua on Fenton Street, is a recommended highlight, as is the nearby Maori Arts and Crafts Institute. Motorcycling speed freaks will no doubt enjoy the Rotorua Luge and the Go-Kart park which is reputed to be one of the best in New Zealand.

The Rotorua Visitor Information Office, Tourism Rotorua, is located at 1167 Fenton Street. Phone (07) 348-5179. Email: gdela@rdc.govt.nz

Lake Tarawera.

The Rotorua Lakes

Lake Rotoiti: *(15 km N.E. of Rotorua on S.H. 30 to/from Whakatane.)* Famous for trout fishing, this pretty lake also hosts several Maori meeting houses and a camping ground at Okere Falls. The 1.5 km 'Hongi's track' linking Lake Rotoiti and Lake Rotoehu is a recommended walk.

Lake Okataina: *(Look for signs off S.H 30 from/to Whakatane, south of Lake Rotoiti, near Ruato 24 km from Rotorua.)* Arguably the prettiest and most natural of Rotorua's lakes, Lake Okataina is also a favoured trout fishing haven.

Lake Tarawera: *(Turn-off S.E. from Lynmore, 18 km from Rotorua.)* Featuring ancient Maori rock drawings found by following the path left from the jetty. The tranquility of the lake today belies the fearsome 1886 eruption which buried the famous Pink and White Terraces.

Tauranga and Mt Maunganui

(80 km from Rotorua; 96 km from Whakatane; 103 km from Hamilton.)

The pleasant seaside retirement town of Tauranga (meaning 'sheltered anchorage') doubles as New Zealand's second largest port. However, the modern commercial hub of Tauranga has a rather more intriguing past. Tauranga's Gate Pa is the site of one of New Zealand's most famous battles, described by historian James Belich in his book *The New Zealand Wars*. In 1864, 1,700 British troops (many from the elite 43rd Light Infantry) and attendant artillery surrounded Gate Pa which contained 230 Maori warriors along with the Ngati-te-Rangi war chief Rawiri Puhirake. After a fierce bombardment which consisted of over 30 tons of shot fired from distances as close as 350 to 800 metres, and lasting over a day and a half, the British attacked. What happened next, highlighted the Maori fighting courage and provided the British troops with a forerunner to World War One trench warfare. As one witness reported: *'The defenders... concealed themselves in chambers dug out in the ground... covered with boughs of trees and earth... (then suddenly) they opened a destructive fire... . The effect was... as if a volcano had suddenly opened beneath their [the British Troop's] feet, and ... many... were killed and wounded at the first discharge.'* (*The Times*, 14 July 1864.) Thus the Maori achieved a remarkable victory against the British forces. The battle of Gate Pa was also notable for the compassion of Heni te Kirikaramu (a.k.a. Jane Foley) who carried water to treat fallen 'enemy' soldiers.

Modern Tauranga shows little of this bloody past, but Gate Pa can be visited on Cameron Road, 5 km from the city centre, and nearby St George's Church hosts several memorials to the battle.

A harbour bridge today links Tauranga with the scenic holiday and beach resort of **Mt Maunganui**, and a visit is highly recommended. Mt Maunganui offers a stunning viewpoint, a beautiful beach and a pleasant walk (half hour return). The Mt Maunganui Domain Motor Camp has waterfront sites handy to all amenities.

Contact the Tauranga Visitor & Travel Centre: 95 Willow Street.
Phone (07) 578-8103. Email: trgvin@tauranga-dc.govt.nz
Internet: www.visitplenty.co.nz

With thanks to I. Davison of Ulysses Whakatane, who recommended aspects of this run.

SAFETY POINT
Take care with logging trucks and wood chip carriers.

The Waikato Museum of Art and History, Hamilton.

Rush hour at Whangamomona Hotel, eastern Taranaki.
photo: Fred King

The Grand Chateau, Tongariro National Park.

Round Lake Taupo

istant mountains and a host of beautiful lakeside beaches traversed by quality roads with plenty of picnic and refreshment opportunities make this an enjoyable half-day outing.

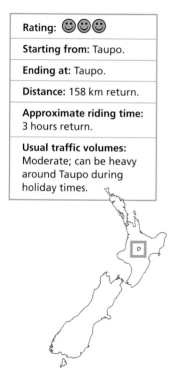

Rating: ☺☺☺	
Starting from: Taupo.	
Ending at: Taupo.	
Distance: 158 km return.	
Approximate riding time: 3 hours return.	
Usual traffic volumes: Moderate; can be heavy around Taupo during holiday times.	

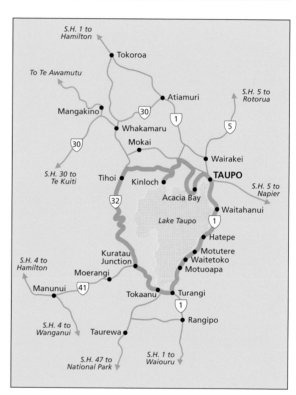

Run Description

- From **Taupo*** head south on **S.H. 1** to **Turangi*** (49 km).
- From Turangi turn right (west) on **S.H. 41** to **Kuratau Junction** (19 km).
- At Kuratau Junction, turn right (north) on **S.H. 32**, 'The Western Bays Highway', signposted to **Tihoi** and **Tokoroa** (41 km).
- 2 km past Tihoi, turn right (east) on **Whangamata Road**, following signs to **Kinloch*** (22 km).
- From Kinloch carry on for 6 km to the junction with **Pohipi Road** and turn right (east).
- Follow Pohipi Road for 1 km and take the next turn right into **Marapara Road**.
- Continue on Marapara Road to Acacia Bay and return to **Taupo*** (20 km).

* *A worthwhile stopover – see Highlights & Diversions.*

Highlights & Diversions

Taupo

(381 km from Wellington; 287 km from Auckland; 84 km from Rotorua.)

The North Island's largest lake is actually the crater of several (hopefully) extinct volcanoes; it is the centre of extensive thermal activity which in turn heats the surrounding waters providing ideal spawning grounds for brown and rainbow trout for which the area is noted. A major eruption circa A.D. 135 deposited the ash that today gives rise to the distinctive pumice landscape of the nearby 'desert road'. Today Lake Taupo is a mecca for anglers and water sport enthusiasts and has in the past attracted such notables as Mark Twain. The area abounds in thermal pools with the more popular being De Brett Pools, 0.5 km from Taupo on the Napier route (S.H. 5); and the A.C. Baths, on Spa Road, which originated as a bath house for the Armed Constabulary over 100 years ago. As befits a major tourist attraction, Taupo offers a variety of restaurants and accommodation, including some splendid camping grounds.

The Taupo Visitor Information Centre is located at 30 Tongariro Street. Phone (07) 376-0027.
Email: taupo@thinkfresh.co.nz
Internet: www.laketaupo.co.nz
www.laketauponz.com

Turangi

(49 km from Taupo; 50 km from National Park.)

Turangi owes its origins largely as a workers' village for the nearby hydroelectric schemes, and as such the architecture has a distinctive 'Ministry of Works' flavour. Today Turangi doubles as a holiday resort and trout fishing base. The Turangi Information Centre on Ngawaka Place has much information on the hydro electricity scheme, while the Tongariro National Trout Centre will be of interest to keen anglers (3.5 km south of Turangi on S.H. 1, open daily between 9.00 am and 4.00 pm).

Kinloch

(131 km from Taupo via this route; 27 km via the direct route.)

A sleepy lakeside village whose main claim to fame is that it once hosted former Prime Minister Keith Holyoake's holiday home.

Acacia Bay

(152 km from Taupo via this route; 6 km via the direct route.)

Once a 'who's who' area of Taupo, Acacia Bay is in danger of becoming very suburban.

View across Lake Taupo.

SAFETY POINT
Beware of frosts and ice on shaded parts of the road in winter.

With thanks to D. Candy of Ulysses Central Plateau, who recommended aspects of this run.

⑬ Round the Volcanoes

The best of the central North Island mountains can be seen as you traverse around Mt Ruapehu (2,797m), Mt Ngauruhoe (2,291m), and Mt Tongariro (1,967m). The route encompasses the brown tussock highlands of the famed 'desert road' and the native beech forests around National Park. Optional diversions to Whakapapa village and Turoa ski field offer you a heightened alpine perspective.

Rating: ☺☺☺☺
Starting from: either Taupo or Wanganui.
Ending at: either Taupo or Wanganui.
Distance: 174 km for the circuit. Allow more for diversions. Add 98 km (return) ex Taupo; add 200 km (return) ex Wanganui.
Approximate riding time: 4 to 5 hours return ex Taupo. (Allow more for diversions.)
Usual traffic volumes: Moderate; can be heavy around Taupo at holiday times.

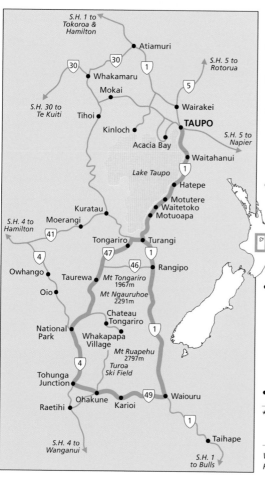

Run Description

- From **Taupo*** head south on **S.H. 1** to **Turangi*** (49 km).

- From Turangi, continue on **S.H. 1** to **Rangipo** and **Waiouru*** (62 km).

- At Waiouru turn west on **S.H. 49** to **Ohakune***, and **Tohunga Junction** (36 km). *An optional diversion from Ohukune is the road up to Turoa ski field* (38 km return).*

- From Tohunga Junction take **S.H. 4** to **National Park*** (26 km). *Note: take care at the Makatote Viaduct, approximately halfway (13 km) between Tohunga Junction and National Park.*

- At National Park turn north-east on **S.H. 47** to **Turangi*** (50 km). *An optional diversion is the 14 km (return) to The Chateau and an additional 12 km (return) to Whakapapa village. (5-star summer riding.)*

- Return to **Taupo*** via **S.H. 1** (49 km).

* *A worthwhile stopover – see Highlights & Diversions.*

With thanks to D. Candy of Ulysses Central Plateau, who recommended aspects of this run.

Highlights & Diversions

Taupo

(381 km from Wellington; 287 km from Auckland; 84 km from Rotorua.)

The North Island's largest lake is actually the crater of several (hopefully) extinct volcanoes; it is the centre of extensive thermal activity which in turn heats the surrounding waters providing ideal spawning grounds for brown and rainbow trout for which the area is noted. A major eruption circa A.D. 135 deposited the ash that today gives rise to the distinctive pumice landscape of the nearby 'desert road'. Today Lake Taupo is a mecca for anglers and water sport enthusiasts and has in the past attracted such notables as Mark Twain. The area abounds in thermal pools with the more popular being De Brett Pools, 0.5 km from Taupo on the Napier route (S.H. 5); and the A.C. Baths, on Spa Road, which originated as a bath house for the Armed Constabulary over 100 years ago. As befits a major tourist attraction, Taupo offers a variety of restaurants and accommodation, including some splendid camping grounds.

The Taupo Visitor Information Centre is located at 30 Tongariro Street. Phone (07) 376-0027.
Email: taupo@thinkfresh.co.nz
Internet: www.laketaupo.co.nz
www.laketauponz.com

Turangi

(49 km from Taupo; 50 km from National Park.)

Turangi owes its origins largely as a workers' village for the nearby hydroelectric schemes, and as such the architecture has a distinctive 'Ministry of Works' flavour. Today Turangi doubles as a holiday resort and trout fishing base. The Turangi Information Centre on Ngawaka Place has much information on the hydroelectricity scheme, while the Tongariro National Trout Centre will be of interest to keen anglers (3.5 km south of Turangi on S.H. 1, open daily between 9.00 am and 4.00 pm).

Waiouru

(111 km from Taupo.)

Waiouru exists primarily to service the nearby military base, and a refuelling stop for the many trucks that ply S.H. 1. A worthy stopping point is the Queen Elizabeth II Army Memorial Museum. The unique architecture of the museum and the realistic displays of our wartime past are superb (even for a pacifist like me!).

Ohakune

(138 km from Taupo; 27 km from Waiouru; 102 km from Wanganui.)

Renowned for its market gardens and particularly tasty carrots, Ohakune is also a winter base for the nearby Turoa skiing resort. There are plentiful walking tracks in the summer, and a ride up the Ohakune Mountain Road to view the Mangawhero waterfalls and the Turoa ski field is well worthwhile.

Contact the Ohakune Visitor Information Office: 54 Clyde Stree. Phone (06) 385-8427

National Park

(35 km from Ohakune; 43 km from Taumarunui; 46 km from Turangi.)

Centre for the Tongariro National Park which in 1991 was accorded World Heritage status in recognition of the unique nature of the surrounding area. Views of the nearby semi-active volcano Mt Ruapehu (2,797m) dominate. Nearby Mt Ngauruhoe (2,291m) last erupted in 1975 and is currently regarded as largely inactive. The park contains notable stands of native forest including red beech, rimu and over 500 other varieties of native flora and fauna.

Whakapapa Village

(Turn-off 9 km east of National Park on S.H. 47; Whakapapa village is 7 km on S.H. 48, and the Whakapapa ski field a further 6 km up the mountain.)

Situated near and somewhat overshadowed by The Grand Chateau luxury hotel, is the Whakapapa Visitor Information Centre from which much information can be gleaned about the Tongariro National Park, including a wide range of bush walks. A skiing museum portrays the history of the nearby Whakapapa ski resort. The 12 km return drive beyond Whakapapa village takes you up to the ski field village, and rates as 5-star riding if the weather conditions are favourable.

Whakapapa Visitor Information Centre:
S.H. 48, Whakapapa. Phone (07) 892-3729.
Email: ruapehuAO@doc.govt.nz

SAFETY POINTS
- Watch for logging trucks and wood chip carriers.
- Beware of frosts and ice on shaded parts of the road in winter.
- Take care on the Makatote Viaduct hairpin bend midway between Tohunga Junction and National Park, especially in winter.

A circuit of Mt Taranaki will give you a variety of vistas featuring this New Zealand volcanic icon, as well as some interesting roads bordering the Egmont National Park. This route can be extended by traversing S.H. 45, 'The Surf Highway', which follows the coastline.

Rating: ☺☺☺ +	
Starting from: New Plymouth (or Wanganui).	
Ending at: New Plymouth (or Wanganui).	
Distance: 140 km return.	
Approximate riding time: 2 to 3 hours	
Usual traffic volumes: Medium on S.H. 3; light elsewhere.	

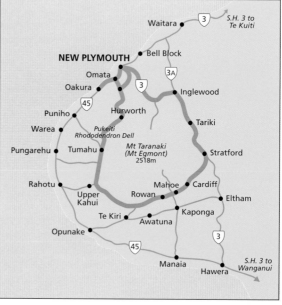

Run Description

- From **New Plymouth*** head south on **S.H. 3** to Inglewood and **Stratford** (40 km).

- At the southern end of Stratford turn right (west) signposted to **Opunake**.

- At **Cardiff** take the left option signposted to Dawson Falls and continue on **Opunake Road** towards Opunake.

- After approx. 25 km take the right fork signposted as **Wiremu Road**.

SAFETY POINT
Beware of frosts and ice on shaded parts of the road in winter.

- Continue on Wiremu Road until it joins **Saunders Road** (58 km).

- At Saunders Road turn right then into **Carrington Road**; follow signs to **Pukeiti* Rhododendron Dell**.

- Continue on Carrington Road via **Hurworth*** into **New Plymouth** (30 km).

*A worthwhile deviation is to turn west on S.H. 45 for 15 km (30 km return) to the seaside holiday resort and surfing mecca of **Oakura***.*

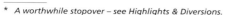

* *A worthwhile stopover – see Highlights & Diversions.*

Highlights & Diversions

New Plymouth

(160 km from Wanganui; 366 km from Hamilton; 163 km from Te Kuiti.)

Mt Taranaki (Mt Egmont) dominates the surrounding countryside.

Very much a rural service town for the rich dairy farmlands that surround Mt Taranaki, in recent times New Plymouth has also become the centre of New Zealand's petroleum and natural gas industry after the Kapuni natural gas field was discovered in 1962. The Taranaki Museum on Ariki Street is well worth a visit, particularly for those interested in the Maori history of the region. The museum houses a superb selection of Te Atiawa wood carvings as well as the fabled anchor stone of the Tokomaru canoe from which it is claimed that early Maori arrived from Polynesia some 600 years ago. For contemporary art lovers the Govett-Brewster Gallery on the corner of Queen and King Streets is a pleasing surprise. Its selection of modern and abstract NZ art is one of the most comprehensive in New Zealand, and seems strangely out of place in the rural hinterland of New Plymouth. Nonetheless it exists, and is a tribute to the area's enlightened art patrons.

The New Plymouth Visitor Information Centre is located on the corner of Leach and Liardet Streets. Phone (06) 759-6080. Email: info@newplymouth.govt.nz Internet: www.newplymouthnz.com

Hawera

(A deviation from this route, 70 km from New Plymouth; 90 km from Wanganui.)

A slice of provincial New Zealand. To my mind no visit to Hawera is complete without visiting the nearby award-winning and privately owned Tawhiti Museum housed in the old Tawhiti cheese factory. This splendid museum uses its remarkable collection of early Maori and colonial memorabilia in novel recreations of past scenes. Check it out: located 4 km north from Hawera on Ohangai Road, open 10.00 am to 4.00 pm Monday to Friday.

The Hawera Visitor Information Office is located at 55 High Street.
Phone (06) 278-8599
Email: visitorinfo@stdc.gov.nz

Pukeiti Rhododendron Dell

The west-facing moist uplands of Mt Taranaki provide an ideal micro climate for rhododendrons and azaleas. Here at Pukeiti over 360 hectares are dedicated to these beautiful shrubs and the result is a world class display at its best from September to November.

Hurworth

A small colonial cottage that was once one of six cottages that housed former NZ Prime Minister, Sir Harry Atkinson. Open 10.00 am to 4.00 pm Wednesday to Sunday (closed noon to 1.00 pm for lunch).

Oakura

(15 km from New Plymouth.)

A small beach resort renowned for its surfing, swimming and wind surfing. Backpacker accommodation is available at The Wave Haven not far from the beach, while the Burnt Toast Diner offers pizzas and snacks.

With thanks to B. Bennetts of Ulysses Taranaki, who recommended aspects of this run.

⓯ *The Ohingaiti Loop*

A deceptively simple and picturesque half-day escape from Palmerston North exploring the upper reaches of the Rangitikei River, providing many challenges and panoramic views as far as Mt Taranaki and Mt Ruapehu. This route can also be accessed from Wellington (allow an extra 290 km or 4 hours, to make a full day). Part of this circuit via Feilding, Cheltenham, Kimbolton, Pemberton to Ohingaiti makes a welcome diversion away from S.H. 1 when travelling either north or south – to and from the Desert Road area and Taupo.

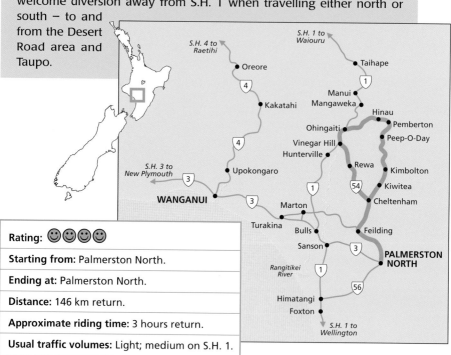

Rating: ☺☺☺☺	
Starting from: Palmerston North.	
Ending at: Palmerston North.	
Distance: 146 km return.	
Approximate riding time: 3 hours return.	
Usual traffic volumes: Light; medium on S.H. 1.	

Run Description

- From **Palmerston North*** head north-west on **S.H. 54** to **Feilding*** (11 km).
- From Feilding continue north on S.H. 54 to **Cheltenham** (13 km).
- At Cheltenham turn right (north-east) following signs to **Kiwitea, Kimbolton*, Peep-o-day, Mangarimu,** to **Pemberton** (34 km).
- Continue on to Pemberton and turn left (west) following signs to **Hinau,** and **Ohingaiti** (24 km).
- At Ohingaiti turn left (south) on **S.H. 1** to return to the **Vinegar Hill*** intersection with S.H. 54 (10 km).
- At Vinegar Hill turn left on **S.H. 54** to Rewa, **Cheltenham, Feilding** and **Palmerston North*** (54 km).

* *A worthwhile stopover – see Highlights & Diversions.*

Highlights & Diversions

Palmerston North

(145 km from Wellington; 74 km Wanganui.)

Palmerston North is a forestry and rural service town which has evolved to become a major centre for agricultural education and research. The emphasis on learning attracts a younger population than is the norm for rural towns and gives Palmerston North a more vibrant selection of bars and cafés, particularly along Broadway Avenue. The arrival of the main north-south railway in 1886 ensured the commercial viability of Palmerston North. The Manawatu River flows nearby and in early history formed the link between Palmerston North and the coast.

The Palmerston North Visitor Information Centre is located in the Civic Complex, in the central square. Phone (06) 354-6593. Email: manawatu.visitor-info@xtra.co.nz

Feilding

(19 km from Palmerston North.)

Primarily a farming service town, Feilding is perhaps more well known to 'motorheads' for the nearby Manfield motor racing circuit. For NZ farmers the huge Feilding sale yards are noted for their stock (farm animal) sales which are held most Fridays.

Ohingaiti

The local hotel is popular amongst motorcyclists.

With thanks to Grant McRae of the BMW Owners Registrar, Rangitikei, who recommended aspects of this run.

Vinegar Hill Junction and Reserve

(8 km north of Hunterville.)

From the Reserve entrance, continue on Rewa Road for 11 km to reach **Stormy Point**, a thoroughly recommended diversion that affords superb views of the Rangitikei River Valley and spectacular surrounding cliffs. The reserve is noted as a picnic and swimming spot.

Kimbolton

(21 km north of Cheltenham.)

A nice stopover for coffee is the old General Store in this charming township. From here to Ohingaiti the road is very challenging.

The old General Store at Kimbolton.

View of the Rangitikei River, near Ohingaiti.

16 *The Rangitaiki Run*

A pleasant one-day romp that can be accessed from either Tauranga, Whakatane, Taupo, Hamilton or Rotorua and offers a diverse range of scenery, from coastal beaches, forests, the Rangitaiki River valley, Rotorua Lakes and the twisty delights of the Kaimai Ranges.

Rating: ☺☺☺	
Starting from: either Tauranga, Whakatane, Rotorua or Taupo.	
Ending at: either Tauranga, Whakatane, Rotorua or Taupo.	
Distance: 305 km return.	
Approximate riding time: 4 to 5 hours return ex Taupo.	
Usual traffic volumes: Moderate. Light in the Rangitaiki River valley.	

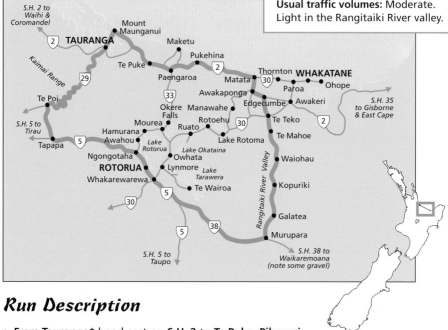

Run Description

- **From Tauranga*** head east on **S.H. 2** to **Te Puke**, **Pikowai**, **Matata**, to **Edgecumbe** (81 km).
- At Edgecumbe turn right (south) onto Te Teko Road to **Te Teko** (9 km).
- At Te Teko turn left (east) to find **Galatea Road**, signposted to **Galatea** and **Murapara** (53 km).
- At Murapara turn right (west) on **S.H. 38** to **Rotorua*** (64 km).
- Continue north-west through Rotorua, picking up **S.H. 5** (to Hamilton) to **Tapapa** (45 km).
- At Tapapa turn right (north), taking the minor road to **Te Poi** (13 km).
- At Te Poi turn right on **S.H. 29** and return to **Tauranga*** (40 km).

* *A worthwhile stopover – see Highlights & Diversions.*

Highlights & Diversions

Tauranga and Mt Maunganui

(80 km from Rotorua; 96 km from Whakatane; 103 km from Hamilton.)

The pleasant seaside retirement town of Tauranga (meaning 'sheltered anchorage') doubles as New Zealand's second largest port. However, the modern commercial hub of Tauranga has a rather more intriguing past. Tauranga's Gate Pa is the site of one of New Zealand's most famous battles, described by historian James Belich in his book *The New Zealand Wars*. In 1864, 1,700 British troops (many from the elite 43rd Light Infantry) and attendant artillery surrounded Gate Pa which contained 230 Maori warriors along with the Ngati-te-Rangi war chief Rawiri Puhirake. After a fierce bombardment which consisted of over 30 tons of shot fired from distances as close as 350 to 800 metres, and lasting over a day and a half, the British attacked. What happened next, highlighted the Maori fighting courage and provided the British troops with a forerunner to World War One trench warfare. As one witness reported: *'The defenders... concealed themselves in chambers dug out in the ground... covered with boughs of trees and earth... (then suddenly) they opened a destructive fire... . The effect was... as if a volcano had suddenly opened beneath their [the British Troop's] feet, and ... many... were killed and wounded at the first discharge.'* (*The Times*, 14 July 1864.) Thus the Maori achieved a remarkable victory against the British forces. The battle of Gate Pa was also notable for the compassion of Heni te Kirikaramu (a.k.a. Jane Foley) who carried water to treat fallen 'enemy' soldiers.

Modern Tauranga shows little of this bloody past, but Gate Pa can be visited on Cameron Road, 5 km from the city centre, and nearby St George's Church hosts several memorials to the battle.

Rotorua

(207 km from Tauranga via this route; 80 km from Tauranga via Te Puke; or 104 km from Hamilton.)

A major tourism icon for the North Island set amidst rolling hills beside a beautiful lake, Rotorua has long been a centre of Maori culture and home to the Arawa tribe, who utilised the naturally occurring thermal pools for bathing, cooking and heating. Early pakeha settlers noted Rotorua's beauty, and were also attracted by its thermal pools and the nearby Pink and White Terraces which, before their destruction by a volcanic eruption in 1886, were considered one of the wonders of the world. The town expanded as a spa resort and in 1908 the imposing Tudor bath house set in the Gardens off Hinemoa Street was built. The bath house now hosts the Rotorua Museum of Art and History. A visit to the famous thermal reserve of Te Whakarewarewa, 2 km south of Rotorua on Fenton Street, is a recommended highlight, as is the nearby Maori Arts and Crafts Institute. Motorcycling speed freaks will no doubt enjoy the Rotorua Luge and the Go-Kart park which is reputed to be one of the best in New Zealand.

The Rotorua Visitor Information Office, Tourism Rotorua, is located at 1167 Fenton Street. Phone (07) 348-5179. Email: gdela@rdc.govt.nz

Fun on the luge track at Rotorua.

A harbour bridge today links Tauranga with the scenic holiday and beach resort of **Mt Maunganui**, and a visit is highly recommended. Mt Maunganui offers a stunning viewpoint, a beautiful beach and a pleasant walk (half hour return). The Mt Maunganui Domain Motor Camp has waterfront sites handy to all amenities.

Contact the Tauranga Visitor & Travel Centre: 95 Willow Street. Phone (07) 578-8103. Email: trgvin@tauranga-dc.govt.nz   Internet: www.visitplenty.co.nz

Geothermal
activity at
Rotorua.

The Rotorua Lakes

Lake Rotoiti: *(15 km N.E. of Rotorua on S.H. 30 to/from Whakatane.)* Famous for trout fishing, this pretty lake also hosts several Maori meeting houses and a camping ground at Okere Falls. The 1.5 km 'Hongi's track' linking Lake Rotoiti and Lake Rotoehu is a recommended walk.

Lake Okataina: *(Look for signs off S.H 30 from/to Whakatane, south of Lake Rotoiti, near Ruato 24 km from Rotorua.)* Arguably the prettiest and most natural of Rotorua's lakes, Lake Okataina is also a favoured trout fishing haven.

Lake Tarawera: *(Turn-off S.E. from Lynmore, 18 km from Rotorua.)* Featuring ancient Maori rock drawings found by following the path left from the jetty. The tranquility of the lake today belies the fearsome 1886 eruption which buried the famous Pink and White Terraces.

Taupo

(381 km from Wellington; 287 km from Auckland; 84 km from Rotorua.)

The North Island's largest lake is actually the crater of several (hopefully) extinct volcanoes; it is the centre of extensive thermal activity which in turn heats the surrounding waters providing ideal spawning grounds for brown and rainbow trout for which the area is noted. A major eruption circa A.D. 135 deposited the ash that today gives rise to the distinctive pumice landscape of the nearby 'desert road'. Today Lake Taupo is a mecca for anglers and water sport enthusiasts and has in the past attracted such notables as Mark Twain. The area abounds in thermal pools with the more popular being De Brett Pools, 0.5 km from Taupo on the Napier route (S.H. 5); and the A.C. Baths, on Spa Road, which originated as a bath house for the Armed Constabulary over 100 years ago. As befits a major tourist attraction, Taupo offers a variety of restaurants and accommodation, including some splendid camping grounds.

The Taupo Visitor Information Centre is located at 30 Tongariro Street. Phone (07) 376-0027.
Email: taupo@thinkfresh.co.nz   Internet: www.laketaupo.co.nz

SAFETY POINT
Beware of frosts and ice on shaded parts of the road in winter.

With thanks to D. Candy of Ulysses Central Plateau, who recommended aspects of this run.

Harrods of Raetihi.
photo: Kennedy Warne

Cruising the Desert Road.
photo: Kennedy Warne

*Twisting hill country
near Kimbolton.*

17 *The Tararua – Puketoi Tour*

The foothills of the Tararua and Puketoi Ranges provide the background to this short escape which can be accessed either from Palmerston North or Wellington.

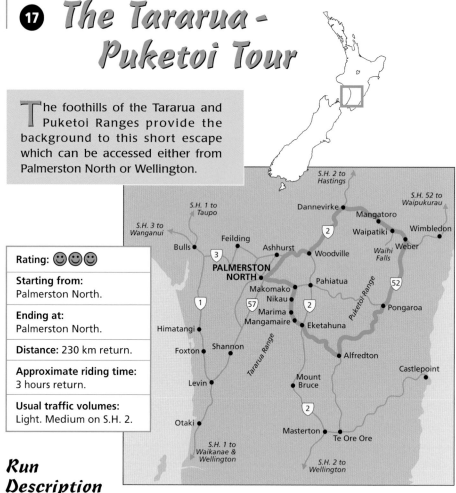

Rating: 😊 😊 😊

Starting from:
Palmerston North.

Ending at:
Palmerston North.

Distance: 230 km return.

Approximate riding time:
3 hours return.

Usual traffic volumes:
Light. Medium on S.H. 2.

Run Description

- From **Palmerston North*** cross the Manawatu River heading south-east towards Massey University and take **S.H. 57** towards Woodville; however, **watch for a minor road on your right** (south-east) signposted from **Aokautere** to the **Pahiatua Track** (8 km).

- From Aokautere follow the Pahiatua Track and signs to **Pahiatua, Nikau, Marima** and **Mangamaire** (31 km).

- After Mangamaire join **S.H. 2**, turn right (south) to **Eketahuna*** (14 km).

- At the southern end of Eketahuna take the minor route to **Alfredton** (18 km).

- From Alfredton continue north-east to **Pongaroa** and **Weber** (69 km).

- At Weber turn left (north-west), following signs on the minor road to **Waipatiki***, **Motea, Mangatoro**, to **Dannevirke*** (35 km). Watch for an optional diversion to view **Waihi Falls***, signposted south at **Waipatiki**.

- From Dannevirke, return on **S.H. 2** to **Palmerston North*** via Woodville (55 km).

* *A worthwhile stopover – see Highlights & Diversions.*

Highlights & Diversions

Palmerston North

(145 km from Wellington; 74 km Wanganui.)

Palmerston North is a forestry and rural service town which has evolved to become a major centre for agricultural education and research. The emphasis on learning attracts a younger population than is the norm for rural towns and gives Palmerston North a more vibrant selection of bars and cafés, particularly along Broadway Avenue. The arrival of the main north-south railway in 1886 ensured the commercial viability of Palmerston North. The Manawatu River flows nearby and in early history formed the link between Palmerston North and the coast. The road through the Manawatu Gorge (15 km N.E. of Palmerston North on S.H. 3) is a challenge for motorcyclists.

The Palmerston North Visitor Information Centre is located in the Civic Complex, in the central square. Phone (06) 354-6593.
Email: manawatu.visitor-info@xtra.co.nz

Pahiatua

(38 km from Palmerston North via this route, or 42 km via S.H.2 & 3.)

Noted for its wider-than-wide main street that still awaits the railway track that was supposed to run down the middle. You are in Tui Beer country here and a diversion to the brewery just 5 km north from Pahiatua at Mangatainoka is possible during business hours in order to sample the legendary 'Tui East India Pale Ale'. A popular swimming and picnicking spot is at the nearby Mangatainoka bridge.

Eketahuna

(24 km from Pahiatua via S.H. 2; 42 km north of Masterton; 144 km from Wellington.)

Eketahuna was once a bush settlement for Scandinavian settlers, along with Dannevirke and Norsewood. Its situation is rather pretty, and the nearby Makakahi River Gorge (signposted 1 km from the town) offers a popular swimming and picnic spot. 16 km south of the town the Mt Bruce National Wildlife Centre breeds rare and endangered native birds (open daily, 9.00 am to 4.00 pm for under $10). It is rated as the best place in NZ to see our native kiwi and also offers tearooms and a picnic area. Phone (06) 375-8004.   www.mtbruce.doc.govt.nz

Dannevirke

(55 km north-east of Palmerston North; 105 km south of Hastings, on S.H. 2.)

As suggested by the name, Dannevirke was originally a Scandinavian settlement, and the name means 'A Dane's work'. The town originated as a bush settlement and owes its origins to the lumber trade which slowly but surely felled the nearby totara forest which was known as 'seventy mile bush'.

Waipatiki and Waihi Falls

(30 km from Dannevirke.)

Signposted near **Waipatiki** these falls are over 18 metres wide, set in a picturesque reserve of native totara and matai, similar to the forests that Dannevirke owes its origins to. A pleasant diversion for a laze and picnic.

Tui Beer country at the Hotel Eketahuna.

SAFETY POINTS
- Take care and look out for farm vehicles and stock (cattle & sheep).
- Take care in windy conditions.

With thanks to Grant McRae of the BMW Owners Registrar, Rangitikei, who recommended aspects of this run.

Waikato and Rotorua Lakes Delight

Rating: ☺☺☺☺

Starting from: either Hamilton, Tauranga, Rotorua or Taupo.

Ending at: either Hamilton, Tauranga, Rotorua or Taupo.

Distance: 300 km.

Approximate riding time: 5 to 6 hours return.

Usual traffic volumes: Moderate.

Featuring the beautiful Waikato River, Lakes Karapiro, Arapuni, Waipapa and Whakamaru plus the thermal delights of the Waikite Valley and Rotorua Lakes. This scenic central North Island run can be easily accessed from either Hamilton, Tauranga, Rotorua or Taupo.

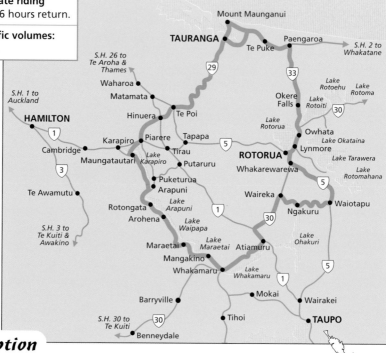

Run Description

- From **Tauranga*** travel south on **S.H. 29** to **Lower Kaimai, Te Poi,** and **Piarere** to the intersection with **S.H. 1** (60 km).
- At Piarere travel towards **Cambridge** and **Hamilton** on S.H. 1 for 2 km.
- On reaching **Lake Karapiro** take the south turn on a minor road signposted to **Maungatautari** and cross Lake Karapiro.
- Continue 4 km and at the Maungatautari turn-off take the left option signposted to Arapuni on **Oreipunga Road**.
- After 13 km take the right turn option signposted **Te Awamutu to Rotongata**.

- At Rotongata take the left option and follow signs to **Mangakino** and **Arohena**, via **Waipapa Road** (46 km).
- From Mangakino continue south on **S.H. 30** to **Whakamaru** (8 km).
- At Whakamaru continue on S.H. 30 to **Atiamuri** (signposted to Taupo) (21 km).
- Near Atiamuri turn north (left) on **S.H. 1** for 6 km. Then turn right (north-east), take **S.H. 30** towards **Horohoro** and **Rotorua**.
- After 18 km on S.H. 30 at Waireka, watch for the **Waikite Valley Road** signposted to **Waikite Valley** (on the right, or south) and follow this road to **Ngakuru, Waikite** and **Waiotapu** (18 km).
- From Waiotapu, take **S.H. 5** to **Whakarewarewa** (and **Rotorua*** if desired) (22 km).
- From Whakawarewa, take **S.H. 30** to **Lynmore, Owhata** (12 km). After Owhata, take the left fork (S.H. 33) to **Mourea, Okere Falls** and **Paengaroa** (34 km).
- From Paengaroa, take **S.H. 2** to **Te Puke** and back to **Tauranga*** (36 km).

* *A worthwhile stopover – see Highlights & Diversions.*

A glimpse of the Waikato River near Atiamuri.

Highlights & Diversions

Tauranga and Mt Maunganui

(80 km from Rotorua; 96 km from Whakatane; 103 km from Hamilton.)

The pleasant seaside retirement town of Tauranga (meaning 'sheltered anchorage') doubles as New Zealand's second largest port. However, the modern commercial hub of Tauranga has a rather more intriguing past. Tauranga's Gate Pa is the site of one of New Zealand's most famous battles, described by historian James Belich in his book *The New Zealand Wars*. In 1864, 1,700 British troops (many from the elite 43rd Light Infantry) and attendant artillery surrounded Gate Pa which contained 230 Maori warriors along with the Ngati-te-Rangi war chief Rawiri Puhirake. After a fierce bombardment which consisted of over 30 tons of shot fired from distances as close as 350 to 800 metres, and lasting over a day and a half, the British attacked. What happened next, highlighted the Maori fighting courage and provided the British troops with a forerunner to World War One trench warfare. As one witness reported: *'The defenders... concealed themselves in chambers dug out in the ground... covered with boughs of trees and earth... (then suddenly) they opened a destructive fire... . The effect was... as if a volcano had suddenly opened beneath their [the British Troop's] feet, and ... many... were killed and wounded at the first discharge.'* (*The Times*, 14 July 1864.) Thus the Maori achieved a remarkable victory against the British forces. The battle of Gate Pa was also notable for the compassion of Heni te Kirikaramu (a.k.a. Jane Foley) who carried water to treat fallen 'enemy' soldiers.

Modern Tauranga shows little of this bloody past, but Gate Pa can be visited on Cameron Road, 5 km from the city centre, and nearby St George's Church hosts several memorials to the battle.

A harbour bridge today links Tauranga with the scenic holiday and beach resort of **Mt Maunganui**, and a visit is highly recommended. Mt Maunganui offers a stunning viewpoint, a beautiful beach and a pleasant walk (half hour return). The Mt Maunganui Domain Motor Camp has waterfront sites handy to all amenities.

Contact the Tauranga Visitor & Travel Centre: 95 Willow Street. Phone (07) 578-8103.
Email: trgvin@tauranga-dc.govt.nz   Internet: www.visitplenty.co.nz

The Waikato River Lakes

The Waikato River is New Zealand's longest river (354 km), and prior to the building of hydroelectricity dams was a major trade and access route for both Maori and pakeha settlers. The river and its lakes are extremely scenic, with many picturesque picnic and fishing spots. The Waikato is world renowned for brown and rainbow trout fishing. The following details the lakes as you travel south:

Lake Karapiro was formed in 1948 when the Karapiro hydro electricity dam was built. The picturesque lake is noted for its calm waters which attracted the 1978 World Rowing Championships. Karapiro continues today as the favoured North Island venue for New Zealand Rowing Championships. At Karapiro a small museum depicts the history of hydroelectric dam building on the Waikato River.

Lake Arapuni, the oldest and second largest of the Waikato hydroelectricity dams, was formed in 1929.

Lake Waipapa was formed in 1961.

Lake Maraetai, formed in 1952, reaches some 76 metres in depth over what must have been a very spectacular valley.

Lake Whakamaru, formed in 1956, extends 22.5 km to Atiamuri.

Some hazards of rural riding: livestock, on-road effluent and railway crossings.

SAFETY POINTS
- Take care with logging trucks and wood chip carriers.
- Beware of frosts and ice on shaded parts of the road in winter.

Rotorua

(208 km from Tauranga via this route; 80 km from Tauranga via Te Puke; or 104 km from Hamilton.)

A major tourism icon for the North Island set amidst rolling hills beside a beautiful lake, Rotorua has long been a centre of Maori culture and home to the Arawa tribe, who utilised the naturally occurring thermal pools for bathing, cooking and heating. Early pakeha settlers noted Rotorua's beauty, and were also attracted by its thermal pools and the nearby Pink and White Terraces which, before their destruction by a volcanic eruption in 1886, were considered one of the wonders of the world. The town expanded as a spa resort and in 1908 the imposing Tudor bath house set in the Gardens off Hinemoa Street was built. The bath house now hosts the Rotorua Museum of Art and History. A visit to the famous thermal reserve of Te Whakarewarewa, 2 km south of Rotorua on Fenton Street, is a recommended highlight, as is the nearby Maori Arts and Crafts Institute. Motorcycling speed freaks will no doubt enjoy the Rotorua Luge and the Go-Kart park which is reputed to be one of the best in New Zealand.

The Rotorua Visitor Information Office, Tourism Rotorua, is located at 1167 Fenton Street.
Phone (07) 348-5179. Email: gdela@rdc.govt.nz

The Rotorua Lakes

Lake Rotoiti: *(15 km N.E. of Rotorua on S.H. 30 to/from Whakatane.)* Famous for trout fishing, this pretty lake also hosts several Maori meeting houses and a camping ground at Okere Falls. The 1.5 km 'Hongi's track' linking Lake Rotoiti and Lake Rotoehu is a recommended walk.

Lake Okataina: *(Look for signs off S.H 30 from/to Whakatane, south of Lake Rotoiti, near Ruato 24 km from Rotorua.)* Arguably the prettiest and most natural of Rotorua's lakes, Lake Okataina is also a favoured trout fishing haven.

Lake Tarawera: *(Turn-off S.E. from Lynmore, 18 km from Rotorua.)* Featuring ancient Maori rock drawings found by following the path left from the jetty. The tranquility of the lake today belies the fearsome 1886 eruption which buried the famous Pink and White Terraces.

With thanks to Roy Watson of Ulysses Tauranga, who recommended aspects of this run.

Wairarapa - Martinborough Wine Trail

A very pleasant one or two-day escape over the fabled Rimutaka Range to the quaint towns of the Wairarapa provides an excuse to sample some of the increasingly popular Martinborough vineyards, and to travel further and enjoy Castlepoint. The wide range of attractive accommodation options in the region favours an overnight diversion.

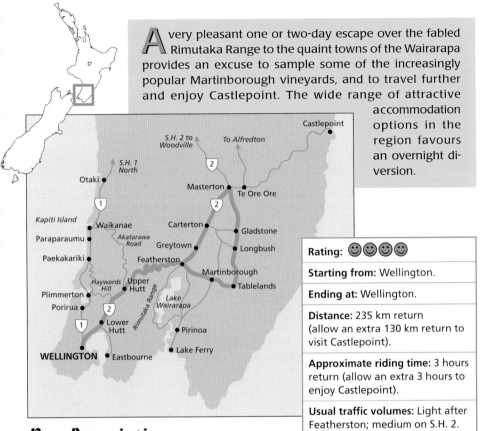

Rating: 😊😊😊😊
Starting from: Wellington.
Ending at: Wellington.
Distance: 235 km return (allow an extra 130 km return to visit Castlepoint).
Approximate riding time: 3 hours return (allow an extra 3 hours to enjoy Castlepoint).
Usual traffic volumes: Light after Featherston; medium on S.H. 2.

Run Description

- From **Wellington*** head north following the harbour on **S.H. 2** to **Lower Hutt** and **Upper Hutt**, and over the Rimutaka Hills to **Featherston*** (65 km).

- At Featherston, turn left (south-east) on S.H. 53 to **Martinborough*** (18 km). *(From Martinborough a diversion south to Lake Ferry is optional and is recommended only in fine, calm weather – allow an extra 70 km return.)*

- From Martinborough continue south-east (initially) on the minor road signposted from the eastern side of the 'square' to Hinakura.

- At Tablelands, 12 km from Martinborough, turn left and follow signs to **Masterton** via Longbush and Gladstone (51 km). *(At Masterton a recommended option is to divert to **Castlepoint*** – allow 130 km return.)*

- From Masterton return to **Wellington*** via S.H. 2, **Carterton*** and **Greytown*** (102 km).

---

* *A worthwhile stopover – see Highlights & Diversions.*

Highlights & Diversions

Te Papa, Museum of New Zealand, Wellington.   photo supplied by Te Papa

Wellington

(658 km from Auckland; 145 km from Palmerston North via S.H. 1.)

New Zealand's high rise harbourside capital city has considerable character and on a fine day is extremely picturesque and benign. Inner city living and cafés are arguably the most vibrant in the country, as is the arts and culture of Wellington. However, on a bad day the weather will test your resolve, and many New Zealanders have their own horror tale of arriving or departing Wellington into one of the gales that 'windy Wellington' is renowned for. The wind is not generated by the hot air of politicians, but rather by Wellington's location on the edge of Cook Strait, the stretch of sea dividing the North and South Islands, which creates a wind funnel effect. For an enjoyable stay in Wellington, pick your weather (or ignore it) and instead revel in the character of this intriguing city.

There is a great variety of accommodation available, with many B&Bs or backpackers providing an opportunity to sample the inner city life. Trekkers Hotel at 216 Cuba Street, phone (04) 385-2153, provides good budget accommodation handy to the best of inner city life. For those seeking motor camp accommodation, it is best to head for the nearby towns of Lower and Upper Hutt (17 km and 30 km north on S.H. 2). Recommended is Hutt Park Holiday Village at 95 Hutt Park Road, Lower Hutt, phone (04) 568-5913, or the Kapiti Coast towns of Paraparaumu or Waikanae (34 km and 45 km north on S.H. 1).

For further information contact the Wellington Visitor Information Centre: 101 Wakefield Street (Civic Square). Phone (04) 802-4860. Email: wgtnvisitors@hotmail.co.nz Internet: www.wellington.net.nz

Featherston

(64 km from Wellington; 127 km from Palmerston North.)

Marking the southern entrance to the Wairarapa region, Featherston grew as a stopping point for coaches after the often arduous climb over the Rimutaka Ranges. (These days, the winding road provides an enjoyable challenge for motorcyclists.) Featherston was originally named Burlings after Henry Burling, who in 1847 opened an accommodation house near the original Maori pa site called Pae-O-Tu-Mokai. The nearby Lake Wairarapa was famed by the Maori for its fishing, particularly for eel. Later the town was more formally named after Dr Isaac Featherston, the first Superintendent of the Wellington province. From 1878, Featherston grew as the railhead for the unique Fell engines which used a third centre rail to climb the 1 in 15 gradient of the Rimutaka Incline. With the opening of the Rimutaka Rail tunnel in 1955, the Fell engines were taken out of service and the remaining engine is now a feature of the Fell Engine Museum, located alongside S.H. 2.

Featherston was known for being the 'hardening up' base camp for NZ soldiers before being sent overseas for service in World War One. Today it is noted for its colonial architecture and antique shops.

Martinborough

(19 km from Featherston; 83 km from Wellington.)

Founded in 1881 by Sir John Martin, Martinborough is noted for its charming central square with streets loyally radiating out in the form of the Union Jack flag of Britain. Once one of New Zealand's earliest sheep farming areas, Martinborough is today noted for its vineyards and fine boutique wineries, of which there are over 20, many within walking distance of the town's central square. The region's Pinot Noir wines have won much international acclaim.

The following are just some of the area's vineyards which welcome visitors:

Ata Rangi: Puruatanga Rd., Martinborough. www.atarangi.co.nz

Chifney Wines: Huangarua Road, Martinborough.

Martinborough Vineyard: Princess Street, Martinborough. www.martinboroughvineyard.co.nz

Murdoch James Estate: Dry River Road (8 km from Martinborough heading towards Lake Ferry). www.martinborough.com

Te Kairanga Wines: Martins Road, Martinborough. www.tkwine.co.nz

Margrain Vineyard: Ponatahi Road, Martinborough.

The restored Martinborough Hotel in the square (www.martinborough.co.nz) offers charming accommodation and a glimpse of our colonial heritage, whilst Margrain Vineyard offers accommodation in a working vineyard. For further accommodation options contact Tourism Wairarapa, P.O. Box 814, Masterton. Phone (06) 378-7373. Email: tourwai@xtra.co.nz

Masterton

(100 km from Wellington; 92 km from Palmerston North.)

Established by Joseph Masters, Masterton and nearby Greytown shared a common agrarian history until the 1870s when the railway reached Masterton (bypassing Greytown), and from that time Masterton has become the commercial centre of the Wairarapa. For further details contact Tourism Wairarapa, P.O. Box 814, Masterton. Phone (06) 378-7373. Email: tourwai@xtra.co.nz
Internet: http://nz.com/travel/wairarapa

Castlepoint

(130 km return diversion from Masterton.)

The resort of Castlepoint rates as a 'must see'. After an entertaining ride to the seaside township, a spectacular beach is revealed. To the south of the main beach and motor camp, a rock shelf stretches precariously out into the sea and is capped by a splendid lighthouse which was built in 1913, and is amongst the tallest in NZ. A walk to the lighthouse reveals a limestone cavern below, and a further sheltered southern bay with a narrow entrance opening to the Pacific Ocean at the base of the spectacular Castle Rock. While the southern bay provides sheltered and safe swimming, the rock 'reef' is noted for its rock fishing; however, great care is needed as rogue waves have claimed lives. Take extreme care, and heed warning signs. Castlepoint motor camp offers camping and some cabins. Fresh fish can sometimes be purchased from local fishermen.

Carterton

(86 km from Wellington; 106 km from Palmerston North.)

A paua shell factory and several nearby vineyards make Carterton worthy of a short stopover, and if visiting during spring you may see why the area is noted as the 'daffodil capital' of New Zealand.

Greytown

(66 km from Wellington; 124 km from Palmerston North.)

Greytown was established in 1853 and is generally regarded as being one of New Zealand's first 'inland' towns. Once a commercial rival to nearby Masterton, the progress of Greytown slowed in the 1870s when it was bypassed by the railway line in favour of Masterton. However, the slower progress has led to the retention of some of the Wairarapa's most charming weatherboard Victorian architecture. There are a range of antique and craft shops as well as some interesting deli-cafés.

SAFETY POINTS
- Take care in windy conditions, particularly over the Rimutaka Hill.
- Take care walking the rock shelves at Castlepoint.
- Take care on single lane sections between Martinborough to Masterton.

Wanganui Round the Block

Heading north from Wanganui the road is full of challenges and twists as it follows the Wanganui River inland. As the road gains altitude the terrain changes and the contrast between the lush coastal lands and the 'desert plateau' becomes apparent. An optional diversion can take you from Ohakune up to the Turoa Ski Field. The return route from Hunterville to Fordell is a gem.

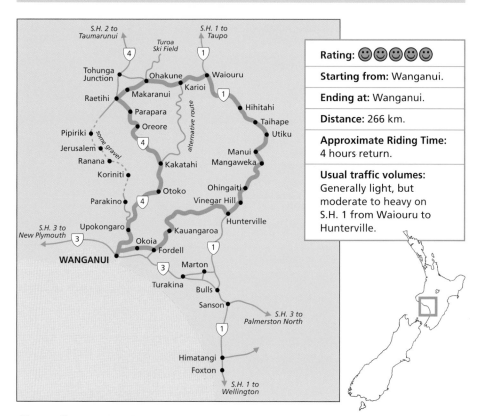

Rating: ☺ ☺ ☺ ☺ ☺

Starting from: Wanganui.

Ending at: Wanganui.

Distance: 266 km.

Approximate Riding Time: 4 hours return.

Usual traffic volumes: Generally light, but moderate to heavy on S.H. 1 from Waiouru to Hunterville.

Run Description

- From **Wanganui*** head north on **S.H. 4** to **Upokongaro, Kakatahi** and **Raetihi*** (91 km).
- At Raetihi turn right (east) on **S.H. 49** to **Makaranui, Ohakune***.
  (Here you can complete an optional diversion to Turoa skifield, 38 km return.)
  Carry on to **Waiouru*** (38 km).

- At Waiouru, turn right (south) on **S.H. 1** to **Taihape***, **Mangaweka** to **Hunterville** (76 km).
- At the northern end of Hunterville turn right (west) on a minor tarsealed road, following signs to **Otairi**; however, after 7 km turn left (south) and follow signs to **Wanganui** via **Kauangaroa**, **Fordell** and **Okoia** (61 km).

* *A worthwhile stopover – see Highlights & Diversions.*

> **SAFETY POINTS**
> - Winter ice on shaded portions of the road can cause danger in the early morning.
> - Some 35 km corners on the Wanganui to Raetihi S.H. 4 are what they say. Take care.

Highlights & Diversions

Wanganui

(195 km north-west of Wellington.)

Before the advent of motorcycles and motorcars the Wanganui River formed a natural highway for water-borne traffic. Legend has it that the Polynesian explorer Kupe discovered the river in A.D. 900 and since that time Maori utilised the Wanganui River as both a food source and a highway to connect the many villages that dotted its banks. The steep cliffs provided easily fortified defensive positions for these villages. With the arrival of the pakeha Wanganui became a flourishing coastal port and grew as a trading centre. Today, while its port has now lost much of its importance Wanganui retains much early colonial charm in a picturesque situation. The Wanganui Regional Museum in Watt Street with its collection of early Maori artifacts is rated one of the best in New Zealand. Art lovers will appreciate a visit to the Sarjeant Gallery by Queens Park, with works by Philip Trusttum and a delightful watercolour by Frances Hodgkins. There is a variety of accommodation and if time allows a river cruise is thoroughly recommended.

The Wanganui Visitor Centre is located at 101 Guyton Street. Phone (06) 349-0508.
Email: info@wanganui.govt.nz

Raetihi

(91 km from Wanganui.)

Once a flourishing saw milling town supplying the upper reaches of the Wanganui River, Raetihi was virtually destroyed by fire in 1918 and survives today as a shadow of its former self, still nourished by logging and farming. River trips on the upper reaches of the Wanganui River can be organised at the motor camp.

Ohakune

(11 km from Raetihi; 27 km from Waiouru.)

Renowned for its market gardens and particularly tasty carrots, Ohakune is also a winter base for the nearby Turoa skiing resort. There are plentiful walking tracks in the summer, and a ride up the Ohakune Mountain Road to view the Mangawhero waterfalls and the Turoa ski field is well worthwhile.

Contact the Ohakune Visitor Information Office:
54 Clyde Stree. Phone (06) 385-8427

Waiouru

(32 km from Raetihi.)

Waiouru exists primarily to service the nearby military base, and a refuelling stop for the many trucks that ply S.H. 1. A worthy stopping point is the Queen Elizabeth II Army Memorial Museum. The unique architecture of the museum and the realistic displays of our wartime past are superb (even for a pacifist like me!).

Taihape

(29 km from Waiouru.)

From its early beginnings as a railway service town, still evident in the architecture, Taihape today is a rural service town. It was made 'famous' by comedian John Clarke (a.k.a Fred Dagg) and hosts an annual 'Gumboot Day' in his honour. Nearby white water rafting on the Rangitikei River offers a challenging and very scenic activity.

Contact the Taihape Visitor Information Centre at 90 Hautapu Street. Phone (06) 388-0350.
Email: rangitikei.tourism@xtra.co.nz

With thanks to John Wakely of Ulysses Wanganui, who recommended aspects of this run.

21 Wellington Round the Block

Rating: ☺☺☺

Starting from: Wellington.

Ending at: Wellington.

Distance: 366 km return.

Approximate riding time: 4 hours return.

Usual traffic volumes: Medium.

Escaping Wellington via S.H. 1 can be a bit of a yawn, as there are limited options. However, this route – more suited to motorcycles – traverses a wide range of terrain and offers interesting diversions: to Castlepoint, the vineyards of Martinborough, or the delights of the Kapiti Coast and Southwards Car Museum.

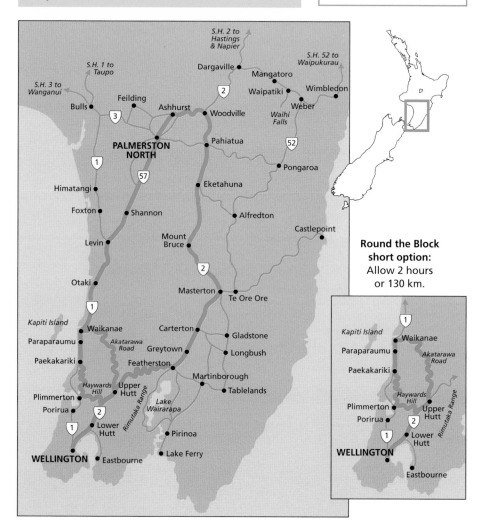

Round the Block short option: Allow 2 hours or 130 km.

Run Description

- From **Wellington*** head north following the harbour on **S.H. 2** to **Lower Hutt** and **Upper Hutt**, and on over the Rimutaka Hills to **Featherston** (65 km).
- Continue via Featherston to **Greytown***, **Masterton*** and **Ekatahuna** to **Pahiatua** and **Woodville** (119 km). *Note: from Pahiatua an alternative route to Palmerston North is via the Pahiatua Track (28 km).*
- At Woodville turn left (west) on **S.H. 3** to **Palmerston North** (27 km).
- From Palmerston North continue south-west on **S.H. 57**, signposted to **Shannon** and **Levin** (48 km).
- From Levin head south on **S.H. 1** to **Otaki** to **Waikanae** (36 km).
- At Waikanae turn inland (south-east) on the minor route signposted to **Upper Hutt** and **Akatarawa** via the Akatarawa River valley (33 km).

  An alternative route is to continue south to Paekakariki, where you turn left (east) and climb up the Paekakariki Hill Road, following signs to Pauatahanui (Whitby) and Lower Hutt via Haywards Hill (20 km).

- From Upper Hutt return to **Wellington** via **S.H. 2** (36 km).

---

* *A worthwhile stopover – see Highlights & Diversions.*

Highlights & Diversions

Wellington

(658 km from Auckland; 145 km from Palmerston North via S.H. 1.)

New Zealand's high rise harbourside capital city has considerable character and on a fine day is extremely picturesque and benign. Inner city living and cafés are arguably the most vibrant in the country, as is the arts and culture of Wellington. However, on a bad day the weather will test your resolve, and many New Zealanders have their own horror tale of arriving or departing Wellington into one of the gales that 'windy Wellington' is renowned for. The wind is not generated by the hot air of politicians, but rather by Wellington's location on the edge of Cook Strait, the stretch of sea dividing the North and South Islands, which creates a wind funnel effect. For an enjoyable stay in Wellington, pick your weather (or ignore it) and instead revel in the character of this intriguing city.

There is a great variety of accommodation available, with many B&Bs or backpackers providing an opportunity to sample the inner city life. Trekkers Hotel at 216 Cuba Street, phone (04) 385-2153, provides good budget accommodation handy to the best of inner city life. For those seeking motor camp accommodation, it is best to head for the nearby towns of Lower and Upper Hutt (17 km and 30 km north on S.H. 2). Recommended is Hutt Park Holiday Village at 95 Hutt Park Road, Lower Hutt, phone (04) 568-5913, or the Kapiti Coast towns of Paraparaumu or Waikanae (34 km and 45 km north on S.H. 1).

For further information contact the Wellington Visitor Information Centre: 101 Wakefield Street, (Civic Square). Phone (04) 802-4860. Email: wgtnvisitors@hotmail.co.nz Internet: www.wellington.net.nz

Martinborough

(19 km from Featherston; 83 km from Wellington.)

Founded in 1881 by Sir John Martin, Martinborough is noted for its charming central square with streets loyally radiating out in the form of the Union Jack flag of Britain. Once one of New Zealand's earliest sheep farming areas, Martinborough is today noted for its vineyards and fine boutique wineries, of which there are over 20, many within walking distance of the town's central square. The region's Pinot Noir wines have won much international acclaim.

The following are just some of the area's vineyards which welcome visitors:

Ata Rangi: Puruatanga Rd., Martinborough. www.atarangi.co.nz

Chifney Wines: Huangarua Road, Martinborough.

Martinborough Vineyard: Princess Street, Martinborough. www.martinboroughvineyard.co.nz

Murdoch James Estate: Dry River Road (8 km from Martinborough heading towards Lake Ferry). www.martinborough.com

Te Kairanga Wines: Martins Road, Martinborough. www.tkwine.co.nz

Margrain Vineyard: Ponatahi Road, Martinborough.

The restored Martinborough Hotel in the square (www.martinborough.co.nz) offers charming accommodation and a glimpse of our colonial heritage, whilst Margrain Vineyard offers accommodation in a working vineyard. For further accommodation options contact Tourism Wairarapa, P.O. Box 814, Masterton. Phone (06) 378-7373. Email: tourwai@xtra.co.nz

Greytown

(66 km from Wellington; 124 km from Palmerston North.)

Greytown was established in 1853 and is generally regarded as being one of New Zealand's first 'inland' towns. Once a commercial rival to nearby Masterton, the progress of Greytown slowed in the 1870s when it was bypassed by the railway line in favour of Masterton. However, the slower progress has led to the retention of some of the Wairarapa's most charming weatherboard Victorian architecture. There is a range of antique and craft shops as well as some interesting deli-cafés.

Carterton

(86 km from Wellington; 106 km from Palmerston North.)

A paua shell factory and several nearby vineyards make Carterton worthy of a short stopover, and if visiting during spring you may see why the area is noted as the 'daffodil capital' of New Zealand.

Masterton

(100 km from Wellington; 92 km from Palmerston North.)

Established by Joseph Masters, Masterton and nearby Greytown shared a common agrarian history until the 1870s when the railway reached Masterton (bypassing Greytown), and from that time Masterton has become the commercial centre of the Wairarapa. For further details contact Tourism Wairarapa, P.O. Box 814, Masterton. Phone (06) 378-7373. Email: tourwai@xtra.co.nz Internet: http://nz.com/travel/wairarapa

SAFETY POINTS
- Take care in windy conditions.
- Take care walking the rock shelves at Castlepoint.

Castlepoint

(130 km return diversion from Masterton.)

The resort of Castlepoint rates as a 'must see'. After an entertaining ride to the seaside township, a spectacular beach is revealed. To the south of the main beach and motor camp, a rock shelf stretches precariously out into the sea and is capped by a splendid lighthouse which was built in 1913, and is amongst the tallest in NZ. A walk to the lighthouse reveals a limestone cavern below, and a further sheltered southern bay with a narrow entrance opening to the Pacific Ocean at the base of the spectacular Castle Rock. While the southern bay provides sheltered and safe swimming, the rock 'reef' is noted for its rock fishing; however, great care is needed as rogue waves have claimed lives. Take extreme care, and heed warning signs. Castlepoint motor camp offers camping and some cabins. Fresh fish can sometimes be purchased from local fishermen.

Eketahuna

(24 km from Pahiatua via S.H. 2; 42 km north of Masterton; 144 km from Wellington.)

Eketahuna was once a bush settlement for Scandinavian settlers, along with Dannevirke and Norsewood. Its situation is rather pretty, and the nearby Makakahi River Gorge (signposted 1 km from the town) offers a popular swimming and picnic spot. 16 km south of the town the Mt Bruce National Wildlife Centre breeds rare and endangered native birds (open daily, 9.00 am to 4.00 pm for under $10). It is rated as the best place in NZ to see our native kiwi and also offers tearooms and a picnic area. Phone (06) 375-8004. www.mtbruce.doc.govt.nz

Kiwi.

Pahiatua

(38 km from Palmerston North via the Pahiatua Track, or 42 km via S.H. 2 & 3; 166 km from Wellington.)

Noted for its wider-than-wide main street that still awaits the railway track that was supposed to run down the middle. You are in Tui Beer country here and a diversion to the brewery just 5 km north from Pahiatua at Mangatainoka is possible during business hours in order to sample the legendary 'Tui East India Pale Ale'. A popular swimming and picnicking spot is at the nearby Mangatainoka bridge.

Woodville

(182 km from Wellington via the Wairarapa; 27 km from Palmerston North.)

Perhaps the name Woodville refers to the 'seventy mile bush' that once attracted early settlers to both fell the timber and clear the bush so that today Woodville is pretty much just another refuelling stop.

Palmerston North

(145 km from Wellington; 74 km Wanganui.)

Palmerston North is a forestry and rural service town which has evolved to become a major centre for agricultural education and research. The emphasis on learning attracts a younger population than is the norm for rural towns and gives Palmerston North a more vibrant selection of bars and cafés, particularly along Broadway Avenue. The arrival of the main north-south railway in 1886 ensured the commercial viability of Palmerston North. The Manawatu River flows nearby and in early history formed the link between Palmerston North and the coast. The road through the Manawatu Gorge (15 km N.E. of Palmerston North on S.H. 3) is a challenge for motorcyclists.

The Palmerston North Visitor Information Centre is located in the Civic Complex, in the central square. Phone (06) 354-6593.
Email: manawatu.visitor-info@nzhost.co.nz

The lighthouse and rock shelves at Castlepoint.

Levin

(94 km north of Wellington.)

Once a railway town during the building of the Wellington to Palmerston North route, Levin is today a rural service town.

Waikanae and Paraparaumu

(58 km north of Wellington.)

The twin attractions of a pretty coastline and a sunny climate has led to the growth of Waikanae which along with nearby Paraparaumu have grown to be suburbs for those wishing to escape Wellington. Southwards Car Museum 3 km south of Waikanae houses one of the most impressive collections of motorcars and motorcycles that you will ever see, and a visit is strongly recommended (open daily 9.00 am to 5.00 pm). Accommodation and dining options are plentiful for those wishing to stay longer in the area. The Paraparaumu Golf Course hosts the NZ Open.

Some of the items on display at Southwards Car Museum, near Waikanae.
photo: Jenny Cooper

Napier,
Art Deco city.

Boat cruise on the Waikato River,
Hamilton.

Gannet colony at Cape Kidnappers,
near Napier/Hastings.
photo: Jenny Cooper

Rating: ☺☺☺☺
Starting from: Wellington.
Ending at: Napier (or vice versa).
Distance: 370 km.
Approximate riding time: 4½ hours one way.
Usual traffic volumes: Light north of Featherston.

This route provides a worthwhile alternative for travel from Wellington to Napier (or vice versa), avoiding much traffic and traversing a wide variety of scenic terrain with twists and turns more suited to the motorcyclist. As an added attraction this route can be treated as a two-day return excursion with the option of returning either via Dannevirke, Palmerston North, Shannon and Levin (allow an additional 325 km or 4 hours), or via Taupo, Turangi and Taihape.

So many good roads and so little time!

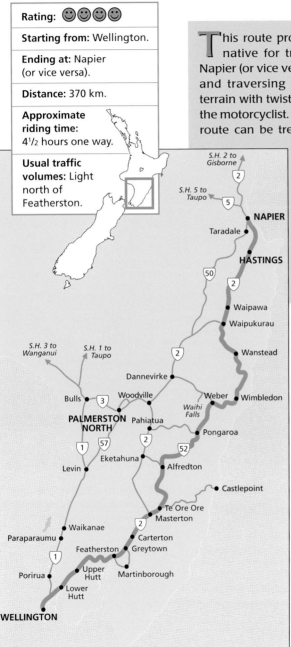

Run Description

- From **Wellington*** head north following the harbour on **S.H. 2** to **Lower Hutt** and **Upper Hutt**, and on over the Rimutaka Hills to **Featherston***, **Greytown*** and **Masterton*** (100 km).

- At Masterton turn right (east) on the minor route signposted to **Te Ore Ore** – also signposted to **Castlepoint** and **Riversdale** (5 km).

Note: Castlepoint* is a recommended 130 km return diversion if time allows.

- At **Te Ore Ore** turn left (north) and follow a minor road to **Alfredton, Pongaroa, Waione, Weber, Ti Tree Point, Wimbledon, Porangahau, Wallingford, Wanstead** to **Waipukurau*** (193 km).
- At Waipukurau, turn right (north-east) on **S.H. 2** to **Hastings*** and **Napier*** (70 km).

* *A worthwhile stopover –*
see Highlights & Diversions.

Highlights & Diversions

Wellington

(658 km from Auckland; 145 km from Palmerston North via S.H. 1.)

New Zealand's high rise harbourside capital city has considerable character and on a fine day is extremely picturesque and benign. Inner city living and cafés are arguably the most vibrant in the country, as is the arts and culture of Wellington. However, on a bad day the weather will test your resolve, and many New Zealanders have their own horror tale of arriving or departing Wellington into one of the gales that 'windy Wellington' is renowned for. The wind is not generated by the hot air of politicians, but rather by Wellington's location on the edge of Cook Strait, the stretch of sea dividing the North and South Islands, which creates a wind funnel effect. For an enjoyable stay in Wellington, pick your weather (or ignore it) and instead revel in the character of this intriguing city.

There is a great variety of accommodation available, with many B&Bs or backpackers providing an opportunity to sample the inner city life. Trekkers Hotel at 216 Cuba Street, phone (04) 385-2153, provides good budget accommodation handy to the best of inner city life. For those seeking motor camp accommodation, it is best to head for the nearby towns of Lower and Upper Hutt (17 km and 30 km north on S.H. 2). Recommended is Hutt Park Holiday Village at 95 Hutt Park Road, Lower Hutt , phone (04) 568-5913, or the Kapiti Coast towns of Paraparaumu or Waikanae (34 km and 45 km north on S.H. 1).

For further information contact the Wellington Visitor Information Centre: 101 Wakefield Street (Civic Square). Phone (04) 802-4860.
Email: wgtnvisitors@hotmail.co.nz
Internet: www.wellington.net.nz

Featherston

(64 km from Wellington; 127 km from Palmerston North.)

Marking the southern entrance to the Wairarapa region, Featherston grew as a stopping point for coaches after the often arduous climb over the Rimutaka Ranges. (These days, the winding road provides an enjoyable challenge for motorcyclists.) Featherston was originally named Burlings after Henry Burling, who in 1847 opened an accommodation house near the original Maori pa site called Pae-O-Tu-Mokai. The nearby Lake Wairarapa was famed by the Maori for its fishing, particularly for eel. Later the town was more formally named after Dr Isaac Featherston, the first Superintendent of the Wellington province. From 1878, Featherston grew as the rail-head for the unique Fell engines which used a third centre rail to climb the 1 in 15 gradient of the Rimutaka Incline. With the opening of the Rimutaka Rail tunnel in 1955, the Fell engines were taken out of service and the remaining engine is now a feature of the Fell Engine Museum, located alongside S.H. 2.

Featherston was known for being the 'hardening up' base camp for NZ soldiers before being sent overseas for service in World War One. Today it is noted for its colonial architecture and antique shops.

Greytown

(66 km from Wellington; 124 km from Palmerston North.)

Greytown was established in 1853 and is generally regarded as being one of New Zealand's first 'inland' towns. Once a commercial rival to nearby Masterton, the progress of Greytown slowed in the 1870s when it was bypassed by the railway line in favour of Masterton. However, the slower progress has led to the retention of some of the Wairarapa's most charming weatherboard Victorian architecture. There is a range of antique and craft shops as well as some interesting deli-cafés.

Carterton

(86 km from Wellington; 106 km from Palmerston North.)

A paua shell factory and several nearby vineyards make Carterton worthy of a short stopover, and if visiting during spring you may see why the area is noted as the 'daffodil capital' of New Zealand.

Masterton

(100 km from Wellington; 92 km from Palmerston North.)

Established by Joseph Masters, Masterton and nearby Greytown shared a common agrarian history until the 1870s when the railway reached Masterton (bypassing Greytown), and from that time Masterton has become the commercial centre of the Wairarapa. For further details contact Tourism Wairarapa, P.O. Box 814, Masterton. Phone (06) 378-7373. Email: tourwai@xtra.co.nz
Internet: http://nz.com/travel/wairarapa

Castlepoint

(130 km return diversion from Masterton.)

The resort of Castlepoint rates as a 'must see'. After an entertaining ride to the seaside township, a spectacular beach is revealed. To the south of the main beach and motor camp, a rock shelf stretches precariously out into the sea and is capped by a splendid lighthouse which was built in 1913, and is amongst the tallest in NZ. A walk to the lighthouse reveals a limestone cavern below, and a further sheltered southern bay with a narrow entrance opening to the Pacific Ocean at the base of the spectacular Castle Rock. While the southern bay provides sheltered and safe swimming, the rock 'reef' is noted for its rock fishing; however, great care is needed as rogue waves have claimed lives. Take extreme care, and heed warning signs. Castlepoint motor camp offers camping and some cabins. Fresh fish can sometimes be purchased from local fishermen.

Waipukurau

(300 km from Wellington via this route; 70 km from Napier.)

'Y-puk' as it is affectionately nicknamed is best approached from the south in order to appreciate its attractive setting. The town signifies the transition from the green interior landscape of Dannevirke to the comparatively dry landscape of the Hawkes Bay area.

SAFETY POINTS
- Take care in windy conditions.
- Take care walking the rock shelves at Castlepoint (a diversion from this route).

Hastings

(350 km from Wellington via this route; 20 km from Napier.)

The southernmost town of Hawkes Bay, Hastings is forever competing with Napier to attract its share of the region's infrastructural assets. Like Napier, Hastings was devastated in a 1931 earthquake and the subsequent rebuilding, influenced by 'art deco' and 'Spanish mission' styles, adds considerable charm to the town. An Art Deco tour guide is available from the Visitor Information Office located in Russell Street, near the Railway Station. Phone (06) 873-5526.
Email: vic@hastingstourism.co.nz

Napier

(370 km from Wellington via this route; 325 km from Wellington via Shannon; 215 km from Gisborne; 143 km from Taupo.)

A jewel of a town well worth a longer stay to maximise enjoyment, Napier occupies a scenic coastal position below Bluff Hill which prior to the 1931 earthquake was an island surrounded by water. The same earthquake led to widespread destruction, and the subsequent rebuilding of Napier in the 1930s has resulted in a town with a unique Art Deco heritage. The equable climate of the area attracts many visitors with the only drawback being a possible shortage of accommodation at peak holiday times. If you are planning to attend the Wine Festival (February) or the Art Deco Weekend (mid-February) it is best to plan well in advance. To absorb the ambience of Napier a visit should not be complete without a cruise along the Marine Parade and a climb to the viewpoint on Bluff Hill (signposted off Lighthouse Road). City centre accommodation is available at the Napier YHA Hostel at 277 Marine Parade, phone (06) 835-7039, or Waterfront Lodge (with off-street motorcycle parking), 217 Marine Parade, phone (06) 835-3429. The centrally located Kennedy Park camping ground is also popular, off Kennedy Road at Marewa. Phone (06) 843-9126.

For further information contact the excellent Napier Visitor Centre, 100 Marine Parade. Phone (06) 834-1911.
Email: info@napiervic.co.nz

23 *Whangamata Wanderings*

Rating: ☺☺☺
Starting from: Hamilton.
Ending at: Hamilton.
Distance: 284 km (including a 12 km return diversion to Thames).
Approximate riding time: 4 hours return.
Usual traffic volumes: Medium and occasionally heavy, particularly during the late December to end of January holiday season when roads between Waihi, Whangamata and Thames require discretion.

Heading North from Hamilton, this one-day escape introduces you to some pretty beaches via the scenic Karangahake Gorge, with contrasting twists that will test your riding skills.

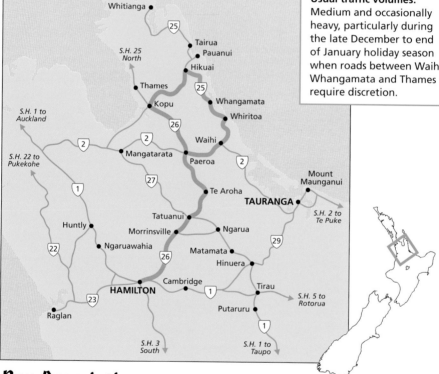

Run Description

- Head north east from **Hamilton*** on **S.H. 26** to **Morrinsville***, **Te Aroha*** and **Paeroa*** (75 km).
- At Paeroa take **S.H. 2** to **Waihi*** (21 km).
- From Waihi take **S.H. 25** to **Whangamata*** (29 km).
- From Whangamata continue on **S.H. 25** and **S.H. 25A** to **Kopu** (45 km). Here you can divert 6 km north on S.H. 25 to **Thames***, or carry on.
- From Kopu head south on **S.H. 26**, returning to **Hamilton*** via Te Aroha and Morrinsville (102 km).

* *A worthwhile stopover – see Highlights & Diversions.*

Highlights & Diversions

Hamilton

(129 km south of Auckland.)

Initially a military settlement on the banks of the Waikato River, Hamilton is now New Zealand's fourth largest city, and a major trading centre for the rich agricultural area of the Waikato. To gain an insight to the region's rich history and the controversial Maori Wars, spend some time at the Waikato Museum of Art and History on the corner of Victoria and Grantham Streets. Hamilton boasts plentiful accommodation and a wide range of restaurants.

The Hamilton Visitor Information Centre is found on the corner of Ward and Angelsea Streets.
Phone (07) 839-3580.
Email: hamiltoninfo@wave.co.nz

Morrinsville

(32 km from Hamilton.)

Centre of the rich and fertile surrounding dairy farm district, Morrinsville is largely a rural service town.

Te Aroha

(52 km from Hamilton.)

Once an elegant Victorian spa town nestled under the Kaimai Ranges, Te Aroha is today primarily another rural service town, but some of its former charm remains. A visit to the Te Aroha domain allows the visitor to imagine its former elegance via the now restored bath-houses.

Paeroa

(75 km from Hamilton.)

The town is 'World famous in New Zealand' for the mineral waters that give rise to the distinctively flavoured soft drink 'Lemon & Paeroa'. A large bottle of the drink appropriately adorns the southern approach to the town; however, as a sign of the times, the drink is now bottled in Auckland. The Historical Maritime Park (4 km north on S.H. 2) is worth a visit to glimpse Paeroa's past prominence as a river port.

SAFETY POINT
Summer holiday crowds can dominate the Coromandel roads. Take care.

With thanks to Greg Bailey of Ulysses Hamilton, who recommended aspects of this run.

Waihi

(96 km from Hamilton; 21 km from Paeroa.)

An 1870s gold rush town, Waihi was the base of the famous Martha Mine which in its heyday produced so much gold that the company's dividends were often 80% per annum. It is claimed that over eight million ounces of gold came from the mine during its 66 years of operations. In 1988 a new gold mine at Martha Hill started producing gold and today produces over 70,000 ounces of gold per annum along with considerable silver ore. The Waihi Gold Mining Company conducts tours over the mine on weekdays. Phone (07) 863-8192 for bookings.

A 25 km return trip to nearby Waihi Beach is well worthwhile. (Look for signs after the western exit to the town heading to Tauranga on S.H. 2.)

The Waihi Visitor Information Centre is located in Seddon Street. Phone (07) 863-6715

Whangamata

(125 km from Hamilton; 29 km from Waihi.)

A sprawling beach side holiday resort, renowned for its white sand and surfing. The Visitor Information Centre is located on Port Road, phone (07) 865-8340. Accommodation is usually plentiful, but make sure you book ahead in the peak holiday season, particularly around New Year's Eve. Gingers Health Food & Café on Port Road is a worthwhile stopping place.

Thames

(170 km from Hamilton via this route; 45 km from Whangamata.)

Providing a gateway to the scenic Coromandel, the architecture of Thames shows its rich gold mining heritage. The Historical Museum on the corner of Cochrane and Pollen Streets is worth a visit in order to appreciate the town's history. The Dickson Holiday camp 3 km north of Thames provides a good overnight stopping point.

On approaching Thames keep an eye out for signs denoting Totara Pa Cemetery (2.5 km south of Thames). This hill-top vantage point provides excellent views of Thames, and is the site of a bloody battle between Hongi Hika and the Ngati Maru tribe.

For further information contact the Visitor Information Office, 206 Pollen Street.
Phone (07) 868-7284. Email: thames@ihug.co.nz

Crossing Cook Strait

Separating the North and South Islands of New Zealand, the waters of Cook Strait must be crossed by ferry if you plan to motorcycle tour both islands. However, the Cook Strait has a deserved reputation for rough seas, and if you are even remotely likely to encounter strong winds then steps should be taken to protect your motorcycle from damage.

Even before you park your motorcycle inside the ferry, there are dangers to be faced. The steel ramps leading onto the ferry can get very slippery from sea spray, rain, diesel and oil spills. Traction is limited, and any braking must be done with extreme caution.

Secondly, cargo decks and entrance ramps may be grooved with railway tracks, which can be deadly traps for motorcycle wheels. Take maximum care.

The ferry staff should offer to strap your motorcycle down, and such strapping usually consists of a large ratchet strap or rope with hooks extending over the seat and fastened to the deck at about 45 degrees out from the centre of the motorcycle. With a bit of luck, padding will be placed over the seat to protect it. The motorcycle is usually placed on its centre stand. Motorcyclists have experienced a wide variation in staff skills and attention to motorcycles, so the following steps are recommended:

1. Instead of using the centre stand, place your motorcycle on its side stand. This gives the motorcycle three points of contact with the steel deck rather than two and is considered more stable.

2. Either leave your motorcycle in first gear or, preferably, strap your hand brake so that it is firmly 'on'. A strong rubber band, an old piece of inner tube (approx. 30mm wide), or even a belt will suffice.

3. Once placed on the side stand, four straps are recommended – two at each end of the motorcycle, fastening the front and rear forks to the deck much as guy ropes fasten a traditional tent. Experienced travellers carry their own adjustable webbing or ratchet straps for this task. When tightening the webbing straps it is advisable to take weight off the side stand by almost pulling the motorcycle upright.

4. The ferry staff may still add their central seat strap for safety, but make sure the seat is protected from damage or pinching.

5. Lastly, make sure all valuables are removed from the motorcycle and taken with you to the passenger area. All saddle bags should be locked, or securely fastened to prevent pilfering.

With a bit of luck, the above should see your beloved motorcycle safely across the Cook Strait.

South Island

Distances Between South Island Main Centres
(in kilometres)

Source: Ministry of Transport Data

	Alexandra	Blenheim	Christchurch	Cromwell	Dunedin	Franz Josef	Geraldine	Gore	Greymouth	Haast	Invercargill	Kaikoura	Milford Sound	Nelson	Oamaru	Picton	Queenstown	Te Anau	Tekapo	Timaru	Twizel	Wanaka	Westport
Alexandra	0	786	455	31	190	370	315	136	550	231	202	657	370	870	223	795	93	270	227	300	169	86	651
Blenheim		0	308	733	670	486	446	821	324	643	887	129	1081	116	555	28	794	960	534	471	592	745	264
Christchurch			0	410	360	390	138	513	250	535	570	185	773	424	247	350	486	650	226	163	284	424	347
Cromwell				0	220	342	273	167	526	200	233	607	336	845	228	761	62	217	196	268	138	55	639
Dunedin					0	560	232	144	563	421	212	545	471	786	115	698	283	290	303	199	261	276	620
Franz Josef						0	481	509	177	148	575	550	678	469	506	531	404	560	485	493	427	287	277
Geraldine							0	387	329	431	449	321	635	562	123	474	346	516	88	35	146	286	432
Gore								0	704	367	66	696	260	937	266	849	169	139	363	350	316	222	804
Greymouth									0	317	769	338	860	290	443	352	583	739	417	352	475	469	101
Haast										0	433	710	539	609	376	671	262	418	343	418	285	145	437
Invercargill											0	762	278	1003	332	915	187	188	429	416	371	285	869
Kaikoura												0	956	245	430	157	669	835	409	346	467	607	340
Milford Sound													0	1146	526	1108	291	121	532	610	474	394	951
Nelson														0	671	117	693	1025	650	587	708	587	226
Oamaru															0	583	319	404	188	84	146	231	580
Picton																0	822	988	562	499	620	773	280
Queenstown																	0	170	258	335	200	117	664
Te Anau																		0	428	489	370	273	830
Tekapo																			0	104	58	198	559
Timaru																				0	162	273	497
Twizel																					0	140	617
Wanaka																						0	558
Westport																							0

Great Escapes

Collingwood
Takaka
Motueka
Karamea
NELSON
Kohatu
Havelock
26
Picton
Blenheim
25
Westport
Murchison
St Arnaud
46
45
Reefton
Springs Junction
Hanmer Springs
28
Kaikoura
GREYMOUTH
33
29
Culverden
Hokitika
34
44
Waipara
Arthur's Pass
Rangiora
35
43
Sheffield
Franz Josef Glacier
Mt Hutt
CHRISTCHURCH
Fox Glacier
27
24
Akaroa
Mount Cook
30
Ashburton
Haast
Lake Pukaki
Tekapo
Geraldine
Fairlie
Temuka
Lake Benmore
TIMARU
31
Lake Wanaka
Lake Hawea
Omarama
Milford Sound
Wanaka
38
37
OAMARU
QUEENSTOWN
Lake Wakatipu
Ranfurly
Lake Te Anau
Cromwell
36
Alexandra
Te Anau
39
Palmerston
Lake Manapouri
Middlemarch
Manapouri
32
DUNEDIN
Lumsden
40
41
Milton
Gore
Balclutha
INVERCARGILL
42
Bluff
Stewart Island

SOUTH ISLAND TOURS

Akaroa - Banks Peninsula Loop

For a quick escape from Christchurch, the Banks Peninsula offers great contrasts, great scenery and challenging riding. The only draw-back is that everyone else may have the same idea, and during weekends things can get a bit busy. Care is needed.

Run Description

- From **Christchurch*** city centre, head to **Moorhouse Avenue** and the intersection with **Lincoln Road** (Hagley Park East). Follow Lincoln Road and the signs to **Akaroa (S.H. 75)**, **Halswell**, and **Taitapu**.

  - Continue with the Port Hills on your left, skirting Lake Ellesmere until you turn inland to the picturesque town of **Little River** (approximately 56 km from Christchurch).

  - Carry on to **Akaroa*** (83 km from Christchurch).

Return to Christchurch:

- Return to **Little River** and back towards Taitapu.

- After Lake Ellesmere, look for a turn-off right (north) to **Gebbies Pass**, **Governors Bay** and Lyttelton.

- Turn right (north) and follow the Gebbies Pass route towards **Lyttelton***.

Optional Return Route:

At the Summit of Gebbies Pass you can turn left and follow the summit road back to Christchurch with stunning views and twists; however, it can be exposed to winds.

Otherwise, continue towards Lyttelton via the scenic Governors Bay.

- From Lyttelton you have the option of heading back to **Christchurch** either through the Lyttelton tunnel, or via Dyers Pass (from Governors Bay), or Evans Pass (from Lyttelton); watch for the respective signs.

* *A worthwhile stopover – see Highlights & Diversions.*

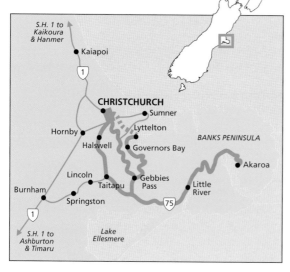

Rating:	☺ ☺ ☺ ☺
Starting from: Christchurch.	
Ending at: Christchurch.	
Distance: 170 km return.	
Approximate riding time: 3 to 4 hours return.	
Usual traffic volumes: Medium. Can be heavy on fine weekends during summer.	

Akaroa Harbour.

Highlights & Diversions

Christchurch

New Zealand's 'Garden City', Christchurch has a distinctly English feel, perhaps due in part to the Avon River which meanders through the city, and the influence of early settlers determined to replicate their home country. Major attractions include the old university Arts Centre on Worcester Boulevard (www.artscentre.org.nz), the nearby Canterbury Museum in Rolleston Avenue, and the bustling restaurant precinct around Oxford and Hereford Streets.

Christchurch Visitor Information Office:
Cnr Worcester Street and Oxford Terrace.
Phone (03) 379-9629.
Email: info@christchurchnz.net
Internet: www.christchurchnz.net

Akaroa

(82 km from Christchurch.)

The sheltered and abundant waters of Akaroa Harbour attracted Maori settlers well before the arrival of the pakeha. The Ngai Tahu's pa site on Onawe Island is still evident, and its chilling history is well documented in Akaroa's interesting museum. European settlement resulted in a French-flavoured town with charming architecture, and a very scenic outlook over the sheltered harbour surrounded by verdant hills. A favoured weekend getaway for Christchurch residents, Akaroa boasts a good selection of craft shops, restaurants, cafés, bars and is an attractive stopover. For a wine and cheese diversion try the Barry's Bay Cheese factory followed by a visit to French Farm vineyard.

If travelling north to south, Akaroa can make an interesting and alternative stopover to Christchurch.

Akaroa Visitor Information Office: 80 Rue Lavaud.
Phone (03) 304-8600. Email: akaroa.info@clear.net.nz.
Internet: http:nz-holiday.co.nz/akaroa

French Farm

(14 km from Akaroa.)

Set in a picturesque valley the French Farm Winery offers fine food and wine in rather exclusive surroundings.

Governors Bay

(10 km from Lyttelton; 21 km from Christchurch.)

An appealing harbour-side town, with lush market gardens and orchards. The Governors Bay Café & Bar at 79 Main Road is a welcome visit.

Lyttelton

(10 km from Christchurch.)

The sea port that serves Christchurch, and the point of arrival for the early settlers in 1850, Lyttelton has a charm which seems to survive despite the reclamation and commercial activity associated with the modern port and railway. There is an assortment of good cafés, pubs and antique or craft shops well worth closer inspection. The Volcano Café and Lava Bar give a hint to the origins of Banks Peninsula as well as providing funky food and surroundings.

Blenheim
Round the Block

Rating: ☺☺☺☺☺
Starting from: Blenheim.
Ending at: Blenheim.
Distance: 648 km return (including an 18 km diversion to Hanmer Springs).
Approximate riding time: 8 hours return. Best as a two day trip.
Usual traffic volumes: Generally light on all roads.

The Blenheim Round the Block run offers superb variety in both roads and scenery with a mixture of mountain, native bush, forest, and coastal scenery. There are opportunities to soak your weary bones in several thermal springs along the route.

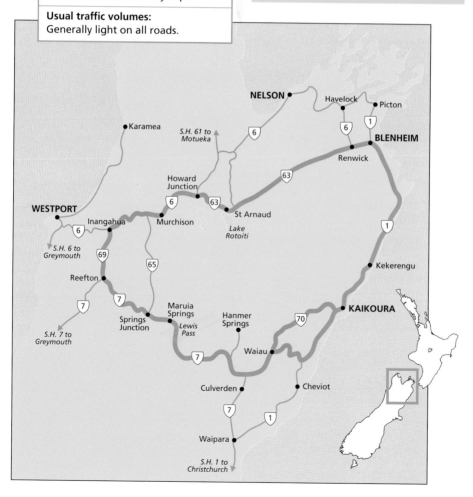

Run Description

- Depart **Blenheim*** on **S.H. 63** signposted to **Renwick, St Arnaud*, Lake Rotoiti*** and carry on until your reach S.H. 6 at Howard Junction (127 km).
- Follow **S.H. 6** to **Murchison** and **Inangahua** (214 km).
- After Inangahua turn left (south) on **S.H. 69** to **Reefton*** (248 km).
- Left at Reefton on **S.H. 7** to **Springs Junction, Maruia Springs*, Lewis Pass*** and on to the Hanmer Springs junction.
- Here you can **divert to Hanmer Springs***, 18 km return, or carry on S.H. 7 for 24 km past the Hanmer Springs turn off and turn left (north) to **S.H. 70** to **Waiau***.
- At Waiau either turn right via the **Leader Valley** to **S.H. 1** and thence to **Kaikoura*** (79 km to Kaikoura via this option), or another scenic and less crowded option is to carry on to Kaikoura via **S.H. 70** (83 km).
- From **Kaikoura** return to **Blenheim*** on **S.H.1**.

* A worthwhile stopover – see Highlights & Diversions.

Highlights & Diversions

Tophouse

(97 km from Blenheim; 4 km before St Arnaud.)

An historic old cob-walled former coach stop and hotel now providing great coffee, and scones with lashings of fresh cream. Take care on gravel approaches.

Lake Rotoiti and St Arnaud

(101 km from Blenheim via S.H. 63.)

St Arnaud acts as headquarters for the Nelson Lakes National Park, and the Department of Conservation visitor centre is a useful stopping point for information. There are numerous camping sites and accommodation houses, plus some pleasant lakeside walks. However, insect repellent should be carried if you are planning to stopover here.

Reefton

(248 km from Blenheim via S.H. 63 & 6.)

Once a wealthy gold-mining town, nicknamed 'Quartzopolis' for its link to the mineral quartz and resulting gold, Reefton is now a local centre for coal mining and farming set in a picturesque valley junction. Links to the mining past are never far away: the nearby hills are littered with old gold mines and the 1886 School of Mines can still be found in its original building in Shiel Street. Indicative of its early gold wealth, Reefton gained fame as being the first New Zealand town to be lit by electricity in 1888.

SAFETY POINTS

- Ice on the shaded areas and high spots of the road during winter.
- Take care with the one-lane bridges between St Arnaud and Howard Junction. Each of the 3 bridges follows rather long straights and is accompanied by tight corners.
- Insect repellent should be carried for any stopovers west of the Alps and in the Nelson Lakes National Park.

Maruia Springs

(308 km from Blenheim.)

An opportunity to relax from your travels in hot mineral pools surrounded by alpine splendour. Clear starry nights make an overnight diversion here hard to beat. There are several good bush walks nearby.

Lewis Pass

Climbing to a height of 863m above sea level, this scenic twisting and undulating route follows that used by the Maori Ngai Tahu tribe as they travelled to and from the West Coast in search of the precious pounamu (greenstone or jade). The area offers many pleasant picnic spots and bush walks. The pass is named after the explorer Henry Lewis, who first detailed the route for other European settlers in 1860.

Hanmer Springs

(An 18 km return diversion from S.H. 7; 376 km from Blenheim via S.H. 7 & 69 & 6 & 63; 133 km from Christchurch.)

A leafy spa town with public thermal pools to ease any aches and pains. Set amongst forest clad foot-hills, there are plenty of local walks – at their best in autumn. A charming town, well worth the diversion. The Forest Trust Motor Camp on Jacks Pass Road offers cabins from $15.00 per night.

Sampling crayfish at Kaikoura.
photo: Len Chilcott

Hurunui Visitor Information Centre: Amuri Drive. Phone 0800-733-426. Email: hanvin@nzhost.co.nz

Waiau

(80 km from Kaikoura; 126 km from Christchurch.)

The Waiau Hotel is a favoured watering-hole for motorcyclists, while the old (1878) cob cottage and museum is worth a visit.

Kaikoura

(516 km from Blenheim via Lewis Pass, Reefton, etc; 132 km from Blenheim via S.H. 1; 196 km from Christchurch (via S.H.1); 129 km from Blenheim.)

Named by early Maori who recognised the bountiful sea harvest potential of the area ('kai' meaning food, and 'koura' meaning crayfish). The importance of the sea catch continues in numerous tasty restaurants such as The Mussel Boys and Lobster Inn. Early European settlers plundered the then-plentiful seals and whales, driving them close to extinction. Today, as a reward for more sympathetic wildlife conservation practices, Kaikoura has evolved to be the heart of a whale and dolphin watching industry (www.whalewatch.co.nz or www.dolphin.co.nz). While fishing and farming are still important to the local economy, they are rapidly being overtaken by the growth of tourism. The Kaikoura peninsula with its early Maori pa site, and port (south of the main town) is well worth exploring. The motor camp at Puketa on South Bay, 2 km south of Kaikoura, is a popular stopover.

Kaikoura Visitor Information Centre:
Phone (03) 319-5641. Email: info@kaikoura.co.nz
Internet: www.kaikoura.co.nz

Kekerengu

(Mid way between Kaikoura and Blenheim; 60 km from Kaikoura; 69 km from Blenheim.)

A favoured stopover for motorcyclists travelling the scenic Kaikoura Coast is 'The Store', located on the coast side of the road and well worth the stop for a good cup of tea, fine food, wines or ale which are served in superb surroundings overlooking the beach.

Blenheim

(28 km from Picton; 138 km from Nelson (via Picton); 116 km from Nelson via S.H. 6.)

Blessed with more sunshine hours than almost any other region of New Zealand, Blenheim has won worldwide recognition as a major wine producing region (and more recently for olive oil). A ride along Rapaura Road, linking S.H. 6 (Nelson) to S.H. 1 (Picton) just north of Blenheim, will introduce you to just a few leading vineyards such as Hunters Wines, Huia Wines and Shingle Peak. The rich Wairau plains are now dotted with wineries, and their associated restaurants. The local information office, or indeed any winery, will give you a 'wine trail' map to explore the area by, and what better way to spend a day or two. The annual Marlborough Wine and Food Festival attracts hordes during the second weekend in February and provides a great excuse for a visit, but make sure you have arranged accommodation beforehand.

Blenheim Visitor Information Centre:
2 High Street. Phone (03) 578-9904.
Internet: www.marlbourgh.co.nz
www.nz-wine.co.nz/marlborough/festival

With thanks to John Mears of Ulysses Marlborough who recommended aspects of this run.

Blenheim and Nelson Round the Block

The Blenheim and Nelson Round the Block run offers superb variety in both roads and scenery with a mixture of mountain, native bush, forest, and coastal scenery. There are numerous opportunities for stopovers.

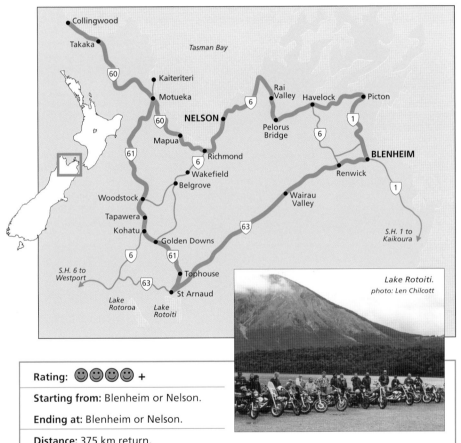

Lake Rotoiti.
photo: Len Chilcott

Rating: ☺☺☺☺ +

Starting from: Blenheim or Nelson.

Ending at: Blenheim or Nelson.

Distance: 375 km return.
(A return diversion to Takaka and Collingwood will add 3 leisurely hours and 160 km.)

Approximate riding time: 5 hours return.

Usual traffic volumes: Light to medium; occasionally heavy from Motueka to Nelson, and between Nelson and Havelock. Traffic between Picton and Blenheim is often heavy. The Takaka Hill can be very busy during holidays, particularly at the time of the annual 'Gathering' (4 to 5 days either side of New Year's Eve).

Run Description

(To start this route from Nelson, follow instructions from the section marked #.)

- Depart **Blenheim*** on **S.H. 63** signposted to **Renwick, St Arnaud, Lake Rotoiti**.
- At the old **Tophouse** (97 km from Blenheim) turn right (north) following **S.H. 61** signs to **Tapawera** (and Nelson).
- At Golden Downs turn left (signposted to **Tapawera**.)
- Continue north on **S.H. 61** to **Tapawera, Woodstock** and on to **Motueka***.
- From Motueka follow **S.H. 60** via **Richmond**. Then left to **S.H. 6** and **Nelson***.
- # Travel out of Nelson following the coast before turning inland to the **Rai Valley, Pelorus Bridge*** and **Havelock** on **S.H. 6**.
- Just after Havelock turn left and take the scenic coastal route to **Picton***.
- From Picton follow **S.H. 1** back to **Blenheim***.

* *A worthwhile stopover – see Highlights & Diversions.*

> **SAFETY POINTS**
> - Ice on the shaded areas and high spots of the road during winter.
> - Traffic congestion on the Takaka Hill at holiday times.

Highlights & Diversions

Tophouse

(97 km from Blenheim; 4 km before St Arnaud.)

An historic old cob-walled former coach stop and hotel now providing great coffee, and scones with lashings of fresh cream. Take care on gravel approaches. An alternative stopover is nearby picturesque Lake Rotoiti and St Arnaud (4 km from Tophouse).

Motueka

(190 km from Blenheim via this route.)

Set in a fertile valley with an equable climate, Motueka is blessed with an abundance of fruit. Major crops include hops, kiwi fruit, raspberries and apples. Accommodation is plentiful, but during January reservations are recommended. During the fruit season there are ample casual employment opportunities.

Motueka Visitor Information Centre: Wallace Street.
Phone (03) 528-6543. Email: mzpvin@xtra.co.nz

Mapua

Situated just off S.H. 60 between Nelson and Motueka, the coastal village of Mapua offers a nice restaurant and tavern opposite the dairy on Aranui Road, but is better known for the Mapua Leisure Park. The Park provides sheltered camping by a beautiful estuary and is a good base from which to explore the region, although its 'clothes optional' choice will either repel or attract depending on your inclinations. Keep an open mind and you will find one of the best camping grounds in the region.   www.nelsonholiday.co.nz

Kaiteriteri Diversion

(28 km return diversion from Motueka.)

From Motueka take S.H. 60 towards Riwaka and Takaka. Just past Riwaka at the foot of the Arthur Range (7 km from Motueka) turn right (north) to Kaiteriteri, another 7 km away. Kaiteriteri is noted for its pristine white beaches, surrounding bush-clad hills and superb bathing and fishing. There is a motor camp site here, and a stopover is highly recommended outside of the crowded January period. Bookings are advisable. A further 9 km will bring you to Marahau where there is a more peaceful motor camp and cabins, as well as the entrance to the famed Abel Tasman Park walk.

Takaka and Golden Bay Diversion

(160 km return; allow an extra 3 hours.)

Another wonderful diversion, the tortuous Takaka Hill offers stunning 5-star riding and scenery as the road climbs 800 metres above sea level before dropping down to Upper Takaka and on to Golden Bay via a series of tight hairpin bends. Take care as this route can be very busy during January. Beautiful coastal scenery awaits as you approach Golden Bay and Collingwood. A stop at the Waikoropupu (or Pupu) Springs is highly recommended (12 km north-west from Takaka). At Collingwood there is a motor camp with cabins.

The Gathering

Set high on Takaka Hill, The Gathering is a 3-day dance rave which draws up to 10,000 young hopefuls to the area and clogs the road for 4 to 5 days each side of New Year's Eve.

Nelson

(237 km from Blenheim via Tophouse and Motueka; 138 km from Blenheim via the return route.)

Surrounded by bush-clad hills and blessed by a kind climate, Nelson offers a delightful mix of cafés, arts and crafts, combined with quaint old buildings and an attractive sea-side location. Nelson is also home to a thriving fishing industry, and an opportunity to sample some of its delights should not be missed. The Suter Art Gallery at 208 Bridge Street is one of my favourite galleries, and the Nelson Provincial Museum is full of interesting items. Favoured refreshment stops are the various restaurants and cafés in Trafalgar Street (unfortunately the favourite Chez Eelco coffee house has shut its doors after 38 years); however, the legacy remains. Another option to try is The Honest Lawyer (for the name alone!) at 1 Point Road, Monaco, Nelson.

Nelson Visitor Information Centre:
Cnr Trafalgar and Halifax Streets. Phone (03) 548-2304.
Email: vin@tourism-nelson.co.nz

Pelorus Bridge

(19 km from Nelson.)

A spectacular river crossing point well worth a stopover. The river offers a refreshing summer swimming spot, and there are numerous bush walks and a very good café, plus a nearby camping ground. Take care to avoid wasps and mosquitoes.

With thanks to John Mears of Ulysses Marlborough and Peter Shaw of Ulysses Nelson who recommended aspects of this run.

Havelock

(75 km from Nelson; 63 km from Blenheim via Picton and the coastal route.)

A picturesque village set on the shores of the Pelorus Sounds, Havelock is now the centre of a large and prosperous green-lipped mussel sea farming industry. As a result there are some lovely cafés which specialise in this delicacy. The Rutherford Youth Hostel set in the old Havelock school is a good venue for a stopover.

Picton

(110 km from Nelson; 28 km from Blenheim.)

The arrival and departure point for the majority of the Cook Strait ferries, Picton is a busy little town with considerable charm. As a necessary stopover point for those crossing the Cook Strait to Wellington, it boasts numerous cafés and plentiful accommodation of all types. Currently there are plans for Tranz Rail to shift its ferry terminus to Clifford Bay (30 km east of Blenheim) which will shorten travelling times by up to an hour, but deprive Picton of much through traffic. As yet, no completion date has been set for these plans.

Picton Visitor Information Centre is located on the foreshore. Phone (03) 573-7477.

Blenheim

(28 km from Picton; 138 km from Nelson (via Picton); 116 km from Nelson via S.H. 6.)

Blessed with more sunshine hours than almost any other region of New Zealand, Blenheim has won worldwide recognition as a major wine producing region (and more recently for olive oil). A ride along Rapaura Road, linking S.H. 6 (Nelson) to S.H. 1 (Picton) just north of Blenheim, will introduce you to just a few leading vineyards such as Hunters Wines, Huia Wines and Shingle Peak. The rich Wairau plains are now dotted with wineries and their associated restaurants. The local information office, or indeed any winery, will give you a 'wine trail' map to explore the area by, and what better way to spend a day or two. The annual Marlborough Wine and Food Festival attracts hordes during the second weekend in February and provides a great excuse for a visit, but make sure you have arranged accommodation beforehand.

Blenheim Visitor Information Centre:
2 High Street. Phone (03) 578-9904.
Internet: www.marlbourgh.co.nz
www.nz-wine.co.nz/marlborough/festival

Christchurch Bypass

The approaches to Christchurch – particularly from the south – make for rather boring motorcycle riding, with long straight roads, heavy traffic, and a plethora of speed cameras to contend with. This alternative route provides a less crowded, scenic, and more twisty route, avoiding Christchurch and opening up the interesting S.H. 79 route to Mt Cook (Aoraki), Lake Tekapo, and the Southern Lakes district via the 5-star Lindis Pass. This bypass is 40 km longer and takes much the same time as the S.H. 1 option.

Rating: ☺☺

Starting from: Temuka.

Ending at: Woodend (26 km north of Christchurch).

Distance: 197 km.

Approximate riding time: 2 hours.

Usual traffic volumes: Light.

Run Description

- Turn inland (west) at **Winchester**, 6 km north of **Temuka** (S.H.1 18 km north of Timaru; 145 km south of Christchurch) and follow **S.H. 72** to **Geraldine*** (11 km). *From Geraldine there is a 5-star route through to Lake Tekapo and Mt Cook (Aoraki) via S.H. 79.*

- From Geraldine follow the 'Inland Scenic Route' S.H. 72 signs to **Mt Hutt, Sheffield/ Waddington, Oxford** and **Rangiora** (173 km). #

- 7 km from Rangiora, turn right onto **S.H. 1** at **Woodend** (26 km north of Christchurch; 32 km south of Waipara), and continue (197 km in total).

Note: the Amberley to Oxford route via the Ashley Gorge is a further enhancement if required.

---

* *A worthwhile stopover – see Highlights & Diversions.*

Highlights & Diversions

Geraldine

(36 km from Temuka; 46 km from Fairlie via S.H. 79; 74 km from Mt Hutt; 138 km from Christchurch via S.H. 1.)

Nestled in green wooded foothills below the Southern Alps, Geraldine has an 'English country village' feel to it. The town, now centre of a thriving agricultural region, also boasts a lively arts and crafts culture, with several galleries offering interesting diversions. Each November the town hosts a Festival of Arts & Plants. South of Geraldine on S.H. 79 to Fairlie is the home of Barkers delicious mulled wines, fruit wines, blackcurrant juice, jams and preserves... worth a visit.

Geraldine Visitor Information Centre:
Talbot Street. Phone (03) 693-1006.
Email: geraldine_info@xtra.co.nz
www.holiday.co.nz/geraldine/index.html

Thompson's Track

(Alternative route from Geraldine to Christchurch)

- From Geraldine head north on S.H. 79 sign-posted to Mt Hutt and Christchurch.

- Just 6 kilometres north of Geraldine, after crossing the Orari bridge, turn left on S.H. 72 and follow the 'Inland Scenic Route' signs north towards **Mt Hutt** via **Arundel** and **Mayfield**.

- Just north of **Mayfield**, look for a right hand turn signposted as **Thompson's Track** to **Rakaia** via **Valletta, Ashburton Forks, Mitcham, Hatfield**. (Follow the Thompson's track and Rakaia signs).

- At Rakaia, continue north on S.H. 1 to Christchurch (50 km).

Note: to connect with Thompson's Track when travelling south from Christchurch, turn right (west, or inland) at Rakaia after crossing the Rakaia River, and follow the Thompson's Track signs to Geraldine.

Mt Hutt

(75 km north of Geraldine; 46 km south of Waddington on S.H. 77.)

Mt Hutt ski field is really of only passing interest to motorcyclists; however, those with a more adventurous bent or who are riding suitable cross country motorcycles may like to attempt the 24 km (return) to the ski field car park.

Rakaia Gorge

(2 km north of Mt Hutt.)

A grand arched bridge marks the point where the Rakaia River leaves the mountains and emerges to the plains via a spectacular gorge which doubles as a popular swimming and picnic spot.

Waddington and Sheffield

(119 km north of Geraldine; 54 km south of Rangiora; 60 km from Christchurch via S.H. 73 and Darfield)

Appealing rural service towns. Sheffield couldn't be further removed from its Yorkshire counterpart.

Waimakariri Gorge

(2 km north of Sheffield and Waddington.)

Spectacular views of the river gorge as it leaves the mountains and sweeps across the plains. There are several picnic and swimming spots.

Oxford

A charming stopover, with the Country Cottage Café favoured for its good coffee and lunches.

Ashley River Gorge

(A 5 km diversion north of Oxford – follow signs from Oxford.)

A sheltered scenic picnic and camping spot overlooking majestic cliffs rising sheer above the Ashley River. Well worth the stopover. Refreshing swimming.

Rangiora

(30 km from Christchurch.)

First established only two years after the foundation of Christchurch, Rangiora is a rather sedate, but nonetheless attractive rural service village which is fast becoming a suburb of Christchurch. There is some interesting architecture and a collection of good cafés.

SAFETY POINT
Wind gusts can be a danger, particularly at the foot of the hills near the gorges. Take care in nor-wester conditions. In this regard you may appreciate why a town is named 'Windwhistle'.

28 Christchurch – Kaikoura Return

A combination of fast plains, hill climbs and winding valleys from the green and rather lush coastal S.H. 1 route, to the spectacular alpine scenes of the inland route. Contrasts and twists with some nice refreshment opportunities make for an enjoyable one-day escape.

Rating: ☺☺☺☺ +

Starting from: Christchurch.

Ending at: Christchurch.

Distance: 389 km return. (185 km Christchurch to Kaikoura via S.H. 1; 204 km return via S.H. 70.)

Approximate riding time: 5 hours return.

Usual traffic volumes: Medium on S.H. 1. Light elsewhere.

Note: For a shorter version of this run, refer to the Leader Valley Loop, page 106.

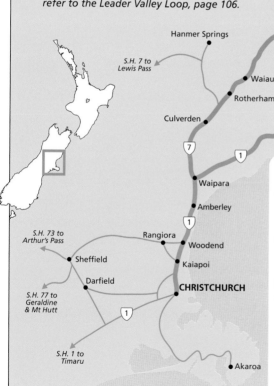

Run Description

- From **Christchurch*** take **S.H. 1** north to **Kaiapoi** (26 km) and **Waipara*** (58 km).
- Follow S.H. 1 north to **Cheviot*** (57 km) and on to **Kaikoura*** (185 km from Christchurch).

Return:

- Return 1 km S.W. from Kaikoura on S.H.1 for the turn-off to **S.H. 70** (signposted as S.H. 70 to Mt Lyford and Waiau) to **Waiau*** (83 km) and **Culverden** (102 km from Kaikoura). This route is part of the 'Alpine Pacific Coast route' and features distinctive signs.
- **S.H. 7** to **Waipara*** (44 km).
- **S.H. 1** to **Christchurch*** (58 km).

---

* *A worthwhile stopover – see Highlights & Diversions.*

Highlights & Diversions

Christchurch

New Zealand's 'Garden City', Christchurch has a distinctly English feel, perhaps due in part to the Avon River which meanders through the city, and the influence of early settlers determined to replicate their home country. Major attractions include the old university Arts Centre on Worcester Boulevard (www.artscentre.org.nz), the nearby Canterbury Museum in Rolleston Avenue, and the bustling restaurant precinct around Oxford and Hereford Streets.

Christchurch Visitor Information Office:
Cnr Worcester Street and Oxford Terrace.
Phone (03) 379-9629.
Email: info@christchurchnz.net
Internet: www.christchurchnz.net

Waipara and Canterbury House Winery

Situated on the right (east) of S.H. 1 just south of the Waipara river crossing and the turn-off to S.H. 7 (to Hanmer Springs and Lewis Pass), the Winery offers an opportunity to sample some of the region's wines in rather splendid surroundings. If this doesn't suit, there are plenty of other vineyards in the vicinity, including: Glenmark Wines, 169 Mackenzies Road, off S.H. 7, Waipara; Torlesse Wines, Loffhagen Drive, Waipara; and Mountford Vineyard, 434 Omihi Road, Waipara.

Cheviot

(121 km from Christchurch.)

A green, tree lined refuge from the dryness of the Canterbury Plains, Cheviot typifies the transition from the comparative dryness of the Canterbury Plains to the lush green foothills that lead over the coastal ranges to Kaikoura. The Magpies Nest is a favoured treat for hungry motorcyclists.

> **SAFETY POINT**
> Ice on the higher stretches, and shaded areas of the road during winter.

With thanks to Ken Beaumont of Ulysses Canterbury who recommended aspects of this run.

Kaikoura

(185 km from Christchurch, via S.H.1; 129 km from Blenheim.)

Named by early Maori who recognised the bountiful sea harvest potential of the area ('kai' meaning food, and 'koura' meaning crayfish). The importance of the sea catch continues in numerous tasty restaurants such as The Mussel Boys and Lobster Inn. Early European settlers plundered the then-plentiful seals and whales, driving them close to extinction. Today, as a reward for more sympathetic wildlife conservation practices, Kaikoura has evolved to be the heart of a whale and dolphin watching industry (www.whalewatch.co.nz or www.dolphin.co.nz). While fishing and farming are still important to the local economy, they are rapidly being overtaken by the growth of tourism. The Kaikoura peninsula with its early Maori pa site, and port (south of the main town) is well worth exploring. The motor camp at Puketa on South Bay, 2 km south of Kaikoura, is a popular stopover.

Kaikoura Visitor Information Centre:
Phone (03) 319-5641. Email: info@kaikoura.co.nz
Internet: www.kaikoura.co.nz

Waiau

(160 km via the Leader Valley, or 126 km via the return route, from Christchurch.)

The Waiau Hotel is a favoured watering-hole for motorcyclists, while the old (1878) cob cottage and museum is worth a visit.

Hurunui

(92 km from Christchurch.)

The restored historic Hurunui Hotel, constructed of limestone in 1869, is a popular refreshment stop.

Hanmer Springs Diversion

(133 km from Christchurch; 33 km return diversion on S.H. 7 – look for the turnoff south of Rotheram.)

A leafy spa town with public thermal pools to ease any aches and pains. Set amongst forest clad foot-hills, there are plenty of local walks – at their best in autumn. A charming town, well worth the diversion. The Forest Trust Motor Camp on Jacks Pass Road offers cabins from $15.00 per night.

Hurunui Visitor Information Centre: Amuri Drive.
Phone 0800-733-426. Email: info@hurunui.com

Christchurch – Leader Valley Loop

L et the scenic and twisting Leader Valley take you inland from the S.H. 1 route to enjoy the twists that abound before you emerge once more into the dry northern Canterbury foothills that are now the centre of a rapidly growing wine industry.

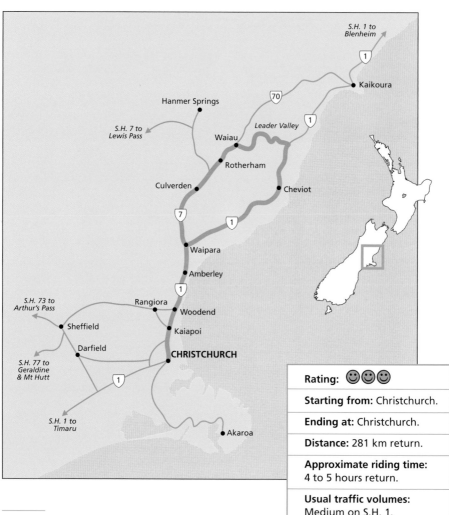

Rating: ☺☺☺
Starting from: Christchurch.
Ending at: Christchurch.
Distance: 281 km return.
Approximate riding time: 4 to 5 hours return.
Usual traffic volumes: Medium on S.H. 1. Light elsewhere.

With thanks to Ulysses Canterbury who recommended aspects of this run.

Run Description

- From **Christchurch*** take **S.H. 1** north to **Kaiapoi** (26 km) and **Waipara*** (58 km).
- Follow S.H. 1 north to **Cheviot*** (57 km).
- After Cheviot continue on S.H.1 towards Kaikoura; however, **15 km north from Cheviot** turn **left** to the Leader Valley, signposted to **Waiau** and **Hanmer Springs*** (30 km).
- **S.H. 70** to **Culverden** (19 km).
- **S.H. 7** to **Waipara** (44 km).
- **S.H. 1** to **Christchurch** (58 km).

* *A worthwhile stopover –*
see Highlights & Diversions.

SAFETY POINTS

- Ice on shaded areas of the road during winter.
- Gravel may be spread to counter ice on parts of the Leader Valley during winter – take care!

Highlights & Diversions

Christchurch

New Zealand's 'Garden City', Christchurch has a distinctly English feel, perhaps due in part to the Avon River which meanders through the city, and the influence of early settlers determined to replicate their home country. Major attractions include the old university Arts Centre on Worcester Boulevard (www.artscentre.org.nz), the nearby Canterbury Museum in Rolleston Avenue, and the bustling restaurant precinct around Oxford and Hereford Streets.

Christchurch Visitor Information Office:
Cnr Worcester Street and Oxford Terrace.
Phone (03) 379-9629.
Email: info@christchurchnz.net
Internet: www.christchurchnz.net

Waipara and Canterbury House Winery

Situated on the right (east) of S.H. 1 just south of the Waipara river crossing and the turn-off to S.H. 7 (to Hanmer Springs and Lewis Pass), the Winery offers an opportunity to sample some of the region's wines in rather splendid surroundings. If this doesn't suit, there are plenty of other vineyards in the vicinity, including: Glenmark Wines, 169 Mackenzies Rd. off S.H. 7, Waipara; Torlesse Wines, Loffhagen Drive, Waipara; and Mountford Vineyard, 434 Omihi Rd., Waipara.

Cheviot

(121 km from Christchurch.)

A green, tree lined refuge from the dryness of the Canterbury Plains, Cheviot typifies the transition from the comparative dryness of the Canterbury Plains to the lush green foothills that lead over the coastal ranges to Kaikoura. The Magpies Nest is a favoured treat for hungry motorcyclists.

Waiau

(160 km via the Leader Valley, or 126 km via the return route, from Christchurch.)

The Waiau Hotel is a favoured watering-hole for motorcyclists, while the old (1878) cob cottage and museum is worth a visit.

Hurunui

(92 km from Christchurch.)

The restored historic Hurunui Hotel, constructed of limestone in 1869, is a popular refreshment stop.

Hanmer Springs Diversion

(133 km from Christchurch; 33 km return diversion on S.H. 7 – look for the turnoff south of Rotheram.)

A leafy spa town with public thermal pools to ease any aches and pains. Set amongst forest clad foot-hills, there are plenty of local walks – at their best in autumn. A charming town, well worth the diversion. The Forest Trust Motor Camp on Jacks Pass Road offers cabins from $15.00 per night.

Hurunui Visitor Information Centre: Amuri Drive.
Phone 0800-733-426. Email: info@hurunui.com

Christchurch to Mt Cook (Aoraki)

This route links Christchurch to the scenic Mackenzie basin, which in turn links to the Southern Lakes via the Lindis Pass. The rather boring sections of the Canterbury Plains south of Christchurch are minimised by utilising the Thompson's Track 'shortcut' from Rakaia to Geraldine. Once south of Geraldine this route is a delight, with beautiful scenery, great roads, and plenty of twists – 5-star riding. For a nice overnight return diversion from Christchurch, stay at either Lake Tekapo, Mt Cook (Aoraki), or Twizel.

Rating: 😊 😊 😊 (5-star south of Geraldine.)	
Starting from: Christchurch.	
Ending at: Mt Cook (or vice versa).	
Distance: 345 km.	
Approximate riding time: 3 to 4 hours.	
Usual traffic volumes: Light.	

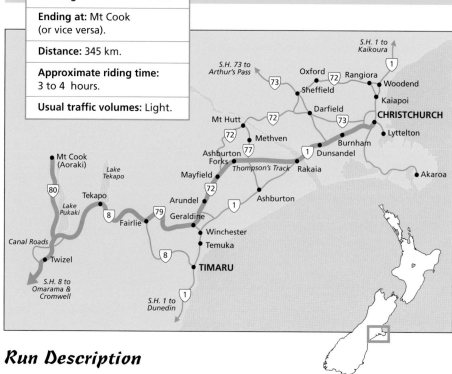

Run Description

- From **Christchurch*** head south on **S.H. 1** to **Rakaia** (47 km).
- At Rakaia, on the south side of the Rakaia River bridge, turn right on minor roads (west, or inland) and follow signs saying **Thompson's Track** to **Geraldine via Hatfield, Ashburton Forks, Valletta** to **Mayfield** (52 km).
- From Mayfield continue south on **S.H. 72** to **Geraldine*** (37 km).
- From Geraldine, follow **S.H. 79** and signs to **Fairlie*** (46 km).

- From Fairlie, continue via S.H. 79 to Burkes Pass and **Lake Tekapo*** (42 km).
- Continue via S.H. 79 for 47 km. to the Mt Cook (Aoraki) turn off (47 km).
- Turn right (west) and continue on **S.H. 80** to **Mt Cook (Aoraki)*** (55 km).

For onward southern travel options refer to the Mackenzie Country Autumn Tour, p.126.

* A worthwhile stopover – see Highlights & Diversions.

Riders returning from a run to Mt Cook, by Lake Pukaki.
photo: Murray Hawke

SAFETY POINTS
- Wind gusts can be a danger.
- Take care with ice on shaded portions of the road, particularly in winter.
- Long, straight, and relatively empty roads encourage speeding – take care!

Highlights & Diversions

Christchurch

New Zealand's 'Garden City', Christchurch has a distinctly English feel, perhaps due in part to the Avon River which meanders through the city, and the influence of early settlers determined to replicate their home country. Major attractions include the old university Arts Centre on Worcester Boulevard (www.artscentre.org.nz), the nearby Canterbury Museum in Rolleston Avenue, and the bustling restaurant precinct around Oxford and Hereford Streets.

Christchurch Visitor Information Office:
Cnr Worcester Street and Oxford Terrace.
Phone (03) 379-9629.
Email: info@christchurchnz.net
Internet: www.christchurchnz.net

Geraldine

(36 km from Temuka; 46 km from Fairlie via S.H. 79; 74 km from Mt Hutt; 138 km from Christchurch via S.H. 1.)

Nestled in green wooded foothills below the Southern Alps, Geraldine has an 'English country village' feel to it. The town, now centre of a thriving agricultural region, also boasts a lively arts and crafts culture, with several galleries offering interesting diversions. Each November the town hosts a Festival of Arts & Plants. South of Geraldine on S.H. 79 to Fairlie is the home of Barkers delicious mulled wines, fruit wines, blackcurrant juice, jams and preserves... worth a visit.

Geraldine Visitor Information Centre:
Talbot Street. Phone (03) 693-1006.
Email: geraldine_info@xtra.co.nz
www.holiday.co.nz/geraldine/index.html

Thompson's Track

(Alternative route from Geraldine to Christchurch. While the Run Description covers the north-to-south traverse of Thompson's Track, the following describes the south-to-north route.)

- From Geraldine head north on S.H. 79 signposted to Mt Hutt and Christchurch.
- Just 6 kilometres north of Geraldine, after crossing the Orari bridge, turn left on S.H. 72 and follow the 'Inland Scenic Route' signs north towards **Mt Hutt** via **Arundel** and **Mayfield**.
- Just north of **Mayfield**, look for a right hand turn signposted as **Thompson's Track** to **Rakaia** via **Valletta, Ashburton Forks, Mitcham, Hatfield** and **Rakaia**. (Follow the Thompson's track and Rakaia signs.)
- At Rakaia, turn north (left) on S.H. 1 to Christchurch (50 km).

Fairlie

(46 km south of Geraldine; 42 km from Lake Tekapo.)

Located amidst the green rolling foothills of the Southern Alps whose snow capped peaks seem enticingly close, Fairlie provides a scenic entrance and exit point to the dry hinterland known as the Mackenzie Country (named after a famous sheep drover, Jock McKenzie [so spelt]). For refreshments, favourite cafés include the Sunflower Centre (for vegetarian and health foods, with yummy cakes) and the Old Library which offers more substantial and conventional fare.

Lake Tekapo

(42 km from Fairlie; 102 km from Mt Cook; 85 km from Omarama.)

An attractive township situated at the southern end of the glacial blue waters of Lake Tekapo. The lake's unique colouring frames the Southern Alp foothills, and makes this township a favourite holiday venue for walking, fishing, hunting, boating and scenic flights. From Lake Tekapo airport (3 km south of the town), scenic flights operate to Mt Cook (Aoraki) and the Tasman Glacier. The unique colour of both Lake Tekapo and nearby Lake Pukaki are reputedly caused by the reflective qualities of eroded rock particles held in suspension in the waters. Tekapo is a favourite stopping point for tour buses which operate between

Church of the Good Shepherd, Lake Tekapo.

Mt Cook

(102 km from Lake Tekapo; 66 km north of Twizel; 93 km north from Omarama.)

With grand views of Mt Cook (3,496m), known by the Maori as Aoraki (the 'cloud in the sky' or 'cloud piercer'), Mt Cook village operates as a centre for alpine pursuits amongst many nearby peaks (14 over 3000m) and scenic flights to the five glaciers within the Mt Cook National Park. The road into Mt Cook offers stunning riding with world-class vistas. However, as most accommodation in the township (and most of the dining facilities) except for the YHA Hostel are operated by one company, the services suffer from lack of competition and prices reflect the area's comparative isolation (in the opinion of this writer). Accommodation options at nearby Twizel (66 km to the south) are cheaper alternatives.

Mt Cook village Department of Conservation Visitor Centre provides useful information at 8778 Bowen Drive. Phone (03) 435-1186. Email: doc.mt.cook@xtra.co.nz

For information on accommodation options at Twizel, contact the Twizel Mt Cook Visitor Information Office:
Phone (03) 435-0801 or (03) 435-0689.
Email: info@mtcook.org.nz
Internet: www.mtcook.org.nz

Christchurch and Queenstown; therefore the town's food outlets are rather 'institutional', catering for convenience rather than quality. I'd recommend a food stop at Fairlie as a better option (if you can wait).

Lake Tekapo Visitor Information Office: State Highway 8. Phone (03) 680-6848. Email: tekapo@xtra.co.nz
Internet: www.tekapo.co.nz

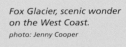

*Fox Glacier, scenic wonder
on the West Coast.*
photo: Jenny Cooper

*On the road to Treble Cone
ski field, near Wanaka.*
photo: Kennedy Warne

*Historic Cardrona Hotel,
on the Crown Range
diversion.*
photo:David Wall

③① *Fox Glacier to Southern Lakes*

Rating: ☺☺☺☺☺
Starting from: Fox Glacier (or Wanaka).
Ending at: Wanaka (or Fox Glacier).
Distance: 266 km one way Fox Glacier to Lake Wanaka. Allow an additional 104 km to Queenstown.
Approximate riding time: 4 hours Fox Glacier to Wanaka (one way). Allow 5 hours to Queenstown.
Usual traffic volumes: Medium. Care needed around Lakes Wanaka and Hawea.

This very scenic one-day escape crosses the Southern Alps to connect with the lakes of Central Otago, providing wonderful diversity. From the lush West Coast native forests, the route traverses the precipitous Haast Pass, with spectacular mountain vistas before proceeding to the comparatively barren golden tussock lands that surround the southern lakes.

Motorcycling doesn't come much better!

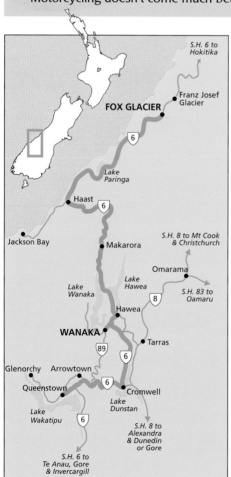

Run Description

- Head south on **S.H. 6** towards **Haast*** (121 km south of Fox Glacier).
- Follow **S.H. 6** inland to **Makarora*** (202 km from Fox Glacier).
- Continue on **S.H. 6** past **Lake Hawea*** and Lake Wanaka.
- After crossing the Clutha River at Albert Town, at the next major intersection...
- turn right on **S.H. 89** for 3 km into **Wanaka*** (266 km from Fox Glacier).
- From Wanaka take either **S.H. 89*** (care required with gravel) or S.H. 6 to **Queenstown** *(see p.122)*.

---

* *A worthwhile stopover – see Highlights & Diversions.*

SAFETY POINTS

- Watch the weather – the West Coast receives up to 5000 mm of rain per year, and more south of Haast (up to 7000 mm). It is no fun riding in adverse conditions, so if the forecast is for rain on the West Coast, simply stay on the east coast side of the Alps (where the annual rainfall averages 330 mm) until the weather clears and you can return to the West Coast.
- Ice in winter on high and shaded portions of this route.

Highlights & Diversions

Salmon Hatchery & Café

(Mid-way between Fox Glacier and Haast, near Jacobs River.)

A welcome stopover – snack on fresh smoked salmon bagels and great coffee overlooking salmon ponds... salmon doesn't come any fresher!

Haast

(121 km from Fox Glacier; 145 km from Wanaka.)

Haast township – the first or the last township on the western side of Haast Pass depending on which way you are travelling – is a stopping point, but not much more. A chance for refreshments and fuel either before or after travelling the very scenic southern-most crossing of the Southern Alps. Accommodation is available both at Haast Beach and Haast Junction. The former THC Hotel, now called the Haast Heritage Hotel, offers ensuite rooms from $40 per person, and although its restaurant is a bit pricey, the public bar provides good value alternatives.

Makarora

(202 km from Fox Glacier; 64 km from Lake Wanaka.)

The first or the last township on the eastern side of the Haast Pass, Makarora boasts a couple of petrol stations, a good motor camp, and an informative National Park Centre. There are numerous bush walks nearby, and the town is the centre of mountain climbing, hunting, and fishing recreational activities. There is a good camping ground, with cheap cabins and backpacking facilities and a limited selection of cafés.

Lake Hawea

(15 km from Wanaka; 247 km from Fox Glacier.)

Somewhat overshadowed by the nearby and more popular Lake Wanaka, Lake Hawea still has plenty to offer, including a very nice lakeside camping ground, just north of the turn-off into Hawea township from S.H. 6. Trout fishing is popular, and Kidds Bush (32 km towards Haast from the township on S.H. 6) and Timaru Creek (on the eastern side of the lake from the township), provide both good fishing and picnic spots.

Wanaka

(262 km from Fox Glacier; 120 km from Queenstown; 57 km from Cromwell.)

An extremely popular holiday resort in both summer and winter, this highly recommended stopover offers plenty of opportunities for swimming, walking, fishing, climbing, canoeing, parapenting and flying. In the winter it serves as a base for the nearby ski resorts of Cardrona, Treble Cone and Waiorau. The town also functions as a base for the nearby Mt Aspiring National Park, and the Park headquarters has some informative displays on the region's natural attractions. There are numerous accommodation facilities and the Glendhu Bay motor camp is a pleasant ride west from the town. Restaurants are plentiful. Stuart Landsborough's Puzzling World with its 'Leaning Tower of Wanaka' offers a fun diversion. 5 km out of Wanaka on the road to Cromwell is an interesting Transport Museum, and the adjoining Fighter Pilots Museum which restores World War Two fighter planes is world renowned. Joyrides are available.

The Wanaka Visitor Information Centre is located by the lakeside. Phone (03) 443-1233.
Email: wpa@wanaka.co.nz
Internet: www.wanaka.co.nz

Crown Range Diversion (S.H. 89)

Linking Queenstown to Wanaka, this 70 km route climbs high over the Crown Range to a height of 1,110 metres above sea level, affording splendid views of the Wakatipu Valley. The climb is ideal motorcycle riding, full of twists and turns, and best done from south to north (Queenstown to Wanaka) to enjoy the hair-pin bends on the climb to the Crown Terrace. The Crown Range is the fastest way to get between the two resorts by motorcycle, but NOTE: some higher portions of the road are still unsealed (gravel). Plans to complete the sealing of this scenic route in 1999 were thwarted by the worst floods in 150 years which caused over $2.2 million damage to the road. It is hoped that sealing will be completed by year-end 2000: check with local garages or the Automobile Association. If you take this route be sure to stop at the historic Cardrona Hotel (25 km from Wanaka), where liquid refreshments and fine food have been served since the gold-rush days. Take care with ice and snow in the winter. The alternative route between the resorts via S.H. 86 including Cromwell and the Kawarau Gorge is also extremely scenic and provides opportunities to bungy jump or sample Central Otago wines. As both routes are such fun, this diversion could be treated as a one-day round trip if you are lucky enough to be staying in either Queenstown or Wanaka.

Utilising little-travelled roads over a variety of scenic and undulating terrain, this route offers a picturesque and challenging half-day break from Dunedin, with a glimpse of modern day open-cast gold mining and some historic country pubs.

Rating: 😊😊😊😊
Starting from: Dunedin.
Ending at: Dunedin.
Distance: 231 km.
Approximate riding time: 4 hours.
Usual traffic volumes: Light.

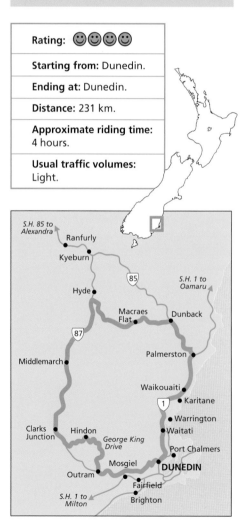

Run Description

Important: set your trip meter at zero from the Octagon (Dunedin's city centre).

- Depart **Dunedin*** heading up Stuart Street from the Octagon (city centre).
- At Kaikorai Valley take the right lane, and follow signs to Wakari and **Three Mile Hill**.
- At the foot of Three Mile Hill, 10 km from Dunedin, turn right on Milner Road, following signs to **Outram**.
- 24 km from Dunedin turn right immediately after you cross the Taieri River at **Outram Glen***.
- Follow the minor road as it heads towards **Hindon** and **Lee Stream**. At all intersections take the left hand option, remaining on tar seal.
- At Lee Stream sale yards and school (58 km from Dunedin) turn right and take **S.H. 87** to **Middlemarch***.
- Continue on S.H. 87 towards Hyde and Kyeburn. 123 km from Dunedin, just before Hyde, take a small right hand road signposted to **Macraes*** and **Palmerston**.

Note: the one lane wooden bridge following this intersection has a centre trough which could be dangerous for motorcycle wheels.

- At the next intersection, take the left option to Macraes.
- After Macraes gold mine the road drops steeply to join **S.H. 85**. At this intersection (176 km) turn right towards **Dunback*** and **Palmerston***.
- At Palmerston turn right and return to **Dunedin*** on **S.H. 1**.

* *A worthwhile stopover – see Highlights & Diversions.*

Highlights & Diversions

Dunedin

Located in a dramatic harbourside position, surrounded by lush green hills, Dunedin is proud of its Scottish heritage (the name Dunedin is Gaelic for Edinburgh, and the city is often called 'Edinburgh of the South'). Blessed by the wealth generated during the 1860s gold rush, Dunedin has a fine collection of Victorian architecture, including its famous railway station and town hall. Today Dunedin is very much a university city, with a lively cultural and artistic scene. It boasts a wide selection of very fine and reasonably priced restaurants. There is plenty of accommodation at most levels, including camping grounds near St Kilda Beach and Leith Valley. The Otago Peninsula offers 4-star motorcycle riding and a circuit is strongly recommended (see p.138), as is a tour of the Albatross Colony, phone (03) 478-0499, and Penguin Place, phone (03) 478-0286, to fully appreciate the natural attractions and unique wildlife.

Dunedin Visitor Information Centre:
The Octagon. Phone (03) 474-3300
Email: visitor.centre@dcc.govt.nz
Internet: www.cityofdunedin.com

Outram Glen

(24 km from Dunedin.)

A favoured summer swimming and picnic spot, with the nearby ridge-top displaying rescued Taieri historical buildings and a vintage machinery museum.

Taieri Historic Park, near Outram Glen.

SAFETY POINTS
- Ice on the shaded areas and high spots of the road during winter.
- Gravel on the road in winter and after storms.
- Wind gusts on exposed heights between Lee Stream and Middlemarch, and between Macraes Mine and Dunback.

The George King Drive

(Outram Glen to Lee Stream, 50 km from Dunedin.)

George King was a local politician known for his persuasive ways, and this little-used tar sealed road must be the epitome of his powers. How he got such a little-travelled road so well constructed and sealed, when such major tourist routes as Glenorchy and the Crown Range road were still unsealed, defies belief. Yet here it is, a testimony to George King and a wonderful motorcyclists' road. Few will fail to enjoy the spectacular descent and subsequent climb out of the Lee Stream Gully (only 34 km from Dunedin).

Middlemarch

(96 km from Dunedin.)

A toilet stop and termination point for the Taieri Gorge railway.

Macraes Mine

(136 km from Dunedin via this route.)

An historic stone hotel and a cluster of stone buildings provide a refreshing stopping point almost midway through this run. However, public tours of the nearby open cast mine – which produces over 110,000 ounces per annum of gold and which in 1999-2000 netted its Australian owners over $NZ15 million in operating profits – are not encouraged.

Dunback

(15 km from Palmerston.)

A restored old hotel offers meals and ale to tempt the weary, while just a few kilometres east of Dunback (towards Palmerston) is a great swimming and picnic spot by the Shag River.

Palmerston

(55 km north from Dunedin.)

An old gold rush town that still serves the nearby Macraes gold mine.

Greymouth – Lake Brunner Return

A quiet (low traffic volume) escape that combines quality road surfaces, idyllic native bush-clad hills with splendid lakeside scenery and plentiful opportunities for picnics (but don't forget the insect repellent).

Rating:	😊😊😊
Starting from:	Greymouth.
Ending at:	Greymouth.
Distance:	150 km.
Approximate riding time:	3½ hours return.
Usual traffic volumes:	Light.

Run Description

- From **Greymouth*** head south on **S.H. 6** towards the **Kumara Junction**. (At Paroa, 8 km from Greymouth, you might wish to turn left and visit **Shantytown***, a replica gold town well worth a visit.

- After Shantytown return to S.H. 6, and on towards the **Kumara Junction**.

Take care on the Kumara road/rail bridge.

- At Kumara Junction, turn left towards **Arthur's Pass** on **S.H. 73**, through **Kumara*** township, and on to the historic coach stop town of **Jacksons** (62 km from Greymouth) where a good cup of tea/coffee or a beer can be found amongst the memorabilia at the last remaining coach inn.

- Just before **Jacksons*** take the road left to **Inchbonnie**, crossing the Taramakau River, and then carry on, following the signs to **Lake Brunner*** and **Moana**, where there is a welcome stopping point at the Brunner Hotel.

- After appropriate refreshments head on through **Kokiri** to **Stillwater***.

- At Stillwater, turn left and return to **Greymouth** on **S.H. 7** via **Dobson**.

* *A worthwhile stopover – see Highlights & Diversions.*

With thanks to Mark Walsh of Ulysses Westland who recommended aspects of this run.

S.H. 6 to Westport
S.H. 7 to Murchison & Nelson
6 Blackball
7
Rapahoe
Runanga Taylorville
Stillwater
GREYMOUTH Dobson Kokiri
Moana
Shantytown
6
Lake Brunner
Ruru
Kumara Junction
Poerua
Inchbonnie
Kumara
Jacksons
73
Otira
6
73
Hokitika
Arthur's Pass
S.H. 73 to Christchurch
S.H. 6 to Haast & the Glaciers

Highlights & Diversions

Greymouth

(342 km from Christchurch; 101 km from Westport.)

Once the site of Mawhera Pa, the largest Maori settlement on the West Coast, Greymouth became a boom town for pakeha settlers when gold was discovered nearby in 1864. Situated at the foot of cliffs carved by the action of the Grey River, Greymouth is the largest town on the West Coast, and clings somewhat precariously to the flood prone Grey River delta. In 1991 'the Great Wall of Greymouth' was completed in an attempt to prevent further flooding, and now forms a pleasant walkway around the town, starting at Cobden Bridge. For a nice alternative to accommodation in Greymouth, refer to **Stillwater** below and pay a visit to The Formerly Blackball Hilton, 19 km from Greymouth off S.H. 7.

Greymouth Visitor Information Centre:
Cnr Herbert and Mackay Streets.
Phone (03) 768-5101. Email: vingm@minidata.co.nz

Shantytown

(Rutherglen, 13 km from Greymouth.)

A visit to Shantytown is strongly recommended. This reconstruction of a typical 1860s gold-town offers historic buildings carefully collected from around the region and reinstated to this location. A collection of memorabilia completes the reconstruction and provides a fascinating picture of the West Coast gold rush. Gold panning is also available, as is horse trekking, a short railway excursion, and refreshments.

Kumara

(24 km from Greymouth.)

Once a booming gold rush town, Kumara was the home of Richard John Seddon (1845-1906), a leading political figure and liberal. Under Seddon's leadership New Zealand led the world in extending the right to vote to women, and introducing welfare benefits such as the world's first Old Age Pensions Bill. He is also reputed to have referred to New Zealand as 'God's own country' and spawned the now common description of New Zealand as 'Godzone'. His Queens Hotel has long since disappeared, but his name and fame remains giving title to Kumara's main street.

Special Note: Many West Coast hotels historically set aside a paddock for travellers' horses and cattle to graze. These facilities can today often be used by motorcyclists to set up a tent and camp for little or no charge.

Jacksons

(62 km from Greymouth.)

The tavern is all that remains of the historic coach stop and watering-hole that once boasted five hotels.

Lake Brunner

The scenic Lake Brunner – known to the Maori as 'Moana Kotuku' or Lake of the Kotuku (White Heron) – offers numerous picnic spots from which to enjoy the views and excellent fishing. The many immaculate holiday homes attest to the area's popularity for Christchurch residents.

Stillwater and Blackball

Stillwater is an old mining town on S.H. 7 which in 1896 achieved notoriety with New Zealand's worst mining tragedy in which 67 miners died. (Their mass grave can be found in the Stillwater cemetery.) From Stillwater you can turn north for a diversion to Red Jacks and then to the town of **Blackball**, made famous by 'The Formerly Blackball Hilton', so named after the London-based Hilton Hotel became upset that an upstart West Coast hotel shared its name. Despite the enforced name change The Formerly Blackball Hilton continues to thrive as visitors share their bemusement. Bed & breakfast or self-catering facilities are provided.

Free phone 0800 4 Blackball (0800 42 52 25)
Email: bbhilton@xtra.co.nz
Internet: www.blackballhilton.co.nz

Blackball is also home to delicious bier sticks and salami via its main street shop and factory.

Dobson

The remains of early coal mines and brick works can still be found near this settlement named after George Dobson, one of the surveyors who detailed and promoted the Arthur's Pass.

SAFETY POINT: Watch the weather – the West Coast receives 5000 to 7000 mm of rain per year, and it is no fun riding in the adverse conditions that arise from time to time. If the forecast is for rain on the West Coast, simply cross one of the several Southern Alp passes and ride on the east coast (where the annual rainfall averages 330 mm) until the weather clears and you can return to the West Coast.

34 *Hokitika Gorge -*
Lake Kaniere return

A half-day run to one of the most photogenic river gorges in New Zealand. Not widely known or visited, this diversion will not disappoint. Take a picnic lunch and enjoy.

Rating: 😊😊😊	
Starting from: Hokitika.	
Ending at: Hokitika.	
Distance: 100 km return.	
Approximate riding time: 3 hours return.	
Usual traffic volumes: Light.	

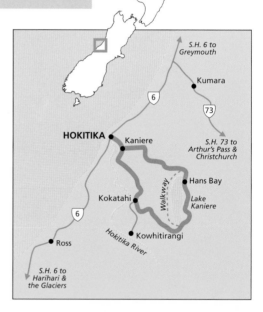

Run Description

- Head east on **Stafford Street** (past the camping ground) and follow the signs to **Kaniere** and **Kokatahi**.

- As the road forks at the end of Kaniere township, take the **right fork** to the **Kokatahi intersection**.

- **Turn right**, and follow the signs to **Hokitika Gorge**. (The last 800m is good gravel.) Park bike.

- Walk down the track to the swing bridge and enjoy the gorge with the Hokitika River below.

- Return to the **Kokatahi intersection**.

- Instead of turning left, turn **right** (more or less straight ahead) towards **Upper Kokatahi**, and **Lake Kaniere**. There is a good camping and picnic spot at **Hans Bay**.

- Continue on and follow the signs round the lake back to **Hokitika***.

* *A worthwhile stopover – see Highlights & Diversions.*

Bevan Climo working with a jade carving.
photo: Mountain Jade Ltd Hokitika

Highlights & Diversions

Hokitika

(164 km north from Fox Glacier; 40 km south from Greymouth.)

Hokitika is the West Coast's centre for the manufacture of greenstone (pounamu or jade) jewellery, and there are several factories worth visiting to learn more about the historical significance of this valuable stone. Hokitika can lay claim to be the epicurean centre of the West Coast: there are numerous restaurants in which to enjoy local delicacies such as whitebait and venison; and an annual Wild Food Festival is held (the second weekend each March), celebrating nature's harvest with rather more exotic delicacies such as 'mountain oysters' and huhu grubs. There is also a wide variety of strange and powerful beverages available to test the palette. At all times of the year the Café de Paris in Tancred Street is renowned for fine food (not your usual pie & pint), while the Filling Station in Revell Street provides more casual dining. The West Coast Historical Museum, at 7 Tancred Street, provides audio visuals and artifacts for those with an interest in the past. The Visitor Information Centre is located in the Carnegie Building, Tancred Street.

Phone (03) 755-6166. Email: hkkvin@xtra.co.nz

SAFETY POINTS
- Compacted gravel from Styx River bridge to Hans Bay (the back of Lake Kaniere) should present no difficulty.
- Watch the weather – the West Coast receives 5000 to 7000 mm of rain per year, and it is no fun riding in the adverse conditions that arise from time to time. If the forecast is for rain on the West Coast, simply cross one of the several Southern Alp passes and ride on the east coast (where the annual rainfall averages 330 mm) until the weather clears and you can return to the West Coast.

With thanks to Mark Walsh of Westland Ulysses who recommended aspects of this run.

Pit stop at the Mahinapua Hotel.

photo: Len Chilcott

35 *Hokitika to the Glaciers*

The West Coast at its wild best: superb roads and scenery interspersed with native bush bluffs and coastal viewpoints. Whether travelling north or south, this run is highly recommended. Savour the ancient forests and mountain vistas.

Rating: ☺☺☺☺☺	
Starting from: Hokitika.	
Ending at: Fox Glacier, or returning to Hokitika.	
Distance: 164 km one way or 328 km return.	
Approximate riding time: 4 hours return. (2 hours one-way)	
Usual traffic volumes: Medium to light.	

Lake Matheson.

Run Description

Heading south:

- Take **S.H. 6** south of Hokitika* to **Franz Josef Glacier*** (139 km from Hokitika).
- Continue on S.H. 6 for another 25 km to **Fox Glacier*** (164 km from Hokitika).

Return, or heading north:

- Simply take S.H. 6 north of Fox Glacier, towards **Franz Josef Glacier** (25 km).
- Continue on S.H. 6 to Hokitika (164 km from Fox Glacier).

* *A worthwhile stopover – see Highlights & Diversions.*

Highlights & Diversions

Hokitika

(164 km north from Fox Glacier; 40 km south from Greymouth.)

Hokitika is the West Coast's centre for the manufacture of greenstone (pounamu or jade) jewellery, and there are several factories worth visiting to learn more about the historical significance of this valuable stone. Hokitika can lay claim to be the epicurean centre of the West Coast: there are numerous restaurants in which to enjoy local delicacies such as whitebait and venison; and an annual Wild Food Festival is held (the second weekend each March), celebrating nature's harvest with rather more exotic delicacies such as 'mountain oysters' and huhu grubs. There is also a wide variety of strange and powerful beverages available to test the palate. At all times of the year the Café de Paris in Tancred Street is renowned for fine food (not your usual pie & pint), while the Filling Station in Revell Street provides more casual dining. The West Coast Historical Museum, at 7 Tancred Street, provides audio visuals and artifacts for those with an interest in the past. The Visitor Information Centre is located in the Carnegie Building, Tancred Street. Phone (03) 755-6166. Email: hkkvin@xtra.co.nz

Franz Josef

(139 km from Hokitika.)

The pretty tourist town of Franz Josef is well worth a stopover, with many cafés and restaurants offering food and refreshments. There is a youth hostel and motor camp plus several hotels/motels for those tempted to stay longer. Visit the National Park information centre before heading 7 km to the south of the town to view the Glacier via a gravel no-exit road, followed by the 1–2 hour return walk to view the glacier more closely. If you can time it, the evening's setting sun shows both glaciers to their best advantage.

Franz Josef Visitor Centre: Main Road, Franz Josef. Phone (03) 752-0796.

A stopover either here or at Fox Glacier is recommended if you are heading south to the Haast Pass, Makarora, and Lakes Hawea and Wanaka, or Queenstown *(see page 112)*, as it makes for a great one-day ride the next day.

Franz Josef Glacier.

Fox Glacier

(25 km south of Franz Josef; 189 km south of Hokitika.)

Another pretty tourist town built around the majesty of the nearby glaciers. Fox Glacier is the largest of the two glaciers, and can be viewed via a diversion south to the Fox River valley and a gravel road, and then a 1 hour walk (return) from the car park.

Beware leaving motorbikes unattended at the glacier car park: the kea (a NZ native parrot) has a destructive liking for chrome work and rubber bungy ties.

Café Neve is recommended as a motorcyclist-friendly stopover, offering appetizing food and great coffee, with outside sun decks for you to absorb the ambience.

Lake Matheson

A 5 km ride west of Fox Glacier will take you to the car park, and the lake made famous for its mirror-like reflections of Mt Cook is then a 1 to 2 hour return walk away.

> **SAFETY POINT**
> Watch the weather – the West Coast receives 5000 to 7000 mm of rain per year, and it is no fun riding in the adverse conditions that arise from time to time. If the forecast is for rain on the West Coast, simply cross one of the several Southern Alp passes and ride on the east coast (where the annual rainfall averages 330 mm) until the weather clears and you can return to the West Coast.

With thanks to Mark Walsh of Westland Ulysses who recommended aspects of this run.

36 Invercargill - Queenstown Round the Block

Rating: ☺☺☺☺	

Starting from: Invercargill.

Ending at: Invercargill.

Distance: 455 km return.
(Allow 30 km extra for diversions into Queenstown and Arrowtown.)

Approximate riding time:
6 hours return.

Usual traffic volumes: Light; can be medium to heavy on the outskirts of Invercargill and Queenstown, and in the Kawarau Gorge.

The world-famous scenery surrounding Queenstown provides a great excuse to escape Invercargill. This run offers plenty of variety in both roads and terrain; although it is a rather long one-day ride, there are opportunities for numerous stopovers and diversions.

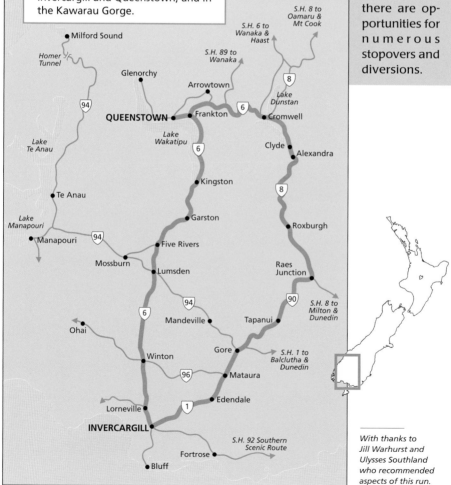

With thanks to Jill Warhurst and Ulysses Southland who recommended aspects of this run.

Run Description

- From **Invercargill*** head north on **S.H. 1** to **Edendale**, **Mataura** and **Gore*** (66 km).
- From Gore continue on S.H.1 towards Balclutha, but 4 km from Gore turn left onto **S.H. 90** to **Tapanui** and **Raes Junction** (67 km).
- At Raes Junction, turn left onto **S.H. 8** to Millers Flat, **Roxburgh**, and on to **Alexandra*** (205 km from Invercargill).
- Continue on S.H. 8 to **Cromwell*** (241 km from Invercargill).
- From Cromwell take **S.H. 6** to **Queenstown*** (294 km from Invercargill).

Queenstown to Invercargill via S.H. 6:

- From **Frankton*** (7 km east of Queenstown town centre) take S.H. 6 to **Kingston***, **Lumsden**, **Winton** and **Invercargill**. (Queenstown is 160 km from **Invercargill*** via S.H. 6.)

To connect to the ***Southern Scenic Route*** *to Dunedin, see page 144; or to* ***Milford Sound***, *see page 130.*

* *A worthwhile stopover – see Highlights & Diversions.*

Highlights & Diversions

Invercargill

(257 km from Dunedin via the Catlins Southern Scenic Route; 186 km from Te Anau via S.H. 99 and Tuatapere.)

New Zealand's southernmost city services the rich grasslands to the north that supply much of New Zealand's dairy and sheep farming wealth. The abundant seas to the south make Bluff (the port of Invercargill) a centre for the famed Bluff oyster. Like Dunedin, Invercargill has a Scottish heritage, and street names and architecture reflect this. There are many motels and camping opportunities, but boutique dining opportunities are (in the view of this writer) limited by a rather staid liquor licensing trust. For me, nearby Riverton is a preferred stopover.

Invercargill Visitor Information Centre:
108 Gala Street. Phone (03) 214-9133.
Email: tourismandtravel.invercargill@thenet.net.nz

Gore

(66 km from Invercargill.)

A rural service town noted for its annual 'Golden Guitar' festival (held each Queen's Birthday weekend in July) has earned Gore the name of NZ's capital of Country Music. Gore is also noted as a centre for trout fishing which is popular in the surrounding rivers and streams. The passionate artistic community has created a local Art Gallery of considerable merit. The nearby 30 km return trip to Mandeville will allow you to see a part of New Zealand's flying history: a factory restores early de Havilland biplanes, and offers sight-seeing flights of the locality. There is a charming nearby restaurant and bar.

Gore Visitor Information Centre:
Cnr Herbert and Mackay Streets. Phone (03) 208-9908.
Email: goreinfo@esi.co.nz

Roxburgh

(165 km from Invercargill.)

Set in an attractive valley Roxburgh is the centre of a major fruit growing region, with many opportunities to buy tasty fresh fruit in season from road-side stalls.

Alexandra

(205 km from Invercargill via this route.)

(191 km from Dunedin via S.H. 8 to Roxburgh and Milton, or 212 km via S.H. 85 to Ranfurly and Palmerston to Dunedin or 224 km via S.H. 85 & 87 to Ranfurly, Middlemarch to Dunedin.)

Set at the junction between the Clutha and the Manuherikia Rivers, Alexandra services the hot dry Central Otago orchard and grape growing region. There are many restaurants and accommodation houses, plus a good camping ground just north of the town on S.H. 85. The vineyards of Black Ridge and Dry Gully just off Earnscleugh Road (turn off south of the Clutha Bridge) make an attractive alternative route to Clyde.

Alexandra Visitor Information Office:
22 Centennial Ave.,
Phone (03) 448-9515.
Email: info@tco.org.nz

Clyde

(A 5 km diversion from Alexandra on the way to Cromwell.)

The old mining town of Clyde at the foot of the huge Clyde hydroelectric dam is a pleasant side-trip from Alexandra, and the preferred stopover for many motorcyclists as it offers some charming historic restaurants and hotels in relatively quiet surrounds. (Olivers Restaurant, and the Old Post Office are recommended.)

Cromwell

(241 km from Invercargill; 60 km from Queenstown.)

A rather characterless modern town in a picturesque setting by Lake Dunstan which overshadows what was (before the advent of the surrounding hydroelectric lake) a charming gold-rush town. Some restored buildings can still be found in the old town, but you have to look hard. The nearby gold-town of Bannockburn is rapidly becoming the centre of a growing wine industry, and has considerable charm. There are good camping grounds in both towns.

Kawarau Gorge

The valley linking Cromwell to Queenstown is full of twists and turns well suited to motorcycling, and the nearby river provides some stunning scenery. However, traffic volumes can be heavy, and portions of the road are prone to ice in winter. Take care.

The Gibbston and Chard Farm Wineries are well worth a visit; Gibbston's pleasant courtyard restaurant serves a variety of tasty food. Nearby is the famous A.J. Hacket bungy jumping operation for those so inclined.

Frankton

On the outskirts 7 km from Queenstown, Frankton serves as the junction to the road heading south to Invercargill. The motor camp here is often less crowded than Queenstown, and is set in a picturesque location beside the lake.

Queenstown

The reasons why Queenstown has become one of New Zealand's premier tourist spots are readily apparent. Set on the wooded shores of a beautiful lake with stunning mountain vistas all around, the town oozes charm, and offers many restaurants and bars which cater to almost all tastes. The mountains, lakes and rivers around Queenstown provide a feast of attractions and activities including fishing, hunting, skiing, climbing, hiking, jet-boating, rafting, bungy jumping, gold panning and much more. No wonder the town is billed as 'NZ's adventure capital'. The transport museum and the nearby Skyline gondola are well worth a visit, or take a cruise on the lake in the historic T.S.S. *Earnslaw.*

Queenstown Visitor Information Centre:
Clock Tower Building, Cnr Shotover and Camp Streets.
Phone (03) 442-4100. Email: qvc@xtra.co.nz

Jet-boating near Queenstown – the Adventure Capital of New Zealand.

Crown Range Diversion

Linking Queenstown to Wanaka this 70 km route climbs high over the Crown Range to a height of 1,110 metres above sea level, affording splendid views of the Wakatipu Valley. The climb is ideal motorcycle riding, full of twists and turns, and best done from south to north (Queenstown to Wanaka) as the hair-pin bends on the climb to the Crown Terrace are stunning. The Crown Range is the fastest way to get between the two resorts by motorcycle, but NOTE: some higher portions of the road are still unsealed (gravel). Plans to complete the sealing of this scenic route in 1999 were thwarted by the worst floods in 150 years which caused over $2.2 million damage to the road. It is hoped that sealing will be completed by year-end 2000: check with local garages or the Automobile Association. If you take this route be sure to stop at the historic Cardrona Hotel (25 km from Wanaka), where liquid refreshments and fine food have been served since the gold-rush days. Take care with ice and snow in the winter. The alternative route between the resorts via S.H. 86 including Cromwell and the Kawarau Gorge is also extremely scenic and provides opportunities to bungy jump or sample Central Otago wines. As both routes are such fun, this diversion could be treated as a one-day round trip if you are lucky enough to be staying in either Queenstown or Wanaka.

Wanaka Diversion

(262 km from Fox Glacier; 120 km from Queenstown; 57 km from Cromwell.)

An extremely popular holiday resort in both summer and winter, this highly recommended stopover offers plenty of opportunities for swimming, walking, fishing, climbing, canoeing, parapenting and flying. In the winter it serves as a base for the nearby ski resorts of Cardrona, Treble Cone and Waiorau. The town also functions as a base for the nearby Mt Aspiring National Park, and the Park headquarters has some informative displays on the region's natural attractions. There are numerous accommodation facilities and the Glendhu Bay motor camp is a pleasant ride west from the town. Restaurants are plentiful. Stuart Landsborough's Puzzling World with its 'Leaning Tower of Wanaka' offers a fun diversion. 5 km out of Wanaka on the road to Cromwell is an interesting Transport Museum, and the adjoining Fighter Pilots Museum which restores World War Two fighter planes is world renowned. Joyrides are available.

The Wanaka Visitor Information Centre is located by the lakeside. Phone (03) 443-1233.
Email: wpa@wanaka.co.nz
Internet: www.wanaka.co.nz

SAFETY POINTS
- Ice on the shaded areas of the road during winter.
- The Cromwell Gorge is prone to sudden wind gusts.
- Heavy traffic volumes in the Kawarau Gorge.

Arrowtown Diversion

(20 km from Queenstown, 40 km return.)

The old gold mining town of Arrowtown set on the banks of the Arrow River has managed to defy 'progress' and retain (with the assistance of heritage protection) an old gold-rush town appearance with considerable charm. The Arrowtown Museum on Buckingham Street is highly recommended, and provides an intriguing insight to the gold-rush era. The nearby library makes clever use of the town's old jail and is worth closer inspection. A walk along the Arrow River from the western end of town will bring you to intriguing ruins and recreations of the historic Chinatown.

Glenorchy Diversion

(50 km from Queenstown, 100 km return – allow 2 to 3 hours.)

Set at the western edge of Lake Wakatipu, surrounded by panoramic mountain vistas, this is a 5-star motorcycling route. Not only is the road challenging, the scenery is some of the best in the world. The Glenorchy motor camp and nearby hotels and restaurants make a pleasant and quiet alternative stopover to Queenstown. A highly recommended diversion.

Kingston

(40 km from Queenstown;119 km from Invercargill.)

Situated at the head of the former railway link between Lake Wakatipu and Invercargill, Kingston is a nice camping spot, and offers rides on an historic steam engine in pleasant surrounds.

Athol

(Mid-way between Kingston and Lumsden.)

A charming cluster of old buildings and a chance for a last coffee before the return run to Invercargill.

Mackenzie Country Autumn Tour

The combination of the vast dryness of the Mackenzie Country, the golden hues of autumn and distant glimpses of the Southern Alps will surely impress. Add to this good, relatively traffic-free roads and numerous glacial blue lakes and the area is a must to visit at any time of the year, but is at its best from March to May. The Lindis Pass is a legend on its own and rates as 5-star riding.

Rating: ☺ ☺ ☺ ☺
Starting from: Dunedin.
Ending at: Dunedin.
Distance: Approx. 768 km (including a 186 km return diversion from Omarama to Mt Cook).
Approximate riding time: 2 days, 4 to 5 hours each day.
Usual traffic volumes: Light.

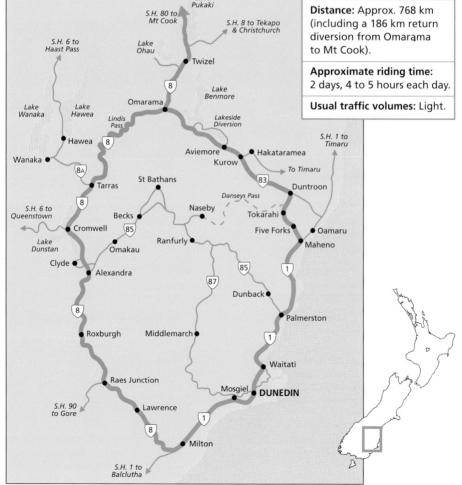

Autumn by Lake Aviemore.
photos: Jenny Cooper

Run Description

- Depart **Dunedin*** on **S.H. 1** heading north to **Waitati** (or alternately take the old main road from North East Valley to Waitati) then on to **Palmerston*** and **Maheno** (11 km short of Oamaru).

- At **Maheno** either turn **left** (west) and follow the winding and picturesque minor road signs to **Five Forks, Tokarahi, Island Cliff,** to **Duntroon**. (Another option is continue on S.H. 1 to Oamaru* and at 8 km north, take S.H. 83 left (west) towards Duntroon, and Omarama.)

- From Duntroon continue on **S.H. 83** to **Kurow*** and **Aviemore**. At Aviemore, cross the dam and continue up the valley past numerous great camping, picnic and fishing spots to the Benmore Dam which you cross to rejoin S.H. 83 to continue on to **Omarama***.

- Turn right on **S.H. 8** to **Lake Ohau, Twizel*, Mt Cook*** or **Lake Tekapo** for a night's stopover.

- Return to **Omarama***, then continue south on **S.H. 8** over the Lindis Pass to **Tarras** and **Cromwell***.

- At Cromwell turn left on **S.H. 8,** to **Alexandra*** where you can return to **Dunedin* either** via S.H. 8 to Roxburgh and Milton (191 km), **or** via S.H. 85 to Ranfurly and Palmerston to Dunedin (212 km), **or** S.H. 85 & 87 to Ranfurly, Middlemarch to Dunedin (224 km). The last 2 options generally have less traffic.

---

* *A worthwhile stopover – see Highlights & Diversions.*

Highlights & Diversions

Dunedin

Located in a dramatic harbourside position, surrounded by lush green hills, Dunedin is proud of its Scottish heritage (the name Dunedin is Gaelic for Edinburgh, and the city is often called 'Edinburgh of the South'). Blessed by the wealth generated during the 1860s gold rush, Dunedin has a fine collection of Victorian architecture, including its famous railway station and town hall. Today Dunedin is very much a university city, with a lively cultural and artistic scene. It boasts a wide selection of very fine and reasonably priced restaurants. There is plenty of accommodation at most levels, including camping grounds near St Kilda Beach and Leith Valley. The Otago Peninsula offers 4-star motorcycle riding and a circuit is strongly recommended (*see p.138*), as is a tour of the Albatross Colony, phone (03) 478-0499, and Penguin Place, phone (03) 478-0286, to fully appreciate the natural attractions and unique wildlife.

Dunedin Visitor Information Centre: The Octagon.
Phone (03) 474-3300. Email: visitor.centre@dcc.govt.nz
Internet: www.cityofdunedin.com

Palmerston

(55 km north from Dunedin.)

An old gold rush town that still serves the nearby Macraes gold mine which currently produces over 110,000 ounces of gold per annum via modern opencast mining methods.

Oamaru

(114 km from Dunedin.)

Although this route can bypass Oamaru, for those who haven't seen Oamaru before, a visit is a must. Oamaru boasts more historic buildings than any other town in New Zealand and the quality of these whitestone buildings is superb. Each November (in the last weekend) the town celebrates with a Victorian festival including such delights as penny-farthing bike races, and stone sawing. There are numerous motels and accommodation houses plus a motor camp; however, a stop at the historic Criterion Hotel in Tyne Street is almost mandatory.

Oamaru Visitor Information Centre: 1 Thames Street.
Phone (03) 434-1656. Email: info@waitaki-dc.govt.nz

Kurow

(66 km from Oamaru; 52 km from Omarama.)

A small fishing and farming centre. The café in the old hall is a popular stopover.

Omarama

(118 km from Oamaru; 117 km from Cromwell; 93 km from Mt Cook; 95 km from Lake Tekapo.)

A bustling junction town with several good restaurants, petrol stations and accommodation houses. Omarama is favoured as a centre for gliding, due to the unique geography of the area creating thermals that rise over the mountains.

Twizel

(38 km from Omarama.)

A former hydro electric construction village, now given over to holiday homes, Twizel offers varied and cheap accommodation as a base to explore the area.

Criterion Hotel, Oamaru.
photo: Reg Graham

SAFETY POINTS
- Ice on the shaded areas and high spots of the road during winter.
- Gravel on the road in winter and after storms.
- Take care with wind gusts around Mt Cook and the Cromwell Gorge.

Mt Cook

(66 km north of Twizel;
93 km north from Omarama.)

With grand views of Mt Cook (3,496m), known by the Maori as Aoraki (the 'cloud in the sky' or 'cloud piercer'), Mt Cook village operates as a centre for alpine pursuits amongst many nearby peaks (14 over 3000m) and scenic flights to the five glaciers within the Mt Cook National Park. There is a motor camp, cabins, hotel, shop and youth hostel; however, prices and service are often a reflection of the relative isolation of the township. The National Park visitor centre is well worth a visit. Nearby Tekapo and Twizel provide alternative accommodation.

Mt Cook National Park Visitor Centre: Bowen Drive. Phone (03) 435-1186. Email: doc.mt.cook@xtra.co.nz Internet: www.mtcook.org.nz

Lindis Pass

(16 km from Omarama to 21 km from Cromwell.)

The route linking the Mackenzie Country and Ahuriri River Valley to the Upper Clutha and Southern Lakes region was travelled by the Ngai Tahu Maori, and became very well known to pakeha in 1861 when gold was found on the Tarras side of the pass. The Lindis Pass is now a major tourist route linking the Southern Lakes to the Christchurch International Airport. The pass climbs to 970m with the gentlest ascent being from the north. The road offers rewarding 5-star riding, but care should be taken during winter in shaded and frost prone areas and after storms when gravel can be washed onto the road.

Cromwell Diversion

(2 km from S.H. 8.)

A rather characterless modern town in a picturesque setting by Lake Dunstan which overshadows what was (before the advent of the surrounding hydro-electric lake) a charming gold-rush town. Some restored buildings can still be found in the old town, but you have to look hard. The nearby gold-town of Bannockburn is rapidly becoming the centre of a growing wine industry, and has considerable charm. There are good camping grounds in both towns.

Alexandra

(191 km from Dunedin via S.H. 8 to Roxburgh and Milton, or 212 km via S.H. 85 to Ranfurly and Palmerston to Dunedin or 224 km via S.H. 85 & 87 to Ranfurly, Middlemarch to Dunedin.)

Set at the junction between the Clutha and the Manuherikia Rivers, Alexandra services the hot dry Central Otago orchard and grape growing region. There are many restaurants, and accommodation houses, plus a good camping ground just north of the town on S.H. 85. The vineyards of Black Ridge and Dry Gully just off Earnscleugh Road (turn off south of the Clutha Bridge) make an attractive alternative route to Clyde.

Alexandra Visitor Information Office:
22 Centennial Avenue. Phone (03) 448-9515.
Email: info@tco.org.nz

For a description of the options for returning to Dunedin from Alexandra, see pages 127 and 134–136.

Near the summit of the Lindis Pass.

The road into Milford Sound rates as one of New Zealand's most scenic; add to this the diversity of the Southern Scenic Route from Invercargill, combined with convenient links to/from Queenstown or Dunedin, and the result is simply the best riding in the region. The only dampener can be Milford Sound's annual rainfall of up to 7 metres. Watch the weather forecasts closely and stay east of the Alps until you are assured of good conditions in the west. Be prepared to bail out (literally!) if the weather turns nasty. The road from Te Anau to Milford Sound is fully sealed.

Rating: ☺☺☺☺☺ (in fine weather)
Starting from: Invercargill.
Ending at: Invercargill.
Distance: 602 km return.
Approximate riding time: *Day 1:* 4 to 6 hours; *Day 2:* 4 hours. (It can be done in one day, but this doesn't do justice to a great escape, so why bother?)
Usual traffic volumes: Light to medium.

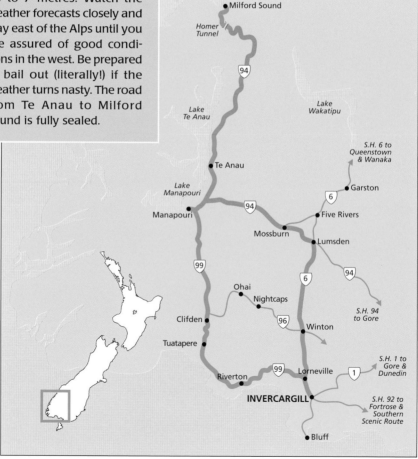

Run Description

- Leave **Invercargill*** on **S.H. 6** towards Winton, Lumsden, Queenstown (8 km).
- 8 km from Invercargill city centre turn left on **S.H. 99** (The Southern Scenic Route), signposted to **Riverton*** (38 km).
- Continue on S.H. 99 to **Tuatapere*** and **Clifden*** and its historic suspension bridge (52 km).
- Continue on to **Manapouri***. From Manapouri take **S.H. 95** to **Te Anau*** (97 km).

MAGIC MILFORD DIVERSION

- From Te Anau take **S.H. 94** to **Milford Sound*** (121 km one way; 242 km return). Take time to stop at the Mirror Lakes and while at Milford Sound perhaps do a trip on one of the many tour boats before returning to Te Anau via the same route.

Return to Invercargill:

- Either return via the Southern Scenic Route, or
- **S.H. 94** to **Mossburn** and **Lumsden** (77 km).
- **S.H. 6** to **Invercargill** (88 km).

* *A worthwhile stopover –*
see Highlights & Diversions.

SAFETY POINTS
- Heavy tour bus traffic from Te Anau to Milford is at its worst from 9.00 to 11.00 am and 1.00 to 3.00 pm.
- Ice on the higher stretches, and shaded areas of the road during winter.
- Tree gum can make road surfaces slippery.

Highlights & Diversions

Invercargill

(257 km from Dunedin via the Catlins Southern Scenic Route; 186 km from Te Anau via S.H. 99 and Tuatapere.)

New Zealand's southernmost city services the rich grasslands to the north that supply much of New Zealand's dairy and sheep farming wealth. The abundant seas to the south make Bluff (the port of Invercargill) a centre for the famed Bluff oyster. Like Dunedin, Invercargill has a Scottish heritage, and street names and architecture reflect this. There are many motels and camping opportunities, but boutique dining opportunities are (in the view of this writer) limited by a rather staid liquor licensing trust. For me, nearby Riverton is a preferred stopover.

Invercargill Visitor Information Centre:
108 Gala Street. Phone (03) 214-9133.
Email: tourismandtravel.invercargill@thenet.net.nz

With thanks to Jill Warhurst of Ulysses Southland who supplied information on aspects of this run.

Riverton

(38 km from Invercargill.)

Turn back the clock to a bygone era. Riverton is the oldest settlement in Southland and started life as a sealing and whaling settlement in the 1830s. Situated on a sheltered estuary with good nearby beaches, Riverton has a charm that makes this my preferred stopover to nearby Invercargill. Good accommodation can be found at the Riverton Rocks (B&B and backpackers) or the motor camp.

Tuatapere

(86 km from Invercargill.)

Situated beside the Waiau River, this former timber town is now a farming service centre, and provides a base for nearby hunting and highly recommended walking opportunities.

Clifden

(99 km from Invercargil; 95 km from Te Anau.)

Presumably named after the nearby limestone cliffs that house extensive cave systems and evidence of early Maori habitation. The town is worth a stopover to view the nearby Clifden Bridge which spans the Waiau River. The bridge, built circa 1900, is claimed to be the largest suspension bridge in New Zealand, and has recently been restored by the Historic Places Trust.

Manapouri

(165 km from Invercargill; 21 km from Te Anau.)

Situated amidst native bush, Manapouri overlooks its namesake lake, and provides a beautiful and peaceful alternative to Te Anau as a stopover travelling to/from Milford Sound. The motor camp is located at the northern end of Manapouri township.

A tour of the Manapouri hydro electric scheme – an amazing feat of engineering – and nearby Doubtful Sound are recommended if time allows (the total tour takes 7 hours). A shorter tour of the vast underground power-house is available.

Te Anau

(121 km from Milford Sound; 186 km from Invercargill.)

Te Anau township, on the shoreline of New Zealand's second largest lake, is a focal point for Fiordland National Park and a gateway to both Milford and Doubtful Sounds.

Mitre Peak at Milford Sound.
photo: TOWANDA women

The name Te Anau means 'cave of rushing water'; it is likely the early Maori named the area for the beautiful limestone caves situated a 30-minute launch trip across the lake from Te Anau.

There is plenty of visitor accommodation. The Te Anau Motor Park, 1 km from Te Anau on the Manapouri Road, offers cosy A-frame cabins for around $35 per double. Phone (03) 249-7457.

If you are heading to Milford Sound, make sure your petrol tank is full before you leave Te Anau, as prices in Milford Sound reflect its relative isolation. I suggest you also take a picnic or a snack, as facilities in Milford are limited, to say the least. Remember to pack insect repellent!

Fiordland Visitor Information Centre: Lake Front Drive. Phone (03) 249-8900.
Email: teanau1@fiordlandtravel.co.nz

Te Anau to Milford Sound

(242 km return, allow 3 hours – more if doing a Milford Sound cruise.)

Mirror Lakes *(56 km from Te Anau.)*
As their name suggests, these small lakes, visible from the roadside, mirror the surrounding mountains to spectacular effect (in calm weather). A short walk runs around the lakes for even better vantage points.

Lake Gunn *(76 km from Te Anau.)*
A 45-minute return loop walk gives access to the bush-clad shores of this splendid alpine lake.

Homer Tunnel *(99 km from Te Anau.)*
Hewn 1.2 km through solid rock, this tunnel takes you in spectacular fashion under the Homer Saddle to emerge truly on the West Coast to an alpine backdrop of waterfalls and native bush. The drive from here down to Milford Sound is truly superb.

The Chasm *(106 km from Te Anau.)*
A short (15 min. return) walk from the roadside takes you through native forest to cross a bridge and view how the Cleddau River has carved through solid rock in its effort to disperse up to 7 metres of annual rainfall.

Milford Sound *(121 km from Te Anau.)*
The fiord has few equals in the world and, if the weather permits, the views of Mitre Peak are wonderful. There are numerous opportunities to cruise the sounds and, if time allows, this is recommended. Whilst both the scenery and walks are world-class, don't expect great service from the rather limited café, bar, and accommodation houses in Milford Sound (back-packer etc.) which have always disappointed this writer.

Cleddau Valley.
photos: Jenny Cooper

Lake Gunn.

*On the eastern side of the
Homer Tunnel.*

❸❾ *Maniototo Big Sky Break*

The 'Big Skies' typified by Grahame Sydney's paintings of the Maniototo, translate to a hot dry climate that makes motorcycle touring of the old North Otago gold towns an extremely pleasant pastime. The route is generally straight and fast rather than curvaceous, but has considerable appeal for its lack of traffic, and interesting diversions.

Rating: ☺☺☺	
Starting from: Dunedin.	
Ending at: Dunedin.	
Distance: 409 km.	
Approximate riding time: 1 day. Allow 6 to 8 hours to include diversions.	
Usual traffic volumes: Light.	

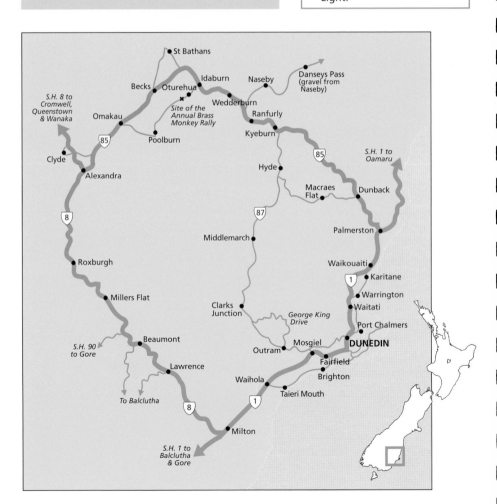

Run Description

- Depart **Dunedin** on **S.H. 1** heading north to **Waitati** and **Palmerston*** (55 km).
- At Palmerston, turn left (nor-west) on **S.H. 85** (known locally as the 'pig-root') to Dunback, Kyeburn and **Ranfurly** (77 km).
- Continue on S.H. 85 towards Alexandra, but look out for diversions firstly to **Naseby***, and later **St Bathans***. Then carry on to **Alexandra*** (87 km). #
- From Alexandra take **S.H. 8** to **Roxburgh***, **Lawrence*** and onwards to the junction with S.H. 1 (131 km)
- Join **S.H. 1** south of **Milton** and continue to **Dunedin** (59 km).

* *A worthwhile stopover – see Highlights & Diversions.*

\# An alternative return route:
via S.H. 85 to Ranfurly and Kyeburn,
then turn south on S.H. 87 to
Middlemarch, Mosgiel and Dunedin.

SAFETY POINTS
- Ice on the road's shaded areas and high spots during winter.
- Gravel on the road in winter and after storms.

Highlights & Diversions

Dunedin

Located in a dramatic harbourside position, surrounded by lush green hills, Dunedin is proud of its Scottish heritage (the name Dunedin is Gaelic for Edinburgh, and the city is often called 'Edinburgh of the South'). Blessed by the wealth generated during the 1860s gold rush, Dunedin has a fine collection of Victorian architecture, including its famous railway station and town hall. Today Dunedin is very much a university city, with a lively cultural and artistic scene. It boasts a wide selection of very fine and reasonably priced restaurants. There is plenty of accommodation at most levels, including camping grounds near St Kilda Beach and Leith Valley. The Otago Peninsula offers 4-star motorcycle riding and a circuit is strongly recommended (see p.138), as is a tour of the Albatross Colony, phone (03) 478-0499, and Penguin Place, phone (03) 478-0286, to fully appreciate the natural attractions and unique wildlife.

Dunedin Visitor Information Centre:
The Octagon. Phone (03) 474-3300.
Email: visitor.centre@dcc.govt.nz
Internet: www.cityofdunedin.com

Trike on display at the Brass Monkey Rally, held annually near Oturehua.

Palmerston

(55 km north from Dunedin.)

An old gold rush town that still serves the nearby Macraes gold mine which currently produces over 110,000 ounces of gold per annum via modern open-cast mining methods.

Naseby

(26 km return diversion from S.H. 85; 37 km from Ranfurly; 145 km from Dunedin.)

Set amidst trees in stark contrast to the nearby dryness of the Maniototo, Naseby is a charming gold field town that has managed to retain much of its character. There is an excellent camping ground, and numerous walks. A swimming dam surrounded by larch trees provides welcome relief from the summer heat.

The open roads
and big skies of
the Maniototo.
photo: David Wall

Danseys Pass Hotel

(A further diversion 15 minutes, or 15 km, from Naseby.)

Getting to this hotel requires navigation of gravel roads, but it is worth it for either accommodation or good food. Restored with clever use of sun dried bricks and demolition timber trusses the building has considerable appeal. (www.danseyspass.co.nz)

St Bathans

(20 km diversion from S.H. 85; 59 km from Alexandra; 153 km from Dunedin.)

Turn back the clock and enter the old gold mining town of St Bathans, set above the beautiful blue lake which often mirrors the surrounding whitestone sculptured cliffs sluiced by early gold miners. The historic (haunted) Vulcan Hotel beckons travellers with a variety of cool ales and snacks. The nearby old post office, local hall, church and cemetery all provide intriguing glimpses of the town's former glory days.

Alexandra

(191 km from Dunedin via S.H. 8 to Roxburgh and Milton, or 212 km via S.H. 85 to Ranfurly and Palmerston to Dunedin, or 224 km via S.H. 85 & 87 to Ranfurly, Middlemarch to Dunedin.)

Set at the junction between the Clutha and the Manuherikia Rivers, Alexandra services the hot dry Central Otago orchard and grape growing region. There are many restaurants and accommodation houses, plus a good camping ground just north of the town on S.H. 85. The vineyards of Black Ridge and Dry Gully off Earnscleugh Road (turn off south of the Clutha Bridge) make an attractive alternative route to Clyde.

Alexandra Visitor Information Office:
22 Centennial Avenue. Phone (03) 448-9515.
Email: info@tco.org.nz

Clyde

(5 km diversion from Alexandra on the way to Cromwell.)

The old mining town of Clyde at the foot of the huge Clyde hydroelectric dam is a pleasant side-trip from Alexandra, and the preferred stopover for many motorcyclists as it offers some charming historic restaurants and hotels in relatively quiet surrounds. (Olivers Restaurant, and the Old Post Office are well worth a visit.) There is also a popular camping ground.

Roxburgh

(40 km from Alexandra; 150 km from Dunedin.)

Set in an attractive valley Roxburgh is the centre of a fruit growing area, and the area abounds with opportunities to buy fresh fruit in season from road-side stalls.

Lawrence

(72 km from Alexandra; 78 km from Dunedin.)

An interesting halfway break on S.H. 8 between Dunedin and Alexandra, Lawrence has lost much of its former charm, but the back streets and the nearby Gabriel's Gully offer some idea of the town's wealth during the gold-rush era. To view some interesting Victorian architecture take a ride around the hill south of the main street.

The historic Vulcan Hotel at St Bathans.
photo: Len Chilcott

Dunedin Railway Station.

Larnach Castle, on the Otago Peninsula.
photo: Neville Peat

Otago Peninsula Natural High

Rating: ☺☺☺☺
Starting from: Dunedin.
Ending at: Dunedin.
Distance: 60 km.
Approximate riding time: 2 hours (allow an afternoon to include diversions).
Usual traffic volumes: Light to moderate.

N o trip to Dunedin is complete without a tour of the Otago Peninsula. It provides a unique opportunity to visit world class nature conservation refuges as well as offering twisting roads tailor-made for motorcycling. All this, plus the intrigue of Larnach Castle, splendid beaches, interesting walks and diverse terrain make Otago Peninsula a memorable escape.

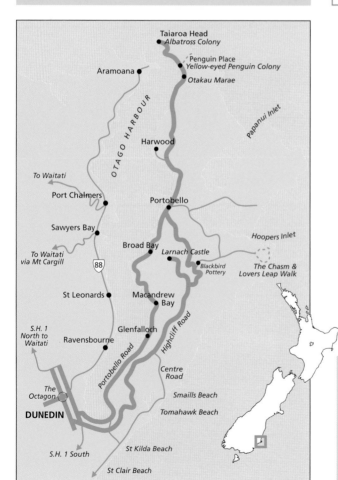

Yellow-eyed penguin.
photo: Neville Peat

SAFETY POINTS

- The tight twisting roads may get a little crowded at weekends and during 'rush-hour' commuting times.
- Look out for loose gravel on some corners after periods of rain.

Run Description

- From the **Octagon** (Dunedin's city centre) travel east down Stuart Street to the historic Railway Station, and turn right onto the one-way street system (**S.H. 1 south**).
- At the Queens Gardens, take the left lane onto an over bridge across the railway lines to **Portsmouth Drive**, and via **Portobello Road** follow the signs around the shores of the peninsula via **Glenfalloch Gardens*** to reach **Portobello*** (28 km).
- A short 10 km return diversion north beyond Portobello will take you to the attractions of **Otakou*, Penguin Place Yellow-eyed Penguin Refuge***, and the **Royal Albatross Colony***.
- Return to **Portobello** and follow signs to **Larnach Castle** (turn left, south-east, at the second street south of the Portobello Hotel).
- Follow the road signs to Larnach Castle. (Near Blackbird Pottery look out for a 5 km return diversion on a gravel road to **Lovers Leap*** and the **Chasm***.)
- At the small township of **Pukehiki**, turn right to **Larnach Castle*** for a 3 km return diversion.
- Return to the Pukehiki intersection and follow **Highcliff Road** back to **Dunedin**, enjoying the views en route.

* A worthwhile stopover – see Highlights & Diversions.

Highlights & Diversions

Glenfalloch Gardens

(Signposted 10 km from Dunedin on the Portobello Road.)

The sheltered valley called Glenfalloch is extensively planted in exotic azaleas, rhododendrons, and maples which are at their colourful best during September and October. At other times of the year the gardens provide a tranquil stopping point and an opportunity for a cup of tea shared with tame doves and peacocks who complement the natural beauty of the woodlands.

Portobello

(28 km from Dunedin.)

A small village which grew as a seaside holiday resort for Dunedin residents and today has become a favourite refreshment stop for the many tourists visiting the Otago Peninsula. Portobello is also home to the 'Happy Hen' craft gallery and the 1908 Restaurant. The Otago University Aquarium is reached via a short 3 km return gravel road and is open to the public most weekends from noon till 4.30 pm. Fletcher House – a restored Victorian villa that played a role in the formation of one of New Zealand's largest building companies, Fletcher Challenge Ltd – can be seen at nearby Broad Bay.

Approaching Taiaroa Head, Otago Peninsula.
photo: David Wall

Otakou

The small township of Otakou was a site of early Maori settlement and its mispronunciation reputedly gave us the name Otago. Today the township retains its strong Maori heritage and is the site of an attractive meeting house. (Please note: permission should be sought before visiting.)

Dunedin nestles at the head of the Otago Harbour, with the Otago Peninsula stretching out to the right.
photo: David Wall

Penguin Place

The first Yellow-eyed Penguin reserve you encounter is the NZ Tourism Award-winning Penguin Place operated by Liz and Howard McGrouther. A late afternoon visit is strongly recommended to see the best of this intriguing 'eco tourism' venture. Phone (03) 478-0286 for bookings.

The Taiaroa Heads Royal Albatross Colony

At the end of the peninsula road lies another NZ Tourism Award-winning conservation project. At the Albatross Centre you can view the world's only mainland breeding colony of the Royal Albatross and gain a unique introduction to this splendid bird whose wing span can measure up to 3 metres from tip to tip, enabling it to circumnavigate the world. Take time to visit Pilots Beach below the Albatross Centre, and walk the cliffs to the north of the upper car park: you will be rewarded by views of a wide range of wildlife including seals, spotted shags (cormorants), terns, and possibly blue penguins.

For those interested in things mechanical or military, the Albatross Centre also offers a trip into the bowels of the old Fort Taiaroa to view the only working Armstrong Disappearing Gun in the world. Phone (03) 478-0499 for bookings and information.

Lovers Leap and Chasm Walk

(Signposted midway between Portobello and Larnach Castle.)

A short (3 km return) gravel diversion takes you to this attractive cliff top walk. Allow an hour and a half for a return walk of 2.5 km which can be completed as a circuit over Sandymount, or as a return trip around the less steep northerly route. (Note: the walk is closed during spring lambing season.)

Larnach Castle

(16 km from Dunedin via Highcliff Road.)

The grand architecture combined with a commanding hill top site and the rather haunting demise of William Larnach combine to make a visit to this Heritage Award-winning castle very memorable. Visitors have the option of either paying a charge to tour the interior of the Castle, or a lesser charge for access to the grounds (and the Tea Rooms located in the former Ballroom).
Phone (03) 476-1616.
Internet: www.larnachcastle.co.nz

This escape offers some exceptional riding on little-used roads, with added benefits for fly fishing exponents as it follows the interesting waterways of the Mataura, Clutha and Waipahi Rivers. From the hills above Heriot there are extensive southerly vistas of the Hokonui Hills and Kaihiku Ranges. This escape can also be easily accessed from Dunedin.

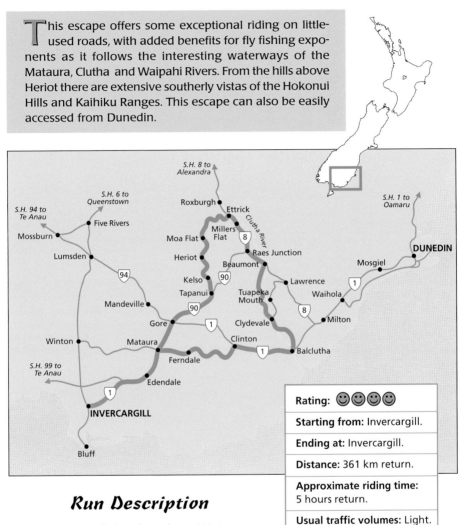

Rating: ☺☺☺☺
Starting from: Invercargill.
Ending at: Invercargill.
Distance: 361 km return.
Approximate riding time: 5 hours return.
Usual traffic volumes: Light.

Run Description

- From **Invercargill*** head North on **S.H. 1** to **Edendale** and **Mataura*** (53 km).

- Turn right at Mataura; leaving S.H. 1 **cross the Mataura River**, and turn left (north) following the old coach road and signs to **Ferndale** and **Clinton*** , by-passing Gore via a scenic and good motorcycling route (45 km).

- At Clinton rejoin **S.H. 1** (turn right) and follow the signs to **Balclutha*** (31 km).

- At Balclutha cross the Clutha River, and look for a left-hand turn signposted to **Clydevale**. Take this minor route, turning left 24 km from Balclutha and crossing the Clutha (as the nearby historic Tuapeka punt, although picturesque, does not operate to the convenience of most motorcyclists).

- From Clydevale turn right and follow the Clutha River via Rongahere Road and signs to **Beaumont** and **Roxburgh.**
- At Beaumont join **S.H. 8** (turn left) and carry on to **Millers Flat** and **Ettrick*** (65 km).
- As you approach **Ettrick**, just past the hotel look for signs to **Heriot** and **Moa Flat**. Then, (after refreshments at either the Ettrick Tavern or the local store which is renowned for its burgers), take the side road to Heriot.
- Follow the minor road (good quality tar sealed) and signs to **Heriot**. From Heriot, at the Kelso forks take the left option to **S.H. 90** and **Tapanui*** (42 km).
- From **Tapanui**, continue on S.H.90 to **Gore*** (35 km).
- From Gore rejoin **S.H. 1** and return to Mataura, and thence to **Invercargill*** (66 km).

* *A worthwhile stopover –*
see Highlights & Diversions.

SAFETY POINT Take care with slippery stock effluent on the road.

Highlights & Diversions

Invercargill

(257 km from Dunedin via the Catlins Southern Scenic Route; 186 km from Te Anau via S.H. 99 and Tuatapere.)

New Zealand's southernmost city services the rich grasslands to the north that supply much of New Zealand's dairy and sheep farming wealth. The abundant seas to the south make Bluff (the port of Invercargill) a centre for the famed Bluff oyster. Like Dunedin, Invercargill has a Scottish heritage, and street names and architecture reflect this. There are many motels and camping opportunities, but boutique dining opportunities are (in the view of this writer) limited by a rather staid liquor licensing trust. For me, nearby Riverton is a preferred stopover.

Invercargill Visitor Information Centre: 108 Gala Street. Phone (03) 214-9133.
Email: tourismandtravel.invercargill@thenet.net.nz

Invercargill clocktower.
photo: Reg Graham

Gore, on the Mataura River, is a renowned trout fishing centre.
photo: David Wall

Mataura

(53 km from Invercargill.)

The home of a meat processing plant and, until recently, a large paper mill which utilised the nearby Mataura River. Despite these intrusions, the waters of the Mataura and its tributaries are noted as world class trout fisheries. Nearby rivers of fishing acclaim are the Waipahi and the Waiwera.

Clinton

(98 km from Invercargill; 111 km from Dunedin.)

Achieving some fame from its namesake American President Clinton, road signs to Clinton and the coincidentally nearby Gore have been the subject of much interest. A hill above the town once marked the border between the Ngai Tahu and Ngati Mamoe tribal lands.

Balclutha

(129 km from Invercargill; 80 km from Dunedin.)

Situated near the mouth of the Clutha River (New Zealand's largest river by volume, and its second longest), Balclutha is primarily a rural service town, but offers a collection of interesting antique and second-hand shops worthy of closer inspection.

Ettrick

(217 km from Invercargill via this route; 134 km from Dunedin.)

A major fruit packing and distribution town, Ettrick has numerous good fruit stalls, but the main reason for inclusion in this guide is the local store which is very popular for its boysenberry sundaes and hamburgers. There is an adjoining park with a sheltered picnic spot. Along the road the 'Seed Farm' at the turn-off to Moa Flat and Heriot offers more substantial fare and is a nice B&B for those turning this escape into an overnighter.

Tapanui

(101 km return to Invercargill or 260 km via this route.)

Surrounded by forests and lush farming country, the rural service town of Tapanui is also famed for the trout fishing attractions of the nearby Pomahaka River, and the hunting attributes of the Blue Mountains.

The Presidential Highway.
photo: Len Chilcott

Gore

(66 km from Invercargill.)

A rural service town noted for its annual 'Golden Guitar' festival (held each Queen's Birthday weekend in July) has earned Gore the name of NZ's capital of Country Music. Gore is also noted as a centre for trout fishing which is popular in the surrounding rivers and streams. A passionate artistic community has created a local Art Gallery of considerable merit. The nearby 30 km return trip to Mandeville will allow you to see a part of New Zealand's flying history: a factory restores early de Havilland biplanes, and offers sight-seeing flights of the locality. There is a charming nearby restaurant and bar.

Gore Visitor Information Centre:
Cnr Hokonui Drive and Norfolk Street.
Phone (03) 208-9908. Email: goreinfo@esi.co.nz

The Seed Farm, near Ettrick.

With thanks to Jill Warhurst and Ulysses Southland who recommended aspects of this run.

Southern Scenic – Catlins Circuit

The journey from Dunedin to Invercargill (or vice-versa) via the scenic Catlins coast offers great riding, with marvellous scenery – the only drawback being 45 km of sometimes tricky gravel between Papatowai and Porpoise Bay. (As this is scheduled for sealing by late 2000, we suggest you check conditions with the local Automobile Association office.) This escape offers a grand link via the Southern Scenic route to Te Anau and Milford Sound *(see page 130).*

Rating: ☺☺☺   (5-star when 100% sealed).
Starting from: Dunedin (or Invercargill).
Ending at: Dunedin (or Invercargill).
Distance: 474 km as a return run to Dunedin (436 km if Invercargill is missed).
Approximate riding time: 7 hours return, but best spread out over 2 days as the scenic opportunities of the Catlins area alone require a full day to enjoy.
Usual traffic volumes: Light. (Medium between Dunedin and Balclutha.)

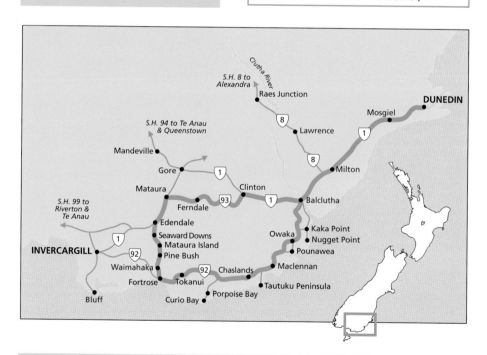

SAFETY POINTS
- Care needed on gravel sections, scheduled to be sealed by end 2000, but check with the Automobile Association.
- Take care with slippery dairy cow effluent on the road between Fortrose and Clinton.

Run Description

- From **Dunedin*** head south on **S.H. 1** to **Milton** and **Balclutha*** (80 km).

- At Balclutha turn left (east) following signs to **Owaka***, via **S.H. 92**, the Southern Scenic Route (35 km).

- After Balclutha take turn left to **Kaka Point*** if you wish to visit the historic **Nugget Point*** lighthouse and nature reserve, otherwise...

- Continue to Owaka, then on to **Maclennan, Papatowai, Chaslands,** (allow for the diversion to **Curio Bay***), **Tokanui and Fortrose** (105 km).

- At Fortrose decide whether you are returning to Dunedin or carrying on via the Southern Scenic route to Invercargill and Te Anau. *(If going to Te Anau, follow S.H. 92 signs to Invercargill and then refer to the Magic Milford run, page 130.)*

- **If returning to Dunedin,** shortly after Fortrose look for a right (north) turn, and follow minor roads signposted to **Waimahaka, Mataura Island, Seaward Downs** and **Edendale** (45 km).

- From Edendale take **S.H. 1 to Mataura*** (15 km).

- Turn right (east) at **Mataura**. Leaving S.H. 1, cross the **Mataura River**, and turn left (north) following the old coach road (S.H. 93) and signs to **Ferndale** and **Clinton***, bypassing Gore via a scenic and relatively quiet motorcycling route (45 km).

- At Clinton rejoin S.H. 1 (turn right) and follow the signs to **Balclutha*** (31 km).

- Continue on S.H. 1 to **Milton** and **Dunedin*** (80 km).

---

* *A worthwhile stopover – see Highlights & Diversions.*

Highlights
& Diversions

University of Otago, Dunedin.

Dunedin

Located in a dramatic harbourside position, surrounded by lush green hills, Dunedin is proud of its Scottish heritage (the name Dunedin is Gaelic for Edinburgh, and the city is often called 'Edinburgh of the South'). Blessed by the wealth generated during the 1860s goldrush, Dunedin has a fine collection of Victorian architecture, including its famous railway station and town hall. Today Dunedin is very much a university city, with a lively cultural and artistic scene. It boasts a wide selection of very fine and reasonably priced restaurants. There is plenty of accommodation at most levels, including camping grounds near St Kilda Beach and Leith Valley. The Otago Peninsula offers 4-star motorcycle riding and a circuit is strongly recommended (*see p.138*), as is a tour of the Albatross Colony, phone (03) 478-0499, and Penguin Place, phone (03) 478-0286, to fully appreciate the natural attractions and unique wildlife.

Dunedin Visitor Information Centre: The Octagon. Phone (03) 474-3300. Email: visitor.centre@dcc.govt.nz
Internet: www.cityofdunedin.com

Balclutha

(129 km from Invercargill; 80 km from Dunedin.)

Situated near the mouth of the Clutha River (New Zealand's largest river by volume, and its second longest), Balclutha is primarily a rural service town, but offers a collection of interesting antique and second-hand shops worthy of closer inspection.

Kaka Point and Nugget Point

(101 km from Dunedin. Turn left (east) 6 km from Balclutha on S.H. 92.)

An intertesting loop detour from S.H. 92, Kaka Point has a pleasant beach and several accommodation options, including a motor camp and Fernlea Backpackers. Following the beach southwards (approximately 5 km gravel) you reach the spectacular Nugget Point wildlife reserve – home to the rare Yellow-eyed Penguins. If you take a walk to the lighthouse and beyond along the rock ridge, you will see an amazing abundance of wildlife. Hookers sea lions and elephant seals cavort in the water and laze on the rocks at most times of the year, while overhead there is a variety of sea birds, including the spotted shag, sooty shearwater, and Australasian gannets. (Allow for a 1-hour return walk from the car-park.)

Owaka and Pounawea

(35 km from Balclutha; 142 km from Invercargill.)

Owaka, the small commercial centre of the Catlins area, has an interesting museum covering the history of the area; however, opening hours are restrictive, and it is best to check with the Visitor Centre by phoning (03) 415-8392.

A short 4 km diversion from Owaka will take you to the sleepy coastal resort of Pounawea. Here there is reasonable accommodation in the seaside motor camp (cabins available, phone (03) 415-8483). The nearby estuary offers safe swimming, and in the evening is a favoured flounder fishing spot. The Pounawea Nature Walk is an interesting outing beginning at the motor camp (30 minutes return).

If staying at Pounawea or Owaka and you are not averse to a short gravel excursion then a visit to Cannibal Bay and Surat Bay is recommended. The rather grizzly name arises from the discovery in 1892 by Dr Hocken of the remains of a Maori feast, and cooking area (midden) containing human bones and skulls.

Purakaunui Falls, Catlins.

Jacks Bay and Blowhole

(44 km from Balclutha; 9 km south of Owaka; 137 km from Invercargill.)

Look for signs on the eastern side of the road just south of Pounawea: Jacks Bay is located on the southern side of the Pounawea estuary. Near the beach is a cliff-top walk to the 60m deep blowhole, located some 200m inland from the coast, and into which the sea crashes with spectacular effect at high tide.

Purakaunui Falls

(52 km from Balclutha; 17 km south of Owaka; 125 km from Invercargill.)

Look for signs to this highly recommended side-trip. A 30-minute (return) easy walk through dense beech forest is required.

Tautuku Beach and Peninsula

(75 km from Balclutha; 40 km south of Owaka; 102 km from Invercargill.)

South of Maclennan and Papatowai the road drops down to the spectacular Tautuku Bay. With native forest edging a long white sand beach the vista that greets you is spectacular. At the northern end of this bay is a picnic and camping spot, with the Tautuku Youth Adventure Trust lodge nearby. At the southern end of the beach, a short diversion from S.H. 92 takes you to a cluster of cribs (holiday homes) that shelter in the sun on the northern side of the peninsula. There is an attractive picnic spot here.

Waikawa, Porpoise Bay and Curio Bay petrified forest

(108 km from Balclutha; 73 km south of Owaka; 70 km from Invercargill.)

As S.H. 92 crosses the Waikawa stream, look for signs directing you south to Waikawa, Porpoise Bay and the Curio Bay petrified forest. This side trip is highly recommended, and the roads are sealed. The sheltered waters of Porpoise Bay attract its namesake as well as the rare Hectors dolphin. (Local boat operators offer dolphin viewing tours.) Carry on for 2 km to reach the Curio Bay petrified forest. Here the sea washes at the remains of a Jurassic forest dated back some 160 million years, which some claim supports the theory that New Zealand was part of the ancient supercontinent of Gondwanaland and was linked to South America.

Invercargill

(257 km from Dunedin via the Catlins Southern Scenic Route; 186 km from Te Anau via S.H. 99 and Tuatapere.)

New Zealand's southernmost city services the rich grasslands to the north that supply much of New Zealand's dairy and sheep farming wealth. The abundant seas to the south make Bluff (the port of Invercargill) a centre for the famed Bluff oyster. Like Dunedin, Invercargill has a Scottish heritage, and street names and architecture reflect this. There are many motels and camping opportunities, but boutique dining opportunities are (in the view of this writer) limited by a rather staid liquor licensing trust. For me nearby Riverton is a a preferred stopover.

Invercargill Visitor Information Centre:
108 Gala St. Phone (03) 214-9133.
Email:tourismandtravel.invercargill@thenet.net.nz

Nugget Point lighthouse. photo: David Wall

Riverton

(A 38 km diversion from Invercargill.)

Turn back the clock to a bygone era. Riverton is the oldest settlement in Southland, and started life as a sealing and whaling settlement in the 1830s. Situated on a sheltered estuary with good nearby beaches Riverton has a charm that makes this my preferred stopover to nearby Invercargill. Good accommodation can be found at the Riverton Rocks (B&B and Backpackers) or the motor camp. Local restaurants are rather good too.

Mataura

(53 km from Invercargill.)

The home of a meat processing plant and, until recently, a large paper mill which utilised the nearby Mataura River. Despite these intrusions, the waters of the Mataura and its tributaries are noted as world class trout fisheries. Nearby rivers of fishing acclaim are the Waipahi and the Waiwera.

Clinton

(98 km from Invercargill; 111 km from Dunedin.)

Achieving some fame from its namesake American President Clinton, road signs to Clinton and the coincidentally nearby Gore have been the subject of much interest. A hill above the town once marked the border between the Ngai Tahu and Ngati Mamoe tribal lands.

Gore

(66 km from Invercargill.)

A rural service town noted for its annual 'Golden Guitar' festival (held each Queen's Birthday weekend in July) has earned Gore the name of NZ's capital of Country Music. Gore is also noted as a centre for trout fishing which is popular in the surrounding rivers and streams. The passionate artistic community has created a local Art Gallery of considerable merit. The nearby 30 km return trip to Mandeville will allow you to see a part of New Zealand's flying history: a factory restores early de Havilland biplanes, and offers sight-seeing flights of the locality. There is a charming nearby restaurant and bar.

Gore Visitor Information Centre:
Cnr Hokonui Drive and Norfolk Street.
Phone (03) 208-9908.
Email: goreinfo@esi.co.nz

A half-day run around the edge of the Canterbury Plain, taking in the splendour and contrasts of the Ashley, Waimakariri, and Rakaia River Gorges. The flat straights at either end of this escape may be a bit 'ho hum'.

Rating: 😊😊
Starting from: Christchurch.
Ending at: Christchurch.
Distance: 246 km return.
Approximate riding time: 3 to 4 hours return.
Usual traffic volumes: Light to Medium. Approaches to Christchurch can get busy in evenings and weekends.

Run Description

- From **Christchurch*** head north on **S.H. 1** to **Kaiapoi** (20 km).
- At Kaiapoi take the left hand fork, **S.H. 73** to **Rangiora** (9 km).
- At Rangiora follow a minor road via the signs to **Ashley***, **Loburn**, **Glentui** and the **Ashley Gorge*** (44 km).
- Carry on towards **Oxford*** (8 km).
- From Oxford continue on **S.H. 77** ('The Inland Scenic Route') towards **Bexley** and **Waddington**, but look for the turn-off on the left to View Hill and the **Waimakariri River Gorge***, which requires a short diversion.
- Continue on S.H. 77 to **Glentunnel, Windwhistle**, and **Mt Hutt**. Between Windwhistle and Mt Hutt you will encounter the **Rakaia River Gorge***.
- From **Mt Hutt**, head for **Methven*** and **S.H. 77**.
- Between Mt Hutt and Methven, opposite the Homestead, look for signs on your left initially to **Methven** and thence to **Highbank, Barrhill**, and **Rakaia** across the plains to link to S.H. 1.
- S.H. 1 to return to **Christchurch*** (50 km).

* A worthwhile stopover – see Highlights & Diversions.

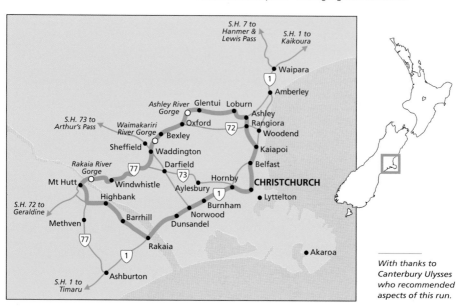

With thanks to Canterbury Ulysses who recommended aspects of this run.

Highlights & Diversions

Christchurch

New Zealand's 'Garden City', Christchurch has a distinctly English feel, perhaps due in part to the Avon River which meanders through the city, and the influence of early settlers determined to replicate their home country. Major attractions include the old university Arts Centre on Worcester Boulevard (www.artscentre.org.nz), the nearby Canterbury Museum in Rolleston Avenue, and the bustling restaurant precinct around Oxford and Hereford Streets.

Christchurch Visitor Information Office:
Cnr Worcester Street and Oxford Terrace.
Phone (03) 379-9629.
Email: info@christchurchnz.net
Internet: www.christchurchnz.net

Ashley River Gorge

A sheltered scenic picnic and camping spot overlooking majestic cliffs rising sheer from the Ashley River. Refreshing swimming.

Oxford

A charming stopover, with the Country Cottage Café favoured for its good coffee and lunches.

Waimakariri Gorge

Stunning views of the river gorge as it leaves the mountains and sweeps across the plains. There are ample picnic and swimming spots.

Rakaia Gorge

A grand arched bridge marks the point where the Rakaia River leaves the mountains and emerges to the plains via a spectacular gorge which doubles as a popular swimming and picnic spot.

Methven

A town of two seasons – in summer Methven is a sleepy rural service town, while in winter it is the centre of après ski for the nearby Mt Hutt ski field, and seldom sleeps. As a result, Methven has some rather good restaurants, bars and plenty of accommodation, but service can depend on the seasons. The Blue Pub is popular with motorcyclists.

SAFETY POINTS
- Wind gusts can be a danger, particularly at the foot of the hills near the gorges. Take care in nor-wester conditions when you may understand why a town is named 'Windwhistle'.
- Ice and grit on shady corners during winter.

Approaching the Rakaia Gorge.   photo: Pat Taylor

44 Twin Passes Run

The two Alpine passes covered by this run – Lewis Pass and Arthur's Pass – combine dramatic contrasts in scenery with superb riding. Travel from the fertile plains of Canterbury to the dry tussock lands east of the alps; from the snow capped mountains of the main divide to the dense native bush and tree-lined roads of the West Coast. Then, as if this is not enough, repeat the experience in reverse on another mountain pass. Surely this route covers some of the best roads in New Zealand.

Rating: ☺☺☺☺☺ +

Starting from: Christchurch or Greymouth (and/or Hokitika)

Ending at: Greymouth or Christchurch.

Distance: Christchurch to Greymouth via Lewis Pass 334 km. Greymouth to Christchurch via Arthur's Pass 251 km. Total Distance 585 km.

Approximate riding time: 8 to 9 hours return. This run can be done in one day, but only by the very keen. If time allows, it should be spread over two days to maximise diversions and to include the Buller Gorge and Westport.

Usual traffic volumes: Medium to light (medium around Christchurch, but generally light elsewhere).

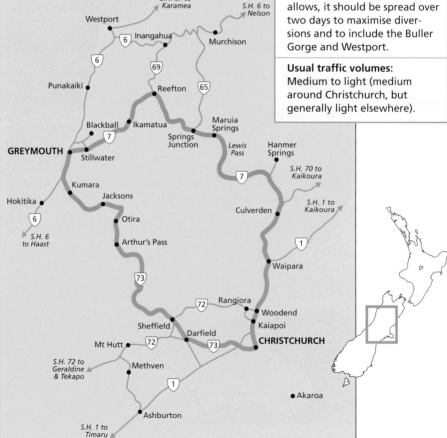

Run Description

DAY 1:

- From Christchurch take **S.H. 1** north to **Kaiapoi** (26 km) and **Waipara*** (58 km).
- After crossing the Waipara River, turn left on **S.H. 7** to **Hanmer Springs*** an 18 km return diversion (135 km from Christchurch and 219 km from Greymouth – see below.)
- Continue on S.H. 7 via Lewis Pass to **Reefton*** (255 km). Turn left (south-west) at Reefton. *A recommended diversion is to turn north at Reefton and proceed to the Inangahua Junction, then west through the Buller Gorge to Westport* then south down the Punakaiki coast to Greymouth. (Allow an extra 183 km or 3 hours.)*
- Continue on S.H. 7 to **Greymouth*** (334 km).

DAY 2:

- From **Greymouth** take **S.H. 6 south** to the **Kumara Junction*** (18 km).
- Turn left on **S.H. 73** to **Kumara*, Jacksons*, Otira*,** and **Arthur's Pass*** (93 km).
- Continue on S.H. 73 via **Sheffield, Waddington, Darfield** and **Aylesbury** to **Christchurch** (251 km).

---

* *A worthwhile stopover – see Highlights & Diversions.*

DANGER POINTS

- Watch the weather – the West Coast receives up to 5000 mm of rain per year, and more south of Haast (up to 7000mm). It is no fun riding in adverse conditions, so if the forecast is for rain on the West Coast, simply stay on the east coast side of the Alps (where the annual rainfall averages 330mm) until the weather clears and you can return to the West Coast.
- Ice (and snow) in winter conditions will effect shaded and high altitude areas of the mountain passes.
- Heavier traffic can be expected during holidays and weekends.

Highlights & Diversions

Waipara Winery

Situated on the right (east) of the S.H. 1 just before the Waipara river crossing and the turn-off to S.H. 7 (to Hanmer Spring and Lewis Pass) the Winery offers an opportunity to sample some of the region's wines in rather splendid surroundings.

Hanmer Springs

(An 18 km return diversion from S.H. 7; 133 km from Christchurch; 209 km from Greymouth.)

A leafy spa town with public thermal pools to ease any aches and pains. Set amongst forest clad foot-hills, there are many local walks – at their best in autumn. A charming town, well worth the diversion. The Forest Trust Motor Camp on Jacks Pass Road offers cabins from $15.00 per night.

Hurunui Visitor Information Centre: Amuri Drive. Phone 0800-733-426. Email: info@hurunui.com

Lewis Pass

Climbing to a height of 863 metres above sea level this scenic twisting and undulating road follows the route used by the Maori Ngai Tahu tribe as they travelled to and from the West Coast in search of the precious pounamu (greenstone or jade). The route offers many pleasant picnic spots and bush walks and is named after the explorer, Henry Lewis, who first detailed the route for other European settlers in 1860.

Maruia Springs

(203 km from Christchurch; 140 km from Greymouth.)

An opportunity to relax from your travels in hot mineral pools surrounded by alpine splendour. Clear starry nights make an overnight stay here hard to beat. There are several good bush walks nearby.

Reefton

(263 km from Christchurch; 79 km from Greymouth.)

Once a wealthy gold mining town, nicknamed 'Quartzopolis' for its link to the mineral quartz and resulting gold, Reefton is now a local centre for coal mining and farming set in an appealing valley junction. Links to the mining past are never far away: the nearby hills are littered with old gold mines and the 1886 School of Mines can still be found in its original building in Shiel Street. Indicative of its early gold wealth, Reefton gained fame as being the first New Zealand town to be lit by electricity in 1888.

Westport Diversion

(81 km from Reefton; 333 km from Christchurch.)

Westport is a good alternative stopping place to Greymouth, and an opportunity to link to Greymouth via the very scenic Buller Gorge and the Grand Loop of the Punakaiki coast route and the Karamea diversion detailed on page 159. Allow an extra 183 km for this diversion, and more if Karamea is included. For details on Westport see page 158.

Ikamatua

Part way between Reefton and Greymouth on S.H. 7 the Ikamatua Hotel is favoured by motorcyclists as a cheap and hearty alternative stopover to Greymouth. Cabins and a bunk-house are available.

All smiles in the Buller Gorge.

Greymouth

(342 km from Christchurch; 101 km from Westport.)

Once the site of Mawhera Pa, the largest Maori settlement on the West Coast, Greymouth became a boom town for pakeha settlers when gold was discovered nearby in 1864. Situated at the foot of cliffs carved by the action of the Grey River, Greymouth is the largest town on the West Coast, and clings somewhat precariously to the flood prone Grey River delta. In 1991 'the Great Wall of Greymouth' was completed in an attempt to prevent further flooding, and now forms a pleasant walkway around the town, starting at Cobden Bridge.

For an intriguing alternative to accommodation in Greymouth, pay a visit to **Blackball** (19 km from Greymouth off S.H. 7), so named after the London-based Hilton Hotel became upset that an upstart West Coast hotel shared its name. Despite the enforced name change The Formerly Blackball Hilton continues to thrive as visitors share their bemusement. Bed & breakfast or self-catering facilities are provided.
Free phone 0800 4 Blackball (42 52 25).
Email: bbhilton@xtra.co.nz
Internet: www.blackballhilton.co.nz

Blackball is also home to delicious bier sticks, and salami via its main street shop and factory.

Greymouth Visitor Information Centre: Cnr Herbert and Mackay Streets. Phone (03) 768-5101
Email: vingm@minidata.co.nz

Kumara Junction

18 km south of Greymouth you leave S.H. 6 and join S.H. 73 up the Taramakau valley to Arthur's Pass. Take care on the road/rail bridge here as rail tracks and motorcycle wheels are not compatible.

Kumara

(24 km from Greymouth; 234 km from Christchurch.)

Once a booming gold-rush town, Kumara was the home of Richard John Seddon (1845–1906), a leading political figure and liberal. Under Seddon's leadership New Zealand led the world in extending the right to vote to women, and introducing welfare benefits such as the world's first Old Age Pensions Bill. He is also reputed to have referred to New Zealand as 'God's own country' and spawned the now common description of New Zealand as 'Godzone'.

WEST COAST HOSPITALITY
Many West Coast hotels historically set aside a paddock for travellers' horses and cattle to graze upon. These facilities can sometimes be used by motorcyclists to set up a tent and camp for little or no charge.

Jacksons

(62 km from Greymouth; 196 km from Christchurch.)

The tavern is all that remains of the historic coach stop and watering hole that once boasted five hotels.

Otira

(81 km from Greymouth; 177 km from Christchurch.)

A small railway and road construction village. Between here and Arthur's Pass the road climbs 400m in less than 5 km via a series of hair-pin bends which used to make enjoyable riding before being somewhat reduced and overshadowed by the spectacular Otira viaduct, opened in November 1999. Place names in this area such as Starvation Point, Death Corner, and Lake Misery attest to the difficulties faced by the early road builders and miners and to the dangers of the road in the winter.

Arthurs Pass Township

(95 km from Greymouth; 163 km from Christchurch.)

Set some 736 metres above sea level, Arthur's Pass offers a variety of refreshments, an informative National Park Visitor Centre, and acts as a gateway to numerous alpine walks.

Arthur's Pass to Sheffield

(Sheffield: 187 km from Greymouth; 60 km from Christchurch.)

Between Arthur's Pass and Sheffield the road follows routes taken by the Maori Ngai Tahu tribe (in search of pounamu – greenstone or jade), as well as early European gold miners. The riding in this country is very scenic, with beautiful alpine views, patches of native bush and rolling tussock country as you follow the Waimakariri River down to the Canterbury Plains.

The Otira Viaduct replaced this precariously placed section of road – not as much fun for motorcyclists, but safer.
photo: Transit New Zealand

photo above: Institute of Geological & Nuclear Sciences

With thanks to Mark Walsh of Ulysses Westland and Ken Beaumont of Ulysses Canterbury who recommended aspects of this run.

Victoria Range Loop

> kirting around Westland's Victoria Forest Park via the picturesque Buller, Inangahua, and Maruia river valleys, this route offers a wide range of alpine and bush scenery, with some charming refreshment stop options. It is accessible as a day escape from Greymouth, Westport, Nelson, and Blenheim, or Christchurch (at a longish stretch).

Rating: ☺☺☺☺	

Starting from: either Nelson, Blenheim, Westport, or Greymouth.

Ending at: either Nelson, Blenheim, Westport, or Greymouth.

Distance: ex Nelson 463 km return. (538 km ex Blenheim.)

Approximate riding time: 1 day. 6 to 7 hours (ex Nelson).

Usual traffic volumes: Light.

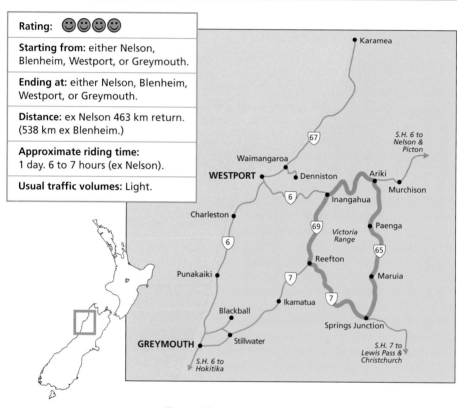

Run Description

- Depart **Nelson*** on **S.H. 6**, south-west to **Richmond**, Wakefield to **Murchison** and the **Inangahua Junction*** (182 km).

- At the Inangahua junction, turn left (south) on **S.H. 69**, to **Reefton***(34 km).

- From Reefton turn left on **S.H. 7**, to **Springs Junction*** (45 km).

- At Springs Junction, turn left on **S.H. 65**, to **Ariki** and Murchison (72 km).

- After Ariki turn right onto **S.H. 6** to **Murchison*** and return to **Nelson*** (130 km).

---

* *A worthwhile stopover – see Highlights & Diversions.*

Highlights & Diversions

Nelson

(116 km from Blenheim via S.H. 6.)

Surrounded by bush-clad hills and blessed by a kind climate, Nelson offers a delightful mix of cafés, arts and crafts, combined with quaint old buildings and an attractive seaside location. Nelson is also home to a thriving fishing industry, and an opportunity to sample some of its delights should not be missed. The Suter Art Gallery at 208 Bridge Street is one of my favourite galleries, and the Nelson Provincial Museum is full of interesting items.

Favoured refreshment stops are the various restaurants and cafés in Trafalgar Street (unfortunately the favourite Chez Eelco coffee house has shut its doors after 38 years); however, the legacy remains. Another option to try is The Honest Lawyer (for the name alone!) at 1 Point Road, Monaco, Nelson.

Nelson Visitor Information Centre:
Cnr Trafalgar and Halifax Streets.
Phone (03) 548-2304.
Email: vin@tourism-nelson.co.nz

Murchison

(130 km from Nelson; 162 km from Blenheim.)

A bustling junction town set amidst native bush-clad valleys, Murchison gained the nation's sympathy when in 1929 it became the centre of a huge earthquake which considerably altered the topography of the area. There are numerous stopover opportunities but top picks are the Beachwoods Café at the southern end of town, the museum, and the riverside domain on Murchison's northern edge.

Inangahua

(51 km from Murchison; 40 km from Westport.)

Another junction and earthquake town, Inangahua lies in the fault zone of the Buller River gorge. The earthquake that hit Inangahua occurred in 1968 and was so severe that the entire town was evacuated. S.H. 69 between Inangahua and Reefton is perhaps the least interesting part of this circuit, but offers some nice straights.

Reefton

(34 km from Inangahua; 79 km from Greymouth.)

Once a wealthy gold-mining town, nicknamed 'Quartzopolis' for its link to the mineral quartz and resulting gold, Reefton is now a local centre for coal mining and farming set in a picturesque valley junction. Links to the mining past are never far away: the nearby hills are littered with old gold mines and the 1886 School of Mines can still be found in its original building in Shiel Street. Indicative of its early gold wealth, Reefton gained fame as being the first New Zealand town to be lit by electricity in 1888. The route between Reefton and Springs Junction is a bush-clad delight.

Springs Junction

(45 km from Reefton; 83 km from Murchison.)

Very much a transit stop, Springs Junction offers a shop, tourist lodge, restaurant and garage.

West Coast native beech forest.

SAFETY POINTS
- Ice on the shaded areas and high spots of the road during winter.
- Insect repellent should be carried for any native bush stopovers west of the Alps.

With thanks to Peter Shaw of Ulysses Nelson who recommended aspects of this run.

West Coast Grand Loop

Rating: ☺☺☺☺☺ +
Starting from: Greymouth.
Ending at: Greymouth.
Distance: 260 to 270 km. (Allow extra for the recommended diversions: Denniston 52 km return; Karamea 194 km return.)
Approximate riding time: 6 hours return. This run can be done in one day, but if time allows is best spread over two days to maximise stopovers and diversions.
Usual traffic volumes: Medium to light.

In fine weather the West Coast Grand Loop surely rates as one of the best motorcycling routes in the world. Riders will find a combination of low traffic volumes, good quality roads and spectacular scenery, varying from coastal to river gorge and native bush. There are enough undulations and twists in the road to test and delight all levels of riding skills.

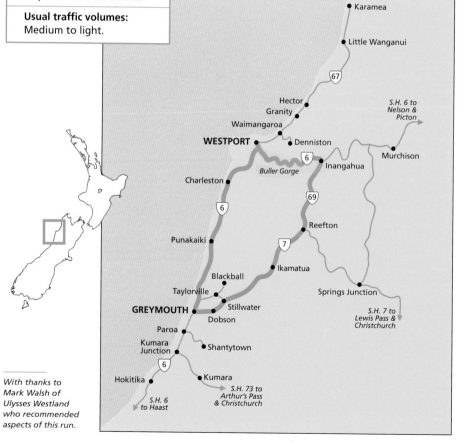

With thanks to Mark Walsh of Ulysses Westland who recommended aspects of this run.

Run Description

- S.H. 6 north of **Greymouth*** to **Westport*** (101 km).

- Stop and enjoy **Punakaiki*** (46 km from Greymouth; 55 km from Westport).

- Continue on S.H. 6, 29 km to **Charleston*** then a further 20 km to the Buller Gorge turnoff (signposted S.H. 6 to Inangahua, Nelson, Reefton).

- At this junction either divert left (north) for a further 6 km to **Westport*** (101 km from Greymouth) for an overnight stop, or for further diversions to **Karamea*** (an option for an overnight stop) or **Denniston*** *(see page 159)*. To carry on...

- From Westport follow **S.H. 6** through the Buller Gorge 47 km to **Inangahua***.

- At Inangahua turn right (south) onto **S.H. 69** travelling 34 km to **Reefton***.

- At Reefton turn right (south) onto **S.H. 7**, 79 km to **Greymouth***.

* *A worthwhile stopover –*
  see Highlights & Diversions.

SAFETY POINTS

- Watch the weather – the West Coast receives 5000 to 7000 mm of rain per year, and it is no fun riding in the adverse conditions that arise from time to time. If the forecast is for rain on the West Coast, simply cross one of the several Southern Alp passes and ride on the east coast (where the annual rainfall averages 330 mm) until the weather clears and you can return to the West Coast.

- Care should be taken with farm stock (cattle and sheep) on the road. The resulting effluent can leave a slippery residue, and this can be a problem on roads approaching Karamea.

Highlights & Diversions

Greymouth

(342 km from Christchurch; 101 km from Westport.)

Once the site of Mawhera Pa, the largest Maori settlement on the West Coast, Greymouth became a boom town for pakeha settlers when gold was discovered nearby in 1864. Situated at the foot of cliffs carved by the action of the Grey River, Greymouth is the largest town on the West Coast, and clings somewhat precariously to the flood prone Grey River delta. In 1991 'the Great Wall of Greymouth' was completed in an attempt to prevent further flooding, and now forms a pleasant walkway around the town, starting at Cobden Bridge.

The strangely named Bonzai Pizzeria at 31 Mackay Street offers tasty baking and pizzas at very reasonable prices.

For a nice alternative to accommodation in Greymouth, pay a visit to 'The Formerly Blackball Hilton' – 9 km from Greymouth: either cross the Grey River on S.H. 6 and turn off to Blackball about 5 km north-east of Greymouth, or take S.H. 7 to Stillwater, and cross the Grey River at that point.

Greymouth Visitor Information Centre:
Cnr Herbert and Mackay Streets.
Phone (03) 768-5101.
Email: vingm@minidata.co.nz

Stillwater and Blackball Diversion

Stillwater is an old mining town on S.H. 7 which achieved notoriety in 1896 when New Zealand's worst mining tragedy claimed the lives of 67 miners. Their mass grave can be found in the Stillwater cemetery.

From Stillwater you can turn north across the Grey River for a diversion to the town of **Blackball**, made famous by 'The Formerly Blackball Hilton', so named after the London-based Hilton Hotel became upset that an upstart West Coast hotel shared its name. Despite the enforced name change The Formerly Blackball Hilton continues to thrive as visitors share their bemusement. Bed & breakfast or self catering facilities are provided.

Free phone 0800 4 Blackball. (0800 42 52 25)
Email: bbhilton@xtra.co.nz
Internet: www.blackballhilton.co.nz

Blackball is also home to delicious bier sticks and salami via its main street shop and factory.

Rapahoe

(11 km north from Greymouth; 90 km south of Westport.)

Here the road joins a rather wild coastline; however, safe bathing can be found north of Rapahoe on Seven Mile Beach. Further north, the road offers plenty of undulations and viewpoints as the route negotiates bluffs and headlands leading north to...

Barrytown

The local tavern is a popular stopping point en route.

Charleston

Continue north towards **Charleston** and Westport, and enjoy more twisty and undulating coastal scenery. North of Charleston the road leaves the coast, with the scenery dominated by undulating 'pakihi' or infertile swamp lands. 20 km from Charleston you will reach the Westport turnoff. To continue the Grand Loop, turn right to the Buller River and Inangahua; however, you may wish to detour the 6 km into Westport.

Punakaiki

(46 km from Greymouth; 57 km south of Westport.)

This is a highly recommended stopover, both to view the Pancake Rocks (stratified limestone blow holes through which the sea crashes to spectacular effect at full tide), and to sample the hospitality of the nearby cafés and craft shops. Nikau Palms Café is a favourite. Punakaiki Camping Ground is a good motor camp if you wish to stay longer.

Punakaiki National Park Visitor Centre: Main Road. Phone (03) 731-1895. Email: punakaikivc@doc.govt.nz

The 'pancake rocks' at Punakaiki.

Westport

(101 km from Greymouth; 81 km from Reefton; 344 km from Christchurch.)

Westport is a town founded on the 'black gold' – coal. A visit to **Coaltown** in Queen Street is strongly recommended as its audio-visual presentations and simulations of underground workings, combined with an interesting collection of historic artifacts provide an understanding of the importance of this industry to the region.

Westport is an ideal stopping-off point for those wanting to stay longer and to sample the diversions of Karamea and Denniston *(see next page)*.

On leaving Westport, return to the Buller Gorge turn-off and take S.H 6 to follow the Buller River as it cuts through the Paparoa Range to **Inangahua**. The **Buller Gorge** road provides some of the best and most scenic motorcycling to be found in New Zealand. The combination of picturesque scenery mixed with the twists of the river make for great riding on a gently undulating route where traffic volumes are usually light to moderate.

At Inangahua, turn right, picking up S.H. 69 towards Reefton. The road between Inangahua and Reefton is a bit of an anti-climax after the delights of the Buller.

Reefton

(263 km from Christchurch; 79 km from Greymouth.)

Once a wealthy gold-mining town, nicknamed 'Quartzopolis' for its link to the mineral quartz and resulting gold, Reefton is now a local centre for coal mining and farming set in a picturesque valley junction. Links to the mining past are never far away: the nearby hills are littered with old gold mines and the 1886 School of Mines can still be found in its original building in Shiel Street. Indicative of its early gold wealth, Reefton gained fame as being the first New Zealand town to be lit by electricity in 1888. Interesting architecture abounds and the town has considerable charm.

Nikau Palms at sunset, West Coast.

Turn right onto S.H. 7 and follow the Grey River from its source as it flows towards Greymouth.

Ikamatua

Part way between Reefton and Greymouth, the Ikamatua Hotel is favoured by motorcyclists as a cheap and hearty alternative stopover to Greymouth. Cabins and a bunk-house are available.

RECOMMENDED DIVERSIONS

Denniston

(Denniston: 26 km north of Westport.)

The old 'ghost town' of Denniston, off the Karamea road (S.H. 67), is well worth a visit. Set on a ridge 600m above Westport, Denniston once boasted a population of 2,000 and from 1880 to 1968 mined over 30 million tons of coal via the precipitous 'incline' (a major engineering feat).

Drive 16 km north of Westport on the Karamea road (S.H. 67) until you reach Waimangaroa, then follow the signs up to Denniston. The twisting climb, the resulting views, the romance of the ghost town plus the engineering skills witnessed in the incline, make this a very enjoyable trip.

Karamea

(Karamea: 98 km north of Westport.)

A glimpse of a sub-tropical or 'winterless' Westland via a 5-star motorcycle touring route can be found north of Westport at Karamea. As the route to Karamea is 'no-exit' you must return to Westport the same way, but the road and scenery are so good that this potential draw-back becomes a feature of the 196 km return journey (allow 3 hours riding time, return). Indeed, Karamea is a recommended option for an overnight stop as an alternative to Westport.

From Westport head north on S.H. 67 towards Granity, Hector, and Karamea. The first 43 km are flat and uneventful; however, 11 km north of Hector the fun starts as you head inland up the attractive Mokihinui River valley and climb bush-clad hills to View Hill Saddle 420m above sea level. From here the road undulates through picturesque scenery and occasional dairy farms (beware of on-road effluent) to Happy Valley Saddle, before winding downward to Little Wanganui and onwards over the lush coastal plain to Karamea.

At Karamea, good accommodation ranging from back-packers to motel units can be found at the appropriately named 'Last Resort' which also arranges numerous local tours. There is good free-camping 15 km north of Karamea at the Kohaihai River, where the Heaphy Track begins and ends.

WEST COAST HOSPITALITY
Many West Coast hotels historically set aside a paddock for travellers' horses and cattle to graze upon. These facilities can today often be used by motorcyclists to set up a tent and camp for little or no charge.

TYPES OF MOTORCYCLES

There are almost as many types of motorcycles as there are types of riders. The following definitions may help you select the motorcycle most suited to your needs. Some categories overlap, so please treat them as broad generalizations.

Motor Scooters: Smaller engined motorcycles, equipped with fairings to keep feet and clothing dry, ideal for round town usage. Wheels are usually small. Engines are up to 250cc and economical.

Commuter: Smaller engined, and therefore economical motorcycles ideal for round town usage. While some will imitate the looks of bigger sports bikes, some are more akin to motor scooters. Usually up to 250cc.

Sports Bikes: Think adrenalin riding. These 'road racers' – designed primarily for fun, speed and cornering – are the favourite of speed cameras. Such bikes are often single seated. Handle bars are low and seating is crouched forward, legs tucked back, with some weight carried on the arms. Some are partly faired, primarily to improve aerodynamics. Rear tyres are often noticeably 'fatter' than front tyres. Engines range from 250cc up to 1,100cc plus.

Sport Tourers: A cross between sports bikes and touring bikes, these will usually feature dual seating to carry a pillion passenger, as well as provision for luggage, a larger capacity fuel tank, and adjustable suspension. Seating is angled forward, legs tucked back, with some weight carried on the arms. Engines range from 500cc up to 1200cc.

Touring Motorcycles: Built to cover big mileages with a minimum of fuss, such bikes offer more comfortable dual seating with provision for luggage, and are often fully or partly faired to protect the rider from the elements. A larger capacity fuel tank is usual, as is load adjustable suspension. The seating position is more upright than the forward crouch of sports bikes. Engines range from 650cc up. Touring motorcycles are often axle or shaft drive for low maintenance.

Cruisers: Think 'Easy Rider'. Handle bars are higher, seating is more upright (even 'laid back'), with feet usually placed forward of the body. Petrol tanks are smaller capacity, as cruisers are generally more for 'show' than distance. Fairings are seldom in evidence. The chrome work will take days to buff, but hey, it's fun. This is the category that Harley Davidson once made its own, but today there are many worthy competitors.

General Sport: GS type bikes are built for dual purpose cross country and general touring. As such, tyres will be less knobbly than cross country ones, ground clearance remains high, but more attention will be paid to comfortable seating, larger fuel capacity, and carrying of luggage. Engine sizes range from 650cc to 1100cc. While some road bikes struggle on gravel surfaces, these bikes will excel on a wide variety of surfaces.

Cross Country: The knobbly tyres usually set these motorcycles apart; they are not generally well suited to tar seal road use. High ground clearance and longer suspension travel is the norm. Engine sizes are usually less than 650cc in order to keep the weight down and make the bike easier to pick up.

What to Pack for Touring

Consider the following gear list as a guideline when touring in New Zealand:

HELMET
It is illegal to ride a motorcycle without a helmet in New Zealand.

CLOTHING
- Leggings (wind and waterproof)
- Jacket (wind and waterproof)
- Gloves (wind and waterproof)
- Boots (wind and waterproof)
- Extra dry and warm socks
- Extra layers of thermal clothing/ underwear
- Extra thermal lining for gloves
- Thermal balaclava
- Casual gear for wearing when not riding, such as:
  - cap to hide your 'bad hair-do' after a day in a helmet.
  - jeans
  - shorts
  - swimming costume
  - t-shirts
  - sweatshirts
  - light sandals/jandals/thongs.
  - socks
  - nightwear

PERSONAL TOILETRIES
- Soap
- Shampoo
- Smellies (aftershave/perfume)
- Shaving gear
- Comb/brush
- Toothbrush and toothpaste
- Insect repellent
- Lip balm (chapstick)
- Sunscreen
- Toilet paper

MISCELLANEOUS
- Drivers licence
- Wallet, money and credit cards
- Sunglasses
- Maps and guide book
- Notebook and pen
- Camera and film
- Ear plugs
- Soft soapy cloth to clean helmet visor
- First aid items
- Portable radio
- Cell phone
- Torch

TOOLKIT
- Adjustable spanner
- Set of allen keys
- Screwdrivers (Phillips type and normal)
- Puncture repair kit
- Chain link tools
- Spare light bulbs
- Spare drive chain
- Spare fuses
- Pliers
- Tyre pressure gauge
- Wheel removal tools
- Spare engine oil

CAMPING EQUIPMENT (optional)
- Lightweight tent, poles and pegs
- Sleeping bag (3 seasons is usually adequate)
- Sleeping mat (rolled foam or air mattress)
- Lightweight stove
- Lightweight cooking pots/pans
- Plates and utensils
- Drinking cup
- Matches or lighter
- Torch
- Food

APPENDIX C

New Zealand National Motorcycle Clubs

> Although there are many regional clubs in New Zealand, this guide only lists national organisations in order to provide a useful starting point for any enquiries. People come, people go ... the following details are subject to change.
>
> Any amendments or new clubs for inclusion should be updated at | www.mcycle.co.nz |

BEARS Motorcycle Club
(British, European, and American Racing & Social)
Contact: PO Box 13-108, Onehunga, Auckland, or PO Box 4007, Palmerston North. Phone (06) 358-0753

BRONZ Inc.
(Bikers Rights Organisation of New Zealand)
PO Box 59, Geraldine. Fax (09) 693-7055

Bimota Club of NZ
Contact: David Coulson, 63 Wainuiomata Rd, Wainuiomata. Wellington.

BMW Owners Register of NZ
PO Box 109-245 Newmarket, Auckland.
Contact: Noel Walker (National President)
Phone (09) 813-2310

Harley Davidson Owners Group (HOG)
Internet: www.hog.com
or contact your local Harley Davidson Sales & Service agent.

Italian Motorcycle Owners Club
Contact: Greg Monahan (President)
Phone (06) 355-2034
Email: greg@bike-italian.com
Internet: www.bike-italian.com

Laverda Owners Register of NZ
Contact: Steve Carr, PO Box 8078, Riccarton, Christchurch. Phone (03) 374-9196
Email: stevecarr@ibm.net

NZ Moto Guzzi Riders
Contact: Jared Scorgie, 12 Cumberland St, Taupo. Phone/Fax (07) 377-6086

NZ Ariel Owners Register
Contact: Bruce Carrad, 28 Menin Road, Napier. Phone (06) 843-6717

NZ BSA Owners Club
(Even if you don't own one now, but did so in the past, you are apparently eligible to join.)
Contact: John Cochrane, PO Box 33-018, Petone, Wellington. Fax (04) 233-2013

NZ Classic Motorcycle Racing Register
(Dedicated to the preservation of pre-1976 British, European and American motorcycles.)
Contact: Norm and Lynda Maddock, PO Box 192, Takanini, Auckland.
Phone (09) 422-5714. Fax (09) 422-5724

NZ Honda Goldwing Riders Inc.
Contact: Brent Saunders, PO Box 723, Manurewa, Manukau City.
Internet: www.ampersand.co.nz/nzgwr

NZ Post Classic Road Race Register
(Dedicated to the preservation of 1962–1982 motorcycles.)
Contact: Sean Donnelly, PO Box 22, Paraparaumu. Phone (04) 297-2630, Fax (04) 297-1343

NZ Classic Scooter Club
Contact: Paul Sheridan, 14 Valley Road, Waiuku, South Auckland.
Phone (09) 235-6335

NZ Royal Enfield Owners Register
Contact: Athalis Clement, c/o Post Shop, Waitara. Phone (06) 754-8836

Participants gather in Dunedin for the annual BRONZ 'toy run' appeal, where toys are collected for distribution to needy children.
photo: William Glendenning

Motorcycle rallies are an enjoyable way for members of various clubs to mingle. Here riders leave the ferry at Waiheke Island for the biennial Snapper Rally.
photo: Judy Voullaire

NZ Vintage Japanese Motorcycle Club
Contact: Ross Charlton, 2 Te Miti St, Paekakariki. Phone (04) 292-8179

Norton Owners Club of NZ
PO Box 721, New Plymouth.

Patriots Defence Force Motorcycle Club
Contact: Shane Wooding.
Phone (09) 489-6458

Talamarkos Motorcycle Club
(For riders aged 16 to 39 years, of all makes of motorcycles. Regional clubs throughout NZ.)
Contact: 118A Waihi Rd, Tauranga.
Phone/Fax (07) 571-1433

Triumph Motorcycle Owners Club
PO Box 18733, Christchurch.
Phone (a/h) (03) 385-6917

Ulysses Club of NZ Inc
(For people aged 40 years and over; all makes of motorcycles. Branches throughout NZ.)
Contact: Don Burrows, 183 Flaxmere Ave., Hastings. Phone (06) 879-9195
Fax (06) 879-4195
PO Box 8712, Havelock North.
Email: ulysses.nz@xtra.co.nz
Internet: www.ulysses.org.nz

Vespa Club of NZ
Contact: Goetz Neugesauer, 94 Newton Rd, Auckland. Phone/Fax (09) 377-2525
Internet: www.scooterhouse.co.nz

Women's International Motorcycling Association (WIMA)
Contact: Lindy Harrison. PO Box 26-110, Newlands, Wellington. Phone (04) 802-4842, or Francis Clarke: (09) 478-7986.

Motorcycle Tour & Hire Agencies

New Zealand Motorcycle Rentals
(New Zealand's largest motorcycle tour and hire agency, and finalist in the 2000 NZ Tourism Awards.)
Internet: www.nzbike.com

AUCKLAND
(for information regarding NZ's North Island.)
Mr Darren Tonar
NZ Motorcycle Rentals
PO Box 106-156
31 Beach Rd.,
Downtown Auckland.

Phone (09) 377-2005
Fax (09) 377-2006
Email: info@nzbike.com

CHRISTCHURCH
(for information regarding NZ's South Island.)
Mr Gordon Lidgard
NZ Motorcycle Rentals
PO Box 13-200
166 Gloucester St.,
Christchurch.

Phone (03) 377-0663
Fax (03) 377-0623
Email: chch@nzbike.com

OTHER USEFUL WEB SITES AND TOUR ORGANISATIONS:

Bike Adventure NZ
Internet: www.banz.co.nz

Edelweiss Bike Travel
Internet: www.edelweissbiketravel.com

Legend Tours (NZ)
Email: legend@legend-tours.co.nz
Internet: www.legend-tours.co.nz

American Motorcycle Association Tours
www.ama-cycle.org/travel/tours.html

GoTourNZ
(Adventure NZ Motorcycle Rentals)
PO Box 674
82 Achilles Ave., Nelson.
Email: mctours@gotournz.com
Internet: www.gotournz.com

Motorcycling Downunder
35 Manchester St.,
PO Box 22-416, Christchurch
Phone (03) 366-0129   Fax (03) 366-7580
Email: bikes@motorcycling-nz.co.nz

NZ Adventures.co.nz.
Phone/Fax (03) 448-7997 or (09) 416-5308
Email: info@nzadventures.co.nz

Riders Hosted Tours of NZ
7 Braileys Track
Port Chalmers, Otago.
Phone (03) 472-7176   Fax (03) 472-7181
Email: riders@earthlight.co.nz

Te Waipounamu Motorcycle Hire & Tours
28b Byron St.,
PO Box 673, Christchurch.
Phone (03) 372-3537   Fax (03) 377-3211
Internet: www.motorcycle-hire.co.nz

Thunderbike Powersports
82 Achilles Ave., Nelson, NZ.
Phone (03) 548-7888   Fax (03) 546-9982
Email: mctours@thunderbike.co.nz
Internet: www.thunderbike.co.nz

TOWANDA women
(Women only motorcycle tour)
Contact: Tina Hartung
2 Scott St., Rangiora, NZ.
Phone (03) 313-2342   Fax (03) 313-2036
Email: towanda@paradise.net.nz
Internet: www.towanda.org

Beaches Motorcycle Adventures (USA)
2763 West River, Grand Island, NY. 14072-2053.
Phone 716-773-4960   Fax 716-773-5227
Email: bma@beaches-mca.com